THE MAYOR OF CASTERBRIDGE

ONE WEEK LOAN

New Casebooks

POETRY

WILLIAM BLAKE Edited by David Punter
CHAUCER Edited by Valerie Allen and Ares Axiotis
COLERIDGE, KEATS AND SHELLEY Edited by Peter J. Kitson
JOHN DONNE Edited by Andrew Mousley
SEAMUS HEANEY Edited by Michael Allen
PHILIP LARKIN Edited by Stephen Regan
PARADISE LOST Edited by William Zunder
VICTORIAN WOMEN POETS Edited by Joseph Bristow
WORDSWORTH Edited by John Williams

NOVELS AND PROSE

AUSTEN: *Emma* Edited by David Monaghan
AUSTEN: *Mansfield Park* and *Persuasion* Edited by Judy Simons
AUSTEN: *Sense and Sensibility* and *Pride and Prejudice* Edited by Robert Clark
CHARLOTTE BRONTË: *Jane Eyre* Edited by Heather Glen
CHARLOTTE BRONTË: *Villete* Edited by Pauline Nestor
EMILY BRONTË: *Wuthering Heights* Edited by Patsy Stoneman
ANGELA CARTER: Edited by Alison Easton
WILKIE COLLINS Edited by Lyn Pykett
JOSEPH CONRAD Edited by Elaine Jordan
DICKENS: *Bleak House* Edited by Jeremy Tambling
DICKENS: *David Copperfield* and *Hard Times* Edited by John Peck
DICKENS: *Great Expectations* Edited by Roger Sell
ELIOT: *Middlemarch* Edited by John Peck
E.M. FORSTER Edited by Jeremy Tambling
HARDY: *Jude the Obscure* Edited by Penny Boumelha
HARDY: *The Mayor of Casterbridge* Edited by Julian Wolfreys
HARDY: *Tess of the D'Urbervilles* Edited by Peter Widdowson
JAMES: *Turn of the Screw* and *What Maisie Knew* Edited by Neil Cornwell and Maggie Malone
LAWRENCE: *Sons and Lovers* Edited by Rick Rylance
TONI MORRISON Edited by Linden Peach
GEORGE ORWELL Edited by Byran Loughrey
SHELLEY: *Frankenstein* Edited by Fred Botting
STOKER: *Dracula* Edited by Glennis Byron
STERNE: *Tristram Shandy* Edited by Melvyn New
WOOLF: *Mrs Dalloway* and *To the Lighthouse* Edited by Su Reid

DRAMA

BECKETT: *Waiting for Godot* and *Endgame* Edited by Steven Connor
APHRA BEHN Edited by Janet Todd
SHAKESPEARE: *Antony and Cleopatra* Edited by John Drakakis
SHAKESPEARE: *Hamlet* Edited by Martin Coyle
SHAKESPEARE: *King Lear* Edited by Kiernan Ryan
SHAKESPEARE: *Macbeth* Edited by Alan Sinfield
SHAKESPEARE: *The Merchant of Venice* Edited by Martin Coyle
SHAKESPEARE: *A Midsummer Night's Dream* Edited by Richard Dutton
SHAKESPEARE: *The Tempest* Edited by R. S. White
SHAKESPEARE: *Twelfth Night* Edited by R. S. White
SHAKESPEARE ON FILM Edited by Robert Shaughnessy
SHAKESPEARE IN PERFORMANCE Edited by Robert Shaughnessy
SHAKESPEARE'S HISTORY PLAYS Edited by Graham Holderness
SHAKESPEARE'S TRAGEDIES Edited by Susan Zimmerman
JOHN WEBSTER: *The Duchess of Malfi* Edited by Dympna Callaghan

GENERAL THEMES

FEMINIST THEATRE AND THEORY Edited by Helene Keyssar
POSTCOLONIAL LITERATURES Edited by Michael Parker and Roger Starkey

New Casebooks Series
Series Standing Order
ISBN 0-333-71702-3 hardcover
ISBN 0-333-69345-0 paperback
(outside North America only)

You can receive future titles in this series as they are published by placing a standing order. Please contact your bookseller or, in case of difficulty, write to us at the address below with your name and address, the title of the series and the ISBN quoted above.

Customer Services Department, Macmillan Distribution Ltd
Houndmills, Basingstoke, Hampshire RG21 6XS, England

New Casebooks

THE MAYOR OF CASTERBRIDGE

THOMAS HARDY

EDITED BY JULIAN WOLFREYS

First published in Great Britain 2000 by
MACMILLAN PRESS LTD
Houndmills, Basingstoke, Hampshire RG21 6XS and London
Companies and representatives throughout the world

A catalogue record for this book is available from the British
Library.

ISBN 0–333–77754–9 hardcover
ISBN 0–333–77755–7 paperback

First published in the United States of America 2000 by
ST. MARTIN'S PRESS, LLC,
Scholarly and Reference Division,
175 Fifth Avenue, New York, N.Y. 10010

ISBN 0–312–23386–8 (cloth)

Library of Congress Cataloging-in-Publication Data

The mayor of Casterbridge / edited by Julian Wolfreys
p. cm. – (New casebooks)
ISBN 0–312–23386–8
1. Hardy, Thomas, 1840–1928. Mayor of Casterbridge.
I. Wolfreys, Julian, 1958– II. Series

PR4750.M3 M38 2000
823'.8–dc21   00-024308

This book is printed on paper suitable for recycling
and made from fully managed and sustained forest sources.

10   9   8   7   6   5   4   3   2   1
09   08   07   06   05   04   03   02   01   00

Printed in China

Contents

Acknowledgements

The editor and publishers wish to thank the following for permission to use copyright material:

Joe Fisher, 'The Mayor of Casterbridge (1886): Made of Money II', in The Hidden Hardy (1992), pp. 115–35 by permission of Macmillan Ltd and St. Martins Press, Inc.; Marjorie Garson for 'The Mayor of Casterbridge: The Bounds of Propriety', reprinted from Hardy's Fables of Integrity: Woman, Body, Text (1991), pp. 94–130 by permission of Oxford University Press, © Marjorie Garson 1991; Simon Gatrell, 'The Mayor of Casterbridge: The Fate of Michael Henchard's Character', in Thomas Hardy and the Proper Study of Mankind (1993), pp. 68–96 by permission of Macmillan Ltd and the University Press of Virginia; Bruce Johnson, material from True Correspondence: A Phenomenology of Thomas Hardy's Novels (1983, Gainseville), pp. 76–83 reprinted with the permission of the University Press of Florida; Robert Langbaum, material from Thomas Hardy in Our Time (1995), pp. 127–41 by permission of Macmillan Ltd and St. Martins Press, Inc.; J. Hillis Miller, material from Thomas Hardy: Distance and Desire (1970, Cambridge MA), pp. 96–102, 144–50. Reprinted by permission of the publisher: Harvard University Press, Copyright © 1970 by the President and Fellows of Harvard College; Michael Valdez Moses, 'Agon in the Marketplace: The Mayor of Casterbridge as Bourgeois Tragedy', South Atlantic Quarterly, 87:2 (Spring 1988), 219–49. Copyright © 1988, Duke University Press. All rights reserved. Reprinted with permission; Tess O' Toole, material from Genealogy and Fiction in Hardy: Family Lineage and Narrative Lines (1997), pp. 17–23 by permission of Macmillan Ltd and St. Martins Press, Inc.

Every effort has been made to trace the copyright holders but if any have been inadvertently overlooked the publishers will be pleased to make the necessary arrangement at the first opportunity.

General Editors' Preface

The purpose of this series of New Casebooks is to reveal some of the ways in which contemporary criticism has changed our understanding of commonly studied texts and writers and, indeed, of the nature of criticism itself. Central to the series is a concern with modern critical theory and its effect on current approaches to the study of literature. Each New Casebook editor has been asked to select a sequence of essays which will introduce the reader to the new critical approaches to the text or texts being discussed in the volume and also illuminate the rich interchange between critical theory and critical practice that characterises so much current writing about literature.

In this focus on modern critical thinking and practice New Casebooks aim not only to inform but also to stimulate, with volumes seeking to reflect both the controversy and the excitement of current criticism. Because much of this criticism is difficult and often employs an unfamiliar critical language, editors have been asked to give the reader as much help as they feel is appropriate, but without simplifying the essays or the issues they raise. Again, editors have been asked to supply a list of further reading which will enable readers to follow up issues raised by the essays in the volume.

The project of New Casebooks, then, is to bring together in an illuminating way those critics who best illustrate the ways in which contemporary criticism has established new methods of analysing texts and who have reinvigorated the important debate about how we 'read' literature. The hope is, of course, that New Casebooks will not only open up this debate to a wider audience, but will also encourage students to extend their own ideas, and think afresh about their responses to the texts they are studying.

John Peck and Martin Coyle
University of Wales, Cardiff

Introduction

JULIAN WOLFREYS

I

At the risk of stating the obvious, *The Mayor of Casterbridge* is complex. This complexity folds and unfolds for the reader the numerous layers and interrelationships of the narrative, its characters, and the places throughout Casterbridge where the fate of Michael Henchard and those associated with him is enacted. In his introduction to the novel, Keith Wilson addresses patterns of doubling, 'and at times tripling and quadrupling', which structure the text and complicate the act of reading.[1] Wilson aptly describes such patterns as 'forming themselves into a dense web'.[2] In the introduction to another edition of the novel, Norman Page also considers the structural and formal complexity: 'In the construction of the narrative, repetition and circularity are ... prominent features'.[3] Furthermore, there is 'a polyphony of different, even contrasting [narrative] voices'.[4]

The two editors see this intricate patterning serving different purposes. For Wilson, the doubling and multiplying folds serve to articulate the rejection of 'absolutist notions of identity'[5] and a proto-modernist exploration of the fragmentation of the self, pursued principally through the character of Henchard, but also through other characters, their 'protean relationships' which serve to relativise identity,[6] and the various doubles they invoke.[7] Page, on the other hand, relates the structural network to Hardy's 'recovery of the past [in the novel's present] both spatially and temporally'.

The novel's complexity, readable by turns as 'difficulty', 'thematic ambiguity' or 'stylistic awkwardness', has provoked a complex of responses since it was published in 1886. As one reviewer expressed it, '[Hardy] is most ingenious in devising problems, and bringing his people into situations of a complicated nature'.[8] This in itself is not peculiar to *The Mayor of Casterbridge*. It is, indeed, a condition of the critical response to Hardy until at least the 1970s, until when criticism was dominated either by aesthetic and formal concerns or with social and historical interests. The interwoven nature of lives, narrative strands and details of *The Mayor* – whether these be topographical, architectural or archaeological, spatial or temporal – produces a matrix of reiterative structures which has troubled critical comprehension. Moreover, Hardy's interlacing of countless aspects of the plot is echoed in the formal levels of the text. The patterns of tension and resistance to easy comprehension suggest that the more we seek a single narrative thread, the more we come to realise how each thread is interwoven with countless others.

II

It is perhaps for such reasons that criticism has tended to focus on Michael Henchard. The attention to this undeniably central character, regarded by Hardy as one of his most complex creations, has served as a means of calming down the play of the text. If we visualise the novel as a wheel, Henchard is often read as its axial figure or identity. To note this critical focus, however, is not to suggest, in a moment of foolhardy contrariety, that he is not important. Nor is it meant to imply that critics have been in error in focusing so strenuously on the man who is so well known for having sold his wife and then, subsequently, rising to a position of some social and political importance.

But, as critics have pointed out, including Simon Gatrell (essay 4), the novel is entitled *The Mayor of Casterbridge*, not *Michael Henchard*. We do the novel an injustice if we do not register fully the implications of this. The title speaks immediately of a certain identity. However, the identity of which it speaks is both a public and an impersonal identity, constructed, not natural. The title is also that of a social position or office, a structure into which any appropriate subject may be located. It names a public office, and a specular role

involved, through the town's hierarchical organisation, with questions of social organisation and society's identity, the economy of the
town in its various relations within itself, and questions of local politics. The mayoral post is a locus of civil organisation and power, to be
filled by successive individuals. Henchard is merely a privileged agent
of an already existing historical and cultural formation, occupying
the position after countless others.

Thus the title names both a social, a communal structuration,
and a position which provides evidence of but one temporal thread,
a continuum or stitch in the social and temporal weave of
Casterbridge itself. Again, it is possible to see, from this brief sketch
of the title's function, the complexity of the novel's structure.

III

Clearly, then, to return to where I started, the novel *is* complex.
Simon Gatrell points out in his essay that the 'narrator of [*The
Mayor*] is a complex organism' (p. 56), speaking with '(at least)
three different accents' (p. 56). Suzanne Keen suggests that the
novel has a 'generically mixed plot',[9] which in part explains both
the levels of complexity and the critical desire to trace a single structure within the heterogeneous whole. Despite the complexities – or,
perhaps, precisely because of them – there has existed what Keith
Wilson calls a 'recurrent critical tendency'[10] to simplify the textual
relations through the act of reading. This act of simplification has
tended, in the past, to reduce Hardy's significance as a novelist.
Terry Eagleton and F. R. Leavis provide us with a suitable starting
point for understanding the critical response to Hardy.

As Eagleton reminds us, Leavis omits Hardy from his 'great
tradition'.[11] Leavis' assessment is a summary dismissal of Hardy.[12]
Making vague allusions to nameless critics whose views of Hardy
are favourable, Leavis, with his customary manipulation of rhetoric,
cites Henry James' condescending assessment ('[t]he good little
Thomas Hardy'), as the authority by which the critic can determine
Hardy's stylistic and philosophical 'clumsiness', along with his not
being either Victorian or modern enough. Indeed, Leavis writes off
critics of the twenties, judging their reading of Hardy as the pre-
eminent writer of 'modern consciousness' as 'comic'.[13] The question
is not one, I would argue, of Hardy's pre-eminence (which merely
serves as the slightly hyperbolic excuse for Leavis' cavalier

disregard). The fact that his writing may be read as struggling to come to terms with a transition between the 'Victorian' and 'modern' in terms of the subject's perception of the world is surely to the point. However, Leavis deflects us from any serious consideration by refusing to take Hardy seriously – or he tries to, at least.

Eagleton sees Leavis' dismissal as symptomatic of certain strains in Hardy criticism, describing it as a 'predominant critical strategy'.[14] In identifying this, Eagleton points to what we might describe as the 'problem of Thomas Hardy', which is, as Eagleton puts it, the novelist's 'blunt disregard for formal consistency, ... [his readiness to] articulate form upon form – to mingle realist narration, classical tragedy, folk-fable, melodrama, "philosophical" discourse, social commentary'.[15] This attempted taxonomy at once points to the difficulty that conventional criticism grounded on formalist and aesthetic criteria has had in making Hardy conform to a single model or identity. At the same time, as Eagleton suggests – and this takes us back to the issue of complexity – Hardy's text resists critical acts of recuperation precisely because of its discursive heterogeneity. Eagleton identifies four 'distinct stages' in the development of Hardy criticism.[16] The first two phases read the novelist as 'anthropologist of Wessex' and, subsequently, 'the melancholic purveyor of late nineteenth-century nihilism'.[17] This particular assessment at least accords Hardy a certain comprehension of the difficulties he encounters in seeking to transcend 'the analytical stage' which he felt novel writing had reached by the 1880s.[18] Moving beyond this early assessment of Hardy, Eagleton describes the response to Hardy in the post-war years. Formalist criticism of the 1940s and 50s reads Hardy's work as 'irreparably violated by ideas'. At the same time, there begins a shift towards 'a more "sociological" reading of Hardy'.[19] This latter phenomenon is not, however, unproblematically positive for Eagleton. For, as he argues, much of such criticism focused sentimentally and mythologically on a safe vision of a lost rural England, while also criticising Hardy for the oddities of his language and style, a critical tendency persisting into the seventies.[20]

IV

Oversimplifying greatly, we might say that criticism of *The Mayor of Casterbridge* falls into two camps. On the one hand, it attempts either directly or indirectly to stay the complex texture of the text through a reading of it as a character study. On the other, there is also the reading, produced most frequently in the 1940s, 50s and 60s, though still in evidence in recent critical studies, which operates more or less thematically, isolating the sociological or tragic aspects of the novel. (More recent critical work has avoided the reductive tendency implicit in thematic analysis.) Reading Hardy's novel as social history or for the influences of Greek or Shakespearean tragedy provided a thematic path, which, in being thematically driven, tended to overlook other aspects of the novel. As early as 1955, James Baker addressed the thematic ambiguity of the novel. Douglas Brown's work in the 1950s and 60s established the sociological approach in a convincing manner. John Patterson was amongst the first critics to explore the tragic dimensions. Lawrence Lerner's *Thomas Hardy's The Mayor of Casterbridge: Tragedy or Social History?* (1975) catches at the principal critical and thematic interests, while also returning to the question of thematic ambiguity explored twenty years earlier by Baker.

Academic criticism of the novel has, then, conventionally stressed and returned to particular kinds of readings, and this critical legacy has been difficult to leave behind. As Suzanne Keen puts it, *The Mayor of Casterbridge* 'has been discussed as tragedy, character study, and as a realistic representation of places, practices and "peasants"'. Michael Valdez Moses (essay 9) also addresses the attempts of '[f]ormalist critics' to seize 'upon those sets of parallels which Hardy developed between his hero and characters such as Oedipus, Lear and Macbeth' (see p. 171). Moses continues to argue that those critics who read the tragic dimension of *The Mayor* persist either in pursuing 'the archetypal equivalence between the dramatic action of Hardy's novel and that of traditional tragic dramas' or otherwise understand 'Henchard according to some universal and transhistorical model of the tragic hero, such as that of existential man facing an indifferent, godless universe' (p. 171).

Marjorie Garson (essay 5) also emphasises the 'common impression' of the novel, guided by the insistence on the part of critical response to read it as shaped by 'the conventions of classical and Shakespearian tragedy' (see p. 80). Reading – or, perhaps, imposing – the 'tragic shape', lends, again in Garson's words, a 'sense of generic decorum [which also] makes it sound somewhat pompous and schematic' (p. 81). Whether pompous or not, the tragic paradigm applied to the reading of the novel *is* schematic, especially if such a context and structurally oriented interpretation is put to work at the expense of other narrative structures, traces, and Hardy's act of generic mixing. Garson's term 'decorum' suggests economically the act of closing down on the novel's play, the domestication of Hardy's novel into a manageable form. It also returns us to Eagleton's understanding of the ways in which criticism has sought to produce particular versions of 'Thomas Hardy' as a manageable product of literary culture. Hardy's writing in general, and *The Mayor of Casterbridge* in particular, has proved particularly resistant to what Eagleton terms the 'literary-ideological process'[21] of recuperation and insertion into a canon formed on ideas of organic wholeness, greatness, beauty or truth. Instead, as Eagleton puts it, 'the significance of Hardy's writing lies precisely in the *contradictory* constitution of his linguistic practice',[22] which in turn, mediates *The Mayor*'s negotiation of social and ideological crisis, as Raymond Williams has so astutely argued.[23]

V

It is precisely the fractured, heterogeneous nature of Hardy's writing, its refusal to be read as a seamless form hinting at a timeless bucolic condition or the universal struggle of humanity in the face of meaninglessness, to which criticism of *The Mayor of Casterbridge* has turned in the last three decades, choosing to emphasise the novel's complexity in resisting the act of critical domestication.

Thus in a positive sense, more recent criticism produced over the last quarter century may be said to *complicate* the novel. It is those essays which complicate and, indeed, challenge our understanding of the workings of *The Mayor* to which I have turned in making the selections for this volume. Each of the critics chosen teases out hitherto 'under-read' aspects of the novel, while acknowledging the debt they have to earlier critics. Some comment directly in the introductions to their studies of the novelist on those aspects of the novel which had previously been judged 'weak', 'awkward', 'clumsy'. In doing so, they make explicit that aesthetic considerations are not the only concerns when reading. If, as Eagleton has argued, the question of Hardy's writing had been, for so many critics, a problem, in more recent assessments this 'problem' is no longer seen as such but is instead the focus of interest.

Marjorie Garson, in her study of subjectivity, suggests that '"Hardy", the realist novelist of "character and environment", is himself a construction', a construction which has led to a distorted reading of the novels.[24] Furthermore, she argues that '[m]any of the instabilities, contradictions, and grotesqueries in the fiction – the "flaws" to which realistically minded readers have always drawn attention – make considerable sense' when the novels are read as the exploration and expression of a 'somatic' anxiety about the dissolution of bodily identity,[25] whether the body is the human body or the figurative bodies of buildings, structures, or indeed towns such as Casterbridge: 'Hardy's fiction expresses certain anxieties about wholeness ... in ways which are fairly consistent, though never simple or predictable'.[26]

Garson's reading, in connecting the human and non-human worlds, shares with the essays by Miller and Johnson a focus on the subject and the world of objects which comprehends more completely the ways in which Hardy's writing functions. Their concern with the text also finds an echo in the essay by Tess O' Toole (3), which considers fictions of genealogy and anxieties surrounding narratives of paternity which surface frequently in Hardy. Although each of the critics addresses different, yet interrelated strands of the text, each acknowledges what Gatrell describes as Hardy's ability 'to sustain ... a multiplicity of causality'.[27] Gatrell's study, which begins with a consideration of Hardy's titles, also acknowledges Hardy's observation of 'individuals in relationship to their non-human environment'[28] and summarises what we can understand as a shared interpretation of Hardy amongst critics since the 1970s that Hardy is never 'single-minded or wholly consistent'. This makes 'the experience of reading his fiction both rich and contradictory'.[29] Whereas this contradictory quality had been seen previously as a problem, Gatrell usefully points to the positive, the 'rich', aspect of such a complex construction. It is for this reason that no one critical approach or 'single line of argument'[30] is ever sufficient.

Robert Langbaum[31] (essay 6) points to the appeal of Hardy to both feminist and 'politically radical critics', as does Joe Fisher (essay 7).[32] Langbaum places Hardy as a transitional writer, arguing that, '[a]lthough Hardy's novels may seem Victorian largely because of their well-made plots, the plots contain exaggerations verging on fantasy that suggest twentieth-century symbolisations of the unconscious'.[33] For Langbaum, whose assessment recalls Garson's in part, Hardy's writing provides a connecting link between George Eliot and D. H. Lawrence. This emerges through the reading of those forms of exaggeration and other 'submerged' elements in Hardy. Fisher also reads the submerged and 'partly concealed patterns' for the force they exert, though his analysis is more explicitly political than Langbaum's. Fisher argues that revealing the submerged patterns suggests 'dangerous subversions of mode and ideology ... which have been critically suppressed in favour of ... the production of an "acceptable" Hardy'.[34]

As Fisher shows so forcefully, the tensions within the competing structures of the novel when read expose 'the essential relationship between prose fiction and the reproduction of ideology'.[35] Michael Valdez Moses also offers a political reading of the novel. Compared with Fisher's radical reading, influenced by the French Marxist Louis Althusser and by British materialist criticism, that of Moses concentrates on the eventual containment of subversion, and thereby shows itself indebted to the New Historicist critical discourse favoured in North America during the 1980s.

VI

Having considered the developments in Hardy criticism in general, and the place of the essays in this collection in that development, I want now to look at some of the essays' features and the particular issues they raise. In part what follows is a summary of the essays, though it is also concerned with their theoretical implications and positions (page numbers refer to this volume).

J. Hillis Miller (essay 1), provides a suitable starting point, inasmuch as he is one of the first critics to avoid the purely thematic reading. He is, in addition, one of the first to address *The Mayor of Casterbridge* from a phenomenological perspective, analysing the interconnectedness between the human subject and the non-human world. Miller also explores the persistence of past moments within the structure of the narrative. The two extracts address the temporal aspects of Hardy's work, its reliance on patterns of repetition across time where the past brings to bear a certain force on the actions of individuals in the present. Such resonance operates in a number of different ways, whether through the impression left by the past on material objects in the present which affect human behaviour; or through the complicating temporal patterns of love affairs, which play themselves out in structurally repetitious forms of behaviour, and which forms return repeatedly through the persistence of desire. Desire makes one act in similar ways, repeatedly, often through the unconscious frustration of the desire by the desiring subject, in order to prolong that self-same desire. Desire thus assumes what Miller describes as a rhythm, a recurring movement of postponement, delay and, thereby, re-enforcement.

This rhythm of insistent recurrence is read at both the human and non-human levels, although the two, it should be stressed, are never separable; each 'contaminates' the other. The question is one of reciprocal oscillation between human consciousness and non-human world, whether this world is the natural world or that of artefacts and objects. Miller therefore begins with the material persistence of the past in the present as the trace of history. Objects bear the trace of those who have used them. This persistence Miller sees as being Proustian, and it demonstrates Hardy's understanding of the interaction between the subject's consciousness and the material world, because the material world and that which haunts it from the past have the power to evoke feelings, rather than feeling being understood as purely subjective. As Miller puts it, the past has a 'coercive power'. Through such an understanding Miller moves on to a reading of *The Mayor* where the imprint of the past causes events to be enacted which are repetitious, which bear a resemblance to acts having occurred in the same place, even though the protagonists are often unaware of this. Hardy's literary allusions also operate in a similar manner. Thus Henchard repeats 'certain archetypal patterns of tragic experience', which are also 'universal patterns of recurrence' (p 24).

Bruce Johnson (essay 2) also speaks of recurrence. Like Miller's, Johnson's essay is phenomenological in orientation, relating the question of tragedy to the figure of the return, in this case initially Hardy's return to 'natural and even rustic identity' (p. 31), as well as the sense of universal recurrence. Johnson also explores the complex relation between past and present. Rather than reading tragedy as the dominant structural form, Johnson helpfully re-reads the novel, showing how Hardy places 'the problems of tragedy in the context of the return, of the correspondence of Man to Nature' (p. 32). Johnson argues that while Hardy can be understood as a writer of tragedies, this view must, of necessity, be complicated through a reading of phenomenological correspondence. No longer simply tragedy, the novel becomes inevitably transfigured by its encounter with the modern. This view is a significant movement forward in criticism of *The Mayor*, for it reads textual relationships as being reciprocal, rather than assuming the tragic text of the past to be merely an interpretable context or determining paradigm, as earlier readers had done.

Hardy's 'return' is also a return to the exploration of the connectedness between the subject and the 'non-human world' (p. 33), which, Johnson argues, is 'forgotten' by the Victorian novel. Henchard's 'tragedy' is that he typifies this Victorian forgetting. As a Victorian of the 1830s and 1840s, Henchard 'forgets' his ontological connectedness to the world in the act of selling his wife. Through this act he enters into the purely commercial and social world, signified by his own 'translation' from 'Michael Henchard' into 'the Mayor of Casterbridge'. Thus the novel is an 'ontological exploration of a social institution' (p. 35), of which the wife-auction is only the first symbolic advertisement. Johnson reads Henchard as a tragic figure inasmuch as Hardy's flawed protagonist provides a vehicle with which to explore the consequences of being blind to or cut off from a sense of Being. In dying, Henchard returns to the non-human world and thus sutures the gap between self and world. For Johnson, Henchard's blindness is Hardy's insight into the phenomenological condition of being-in-the-world.

The emphasis on persistence and return is to be found in Tess O'Toole's extract (essay 3), although given a significantly different orientation, directed towards a consideration of genealogy. Beginning with a consideration of how both genealogy and fiction are 'arts of making' (p. 40), O'Toole directs the reader to family relations and histories, as well as to 'fictions' of paternity, as expressed through Henchard's story maintained for Elizabeth-Jane (Garson also usefully explores the problematic claims of paternity [pp. 101–3], particularly in relation to Elizabeth-Jane's sense of propriety). What returns for O'Toole is a 'spectral' recurrence of a family figure from the past. She reads the wife-sale as effecting the dissolution of the family structure, only to return twenty years later. This reorganisation of the family shapes our reading, as 'family relations ... are integral to the narrative pattern' (p. 43). Such patterns are more closely linked than we may imagine. For the family is not Henchard's, the grown-up Elizabeth-Jane being of course Newson's daughter. Discovering this, Henchard reinvents the family narrative, which fiction is already anticipated in Susan's 'lie' to her first husband. However, as O'Toole makes explicit, Elizabeth-Jane disrupts any simply organised familial or narrative

structures in that the genetically transferred 'spectral' traces readable in her face bring back not paternal but maternal likeness. This
exchange of stories and structures serves a double purpose: it both
speaks of the return of the past – the uncanny likeness readable
being that of the young Susan sold at the fair, who thus 'haunts'
Henchard – and it speaks also of exchange as the dominant mode
of transaction in present-day Casterbridge. Elizabeth-Jane and the
landscape around the town both carry traces of the past in the
present, and this 'archeological' sedimentation (p. 45) reflects a
'deeper structure in the narrative' (p. 45). From this, the extract
concludes by acknowledging the frequency with which 'fictions
intervene in genealogical patterns' in Hardy's novel (p. 46), while,
in turn, genealogical structures and 'genetic product' (p. 44) can
be understood as deeply sedimented, complex textual traces, mis-
recognised and subsequently available for further reading.

VII

Simon Gatrell (essay 4) also turns our attention to the necessity for
further acts of close reading. Beginning with the title and its relation
to tragic convention, Gatrell considers Hardy's cursory treatment of
Henchard's rise to power and his desire for power. It is the rhyth-
mic drive of desire, already discussed, which causes Henchard to
shift his attention from various love-objects, and which unveils
desire, not for a particular character but for power. Henchard fails,
however, and the submissive position he assumes following the fight
with Farfrae 'feminises' him, at least as far as the 'expectations of
the novel's Victorian readership' (p. 53) are concerned.

From this initial consideration, Gatrell turns his attention to the
heterogeneity and complexity of the novel's description of
Casterbridge. The description of the town and the 'reader's experience of Casterbridge' (p. 58) is markedly ambiguous, complicated
by a range of narrative voices. Gatrell's reading of the ambiguity of
urban representation insists on the difficulty of 'pin[ning] down ...
a single definition of Dorchester' (p. 58). The town, too rural to be
properly metropolitan, and not rural enough to be merely an
organic extension or function of the countryside, exists temporally,
spatially, culturally and socially between definable meanings.

The representation of Casterbridge is implicated in the structures
of the entire text. Despite its rural affiliations, one aspect of the

town which is urban is its ability to create currents of 'economic struggle or collapse' (p. 58) as an expression of the modern, in which Henchard is himself ensnared and which operates across the novel, from the narratives of success and failure of individual characters to the lives of the poor in Mixen Lane. The modernity of economic struggle is played out in the trial scene, between Henchard and the furmity woman, where Henchard's supposedly tragic 'flaw' becomes rewritten within the specific economic and social contexts of Casterbridge life.

Moving to the novel's often overlooked subtitle – 'a man of character' – Gatrell considers Henchard in the context of John Stuart Mill's *On Liberty*. From scrutiny of Mill, Gatrell shows how Henchard's character is articulated through what Mill describes as both a 'greater humanity and, equally, a more powerful impulsive nature ... an intensity of desire' (p. 65). Henchard fulfils the description of Mill's 'individual', but fails to live up to his potential, making him dangerous to society because his will to power and desire outstrips his conscience. Gatrell argues that this should not be read just in terms of tragedy, that Henchard's so-called tragic dimension may be read as a rejection of Mill's notions concerning a man of character. Moreover, through this rejection it is possible to read a critique of, and 'fundamental discontent' with, Victorian society (p. 67). Thus the novel's complexities, its ambiguities and elements read by earlier critics as flaws of design or clumsiness, become available to us as the struggle to articulate a position at the limits of a culture which has helped in part to make that very critique possible. Recognition of this allows Gatrell to move to a more general consideration of 'certain unsettling features' (p. 68) of the narrative, which disturb any unequivocal sense of authority, not least of these being the absence of homogeneity, if not 'evidence of radical ambiguity' in the narrative voice, or voices (p. 73).

Marjorie Garson's psychoanalytically inflected analysis (essay 5) seeks to explore the expression of the 'dissolution of the self', the anxiety concerning identity and the fear of 'corporeal dissolution',[36] against which fables of subjectivity are positioned in Hardy's novels, as one particular expression of the negotiation of crisis. Garson examines the roles the principal characters play and the ways in which these characters, according to questions of Victorian and tragic decorum, exist more as textual figures with social and structural connotations, rather than having any somatic depth. The decorum of the text dominates the reading to such an extent that there is always that sense of ambiguity identified by Gatrell, while, on the other hand, there is little of the overt erotic expression – what Langbaum describes as the minimisation of sexuality – which is found in Hardy's other novels. Treating primarily of the tragic dimension, Garson moves through a carefully articulated set of readings of the principal characters, including Casterbridge itself, as she examines the 'gaps and discontinuities' in character delineation alongside the text's constant concern with boundaries and borders, with propriety and decorum.

Describing the novel as a text concerned with exposure – the exposure of truths motivated often enough by the frequently contradictory claims of decorum – Garson's essay is as much concerned with what remains unsaid as with what is explicit. Indeed, the strength of her argument is in the reading of textual surfaces and the silences by which the surface structures are articulated. The 'tragic shape' (p. 80) of the narrative is not simply a dominant structure, one which determines 'the novel's sense of 'generic decorum' (p. 81). Also, the generic parameters are themselves mediated and dependent on both readers' and characters' understanding of discursive and generic boundaries. All of this serves to produce a novel which is simultaneously 'unusually controlled' (p. 81) in comparison with other novels by Hardy, notable for their melodrama and more explicit erotic content, and 'delicate and ambiguous' in expression (p. 81). Indeed, Garson contends that the propriety of the text emerges as a result of Hardy's attention to control, even to the extent that tragic decorum dictates that Henchard will die 'off-stage'.

One of the ways in which Hardy's text is controlled is through the essentially decorous representation of characters' bodies, which have any '*somatic* depth and penetrability' carefully erased (p. 82), and are equally 'carefully subordinated to their thematic function' (p. 82). Farfrae, for example, is 'all surface' (p. 82). The Scot has 'a canny sense of boundaries' (p. 91). He easily assumes roles in his ability to move across various boundaries – social and cultural – and is an explicitly textual character. For as much as he borrows 'bits of speech and song' to construct a persona, he is also 'produced' by Hardy 'in terms of a paradigm' constructed by Sir Walter Scott, as Hardy's narrator makes us aware through allusions to the Scottish novelist (p. 93). We understand therefore that we are in the presence of a character from a novel, rather than some flesh and blood figure, and what is true of Farfrae is true in different ways about the other principal characters. There is, moreover, 'little erotic life' either to Henchard or Farfrae, while the women are even more lacking in any somatic resonance than their male counterparts (p. 83). Garson would doubtless agree with Langbaum that there is a minimisation of sexuality unusual for Hardy in this novel. And Garson goes further, for she analyses the function of clothing, which she reads as being almost wholly absent of 'sexy texture' and serving solely a socially orientated semiotic function, merely one more surface in a novel of surfaces (p. 83).

Tragic decorum and Victorian propriety commingle in the text, conspiring to reduce bodies to surfaces without erotic or somatic oscillation. Clothes, in being primarily socially encoded, provide one more figure of the boundary or border with which the novel is so concerned. 'Spatial boundaries often correspond to social boundaries in this novel', writes Garson (p. 86), yet 'the novel seems to depict ... the mingling of classes and the crossing of boundaries' (p. 87). Moreover, it is this constant play of structuration and mobility across lines of demarcation which serves in the construction of the social and economic aspects of the characters of Henchard and Farfrae. Thus, the novel 'has a powerful investment in the permeable boundary as a positive image' (p. 89). There is a 'flexibility to the social borders' of the novel which suggests that it is readable as strangely ambiguous concerning those tactful and underplayed moments of illicit behaviour which punctuate the narrative. While the characters are strangely de-eroticised, then, the town is not. Indeed, Casterbridge is the only fully realised 'body' in the novel (p. 83), ambiguously articulated through innumerable references to structure, to apparently stable boundaries, while simultaneously endlessly permeable, easily penetrated, and equally constantly eroticised. Casterbridge is a 'splendidly androgynous body' (p. 86), while the land surrounding it is clearly maternal. Such eroticism and corporeality leaves female characters nothing other than their social roles.

Social function expressed as a specular sense of the self is explored through Elizabeth-Jane, defined 'in terms of her clothing and her image in the mirror' (p. 99). Garson's reading suggests that Elizabeth-Jane is always defined in relation to her own sense of propriety, her self-control always being a condition of her awareness of 'the specular nature of the subject' (p. 99). This reflexive sense of propriety as social image is that which kills Henchard. Elizabeth-Jane's construction always refers back to issues of decorum, which is clearly articulated through her attitude towards her dress. Interestingly, she finds ways of justifying first her plain dress and then her more elegant clothing according to her flexible sense of what is fitting. Through Elizabeth-Jane perhaps, Hardy finds a way of exploring the limits of the ideology of Victorian decorum.

Ultimately, and in contradiction to the 'text's more liberal and generous social notions' (p. 103), the function which Elizabeth-Jane serves is one served by all the female characters. The novel operates through the mechanics of exposure, where the guilt of tragedy becomes rewritten as the shame of social revelation. While a 'real man does not expose people' in the novel, '[w]omen are at the bottom of Henchard's exposure' and are seen to have no real objection to exposing one another (p. 104). That which exposure challenges, that which it *exposes*, is the fantasy of integrity. If men such as Henchard desire the integrity of the self, and with that a certain subjective stability, a 'dream of phallic unity' (p. 110), then Susan and Lucetta's deaths expose what Garson calls the 'final impropriety ... the extinction of the subject' (p. 109), and with that the impossibility of the imagined unity of the tragic hero.

VIII

Perhaps the most 'traditional' of the readings, Robert Langbaum's reading of tragedy (essay 6) complicates the perception of the tragic framework by concentrating on the unusual – for Hardy – minimisation of sexuality. The diminishment is necessary, Langbaum argues, in order that, in keeping with the tragic framework, emphasis be placed on the question of 'moral judgement' (p. 117). Langbaum's principal interest, though, is in Henchard, who is almost wholly devoid of sexual feelings. This absence is compensated for and explained by Henchard's extraordinarily determined will to power, along with his desire to control and to possess, whether money or people. Henchard's behaviour towards Susan and Lucetta is governed by 'moral obligation without anticipation of sexual pleasure' (p. 117), as he has chosen 'the pursuit of money over the pleasures of sexuality' (p. 118).

The one sexual aspect of Henchard is his 'passion' for Farfrae. This, Langbaum correctly observes, is touched by the intimation of homoeroticism which, however, never becomes fully worked out, but is instead subordinated to 'male power rivalry' (p. 119).

Henchard's struggle with Farfrae is a sign of the former's tragic flaw, as Langbaum sees it, which is his 'self-destructiveness' (p. 120). This eventually results in Henchard's 'unmanning'. For Langbaum, such excessive 'imaginative and emotional resources [are] too large for success in life' (p. 124; recalling Gatrell's reading of Mill). The excess simultaneously amplifies the idea that character is fate while also resonating with Hardy's indebtedness to *King Lear*.

From Henchard, Langbaum moves to Farfrae and Elizabeth-Jane and their lack of sexuality. While Lucetta is the 'only sexually passionate character' in the novel (p. 125), Farfrae exhibits only 'shallow emotions' (p. 125; recalling Garson's argument); Elizabeth-Jane's character is marked by an 'unromantic rage for respectability' (p. 126). She is asexually intellectual, a woman who 'does not *feel* beautiful and compensates with intellectuality' (p. 127). Langbaum's argument thus complements Garson's analysis of figures living in a social world which, like the text itself, is marked by absence.

Joe Fisher's essay (7), which searches for hidden patterns and structures within Hardy's narratives as potential sites of subversion, trades between two 'texts', two ostensibly different and differing versions of the same narrative within *The Mayor of Casterbridge*, as he builds a materialist critique. Reading for the 'hidden Hardy' and the 'force of ... concealed patterns',[37] Fisher discerns an imminent patterning drawing on 'pre-capitalist myths' and, most significantly, the discourse of witchcraft, first figured in the novel by the mixing of rum and seed (as a form of alchemy), in the furmity woman's 'cauldron'.[38] The submerged discourses of mythology and witchcraft are figured in the text in a number of places, Fisher argues, and pertain throughout to issues of fertility (or its lack) and female sexuality.

The initial scene of 'witchcraft', where Henchard imbibes the adulterated furmity, enacts the planting of the seed by which Henchard is to grow and assume his later temporary power. Thus there is movement or trade between the two texts, between the world of economic exchange, modern market forces and commodity value, and the older, anti-rational world of carefully encoded magic, symbolised not only by the furmity woman but also by Conjuror Fall, the skimmington ride, and the figure of Henchard himself, a manifestation of the rural, medieval myth of the Wild Man, momentarily controlled by the organised social forces of Casterbridge, but eventually to return to the natural world. The binary opposition between natural and social world is not so simply defined, however, as Fisher makes clear. For there are a number of marginal places – Mixen Lane and the fair at Weydon-Priors being the most significant (the Ring is another such, and makes explicit Casterbridge's, and the present moment's relationship with an older, other past) – which undo the opposition.

The fair stands at the limits of both the natural and the civilised worlds, a structure symbolising a 'threatening "low" culture' (p. 136), in opposition to the ostensibly bourgeois culture of Casterbridge (with, once again, the notable exception of Mixen Lane). Henchard, the 'superstitious countryman' (p. 135), enters through the liminal site of the fair and is transformed by it, his transformation effected by the intersection between the old mythical world and the modern one of economic exchange. In entering into economic transactions, Henchard is put into a process of becoming a man of 'character', 'credit' and 'standing', which three figures are virtually synonymous (p. 146–7). So, while there is 'no clear narrative continuity offered to explain' (p. 132) the relationship between the 'two' Michael Henchards (the one who drunkenly sells his wife, and the one who is a solid, respectable pillar of the community), there is a carefully staged '"magical" disruption of 'realism' (p. 138), as well as a disruption of the apparent stability of civilised life as a result of the introduction of 'anti-rational and "superstitious" discourses' (p. 147). The novel thus read maps a struggle for 'hegemonic control' between 'competing discourses, where the mythical and anti-rational displace bourgeois realism from the very start' (p. 147). In the unfolding of this struggle, *The Mayor* is Hardy's most successfully subversive novel, challenging most completely the ideology of stability at the heart of late Victorian bourgeois culture.

The material aspect of the text is only one, however. Miller, O'Toole, and Langbaum variously describe moments of ghostly apparition. No discussion, though, has fully considered the novel's spectral quality. Moreover, while various essays consider the legacy of the past in the novel's present, none has explicitly mobilised the past's return as an expression of ghostly revenance. In my essay (8), I turn precisely to the question of haunting.

Throughout the novel, Hardy draws explicitly on the language of the uncanny, as well as the discourse of the spectral. This occurs in discussion of individual characters, but also in the consideration of the town and its environs, and through particular architectural features. Hardy makes plain that there is always installed in every structure the resonance of earlier structures which haunt the present formations, whether as in the case of the Ring or the keystone over Lucetta's door. Taking each of these temporal oscillations as spectral displacements, I continue by suggesting that the very form of the novel itself is haunted by the trace of other textual structures and that the movement of haunting figures circulates to disrupt any simple identity or generic identification. The identity of the novel, of the town and its inhabitants, the very shape of the novel itself is indelibly traced by spectral energies which displace and make unknowable any single originary point. Seeing tragedy as just a prior textual form is to misrecognise the way in which the structures of the text haunt one another. Instead, it is necessary to redefine the tragic as one manifestation of the spectral trace.

While also redefining the tragic dimension, Michael Valdez Moses (essay 9) reads ideological containment rather than subversion, arguing that Casterbridge is 'a modern bourgeois variant of the *polis*' (p. 174). For Moses, a historicised understanding of the novel, where the 'changing economic and political conditions' (p. 197) inform the reinvention of tragic models, reveals how Henchard's tragic 'fall' merely, in bourgeois fashion, divests him of 'stature and dignity without putting an end to his life' (p. 197). In order to follow this reading, Moses insists that 'an attempt be made to understand the history of tragedy in political terms' (p. 170), and hence his discussion of Greek political and social concepts. Moses not only effectively reinvents and politicises the tragic dimensions, but he also demonstrates how a supposedly aesthetic form such as the novel is indelibly marked by the signs of its own historicity. His reading complicates the comprehension both of tragedy as aesthetic context and of the supposedly timeless rural values on which Hardy draws, unfolding the politics of both contextual and conceptual investment on the part of the novelist, subsequently obscured by critical practice. The possibility of reading the 'superimposition' of the tragic model on the story of Henchard is in one sense 'an ideological feint, an attempt to mask the contradictions in bourgeois existence Hardy had uncovered' (p. 192). Mobilising the politicised reading 'reveals the contradictions of that riddle' (p. 192) although Hardy sought to make these acceptable to his contemporary audience. Henchard's banishment is not just a result of an inevitable tragic plan, but because of 'quickly changing economic and political conditions of Victorian England' (p. 197), which overdetermine the supposedly universal and timeless tragic model. Like the essays as a whole, Moses' re-reading of the text works to unsettle our grasp of the novel and the ideas it raises, the same kind of unsettling that *The Mayor of Casterbridge* itself seems to be about.

NOTES

1. Keith Wilson, 'Introduction', in Thomas Hardy, *The Mayor of Casterbridge*, ed. Keith Wilson (London, 1997), p. xxviii.

2. Ibid.

3. Norman Page, 'Introduction', in Thomas Hardy, *The Mayor of Casterbridge*, ed. Norman Page (Peterborough, Ontario, 1997), p. 23.

4. Ibid., p. 24.

5. Wilson, 'Introduction', p. xxviii.

6. Ibid., p. xxxi.

7. Ibid., p. xxvii.

8. Anon. Review of *The Mayor of Casterbridge*, *Athenaeum* (29 May 1886), rpt. in Hardy, *The Mayor of Casterbridge*, ed. Page, p. 404.

9. Suzanne Keen, *Victorian Renovations of the Novel: Narrative Annexes and the Boundaries of Representation* (Cambridge, 1988), p. 129.

10. Wilson, 'Introduction', p. xxv. Wilson highlights the 'recurrent critical tendency to read Henchard and Farfrae as existing in simple opposition'.

11. Terry Eagleton, *Walter Benjamin, or Towards a Revolutionary Criticism* (London, 1981), p. 127.

12. F. R. Leavis, *The Great Tradition: George Eliot, Henry James, Joseph Conrad* (New York, 1963), pp. 22–3.

13. Ibid., p. 23.

14. Eagleton, *Benjamin*, p. 127.

15. Ibid., p. 126.

16. Ibid., p. 127.

17. Ibid.

18. Florence Emily Hardy, *The Life and Work of Thomas Hardy*, ed. Michael Millgate (London, 1985), p. 183.

19. Eagleton, *Benjamin*, p. 127.

20. Ibid., pp. 127–8.

21. Ibid., p. 129.

22. Ibid., p. 128.

23. Raymond Williams, *The English Novel from Dickens to Lawrence* (London, 1970), pp. 106f.

24. Marjorie Garson, *Hardy's Fables of Integrity: Woman, Body, Text* (Oxford, 1991), p. 1, n. 2.

25. Ibid., p. 1.

26. Ibid., p. 3.

27. Simon Gatrell, *Thomas Hardy and the Proper Study of Mankind* (Basingstoke, 1993), p. 3.

28. Ibid., p. 4.

29. Ibid., p. 6.

30. Ibid.

31. Robert Langbaum, *Thomas Hardy in Our Time* (Basingstoke, 1995).

32. Joe Fisher, *The Hidden Hardy* (Basingstoke, 1992), p. 1.

33. Langbaum, *Thomas Hardy in Our Time*, pp. vii–viii.

34. Fisher, *Hidden Hardy*, p. 2.

35. Ibid., p. 19.

36. Garson, *Fables*, p. 1

37. Fisher, *Hidden Hardy*, p. 1.

38. Ibid., p. 16.

1

The Mayor of Casterbridge, the Persistence of the Past, and the Dance of Desire

J. HILLIS MILLER

I

[...]

The power humans have to transfigure nature by turning it into artifacts and implements is assumed as a given. Hardy's characters are born into a world which has already been made over by past generations. All men and women must live out their lives in a place full of houses, roads, and tools. The parts of nature which man or woman has reshaped in this way are the sedimentation of history. Without the physical world history might disappear without a trace, but as long as any relics of the past remain history need not be dependent on memory or on books. Hardy's people are surrounded by objects which embody the past and bring it before them. In one poem, for example, a collection of old musical instruments is played again by the ghosts of the people who once played them in the past.[1] In another beautiful poem the speaker lovingly describes how the dead are still present in the things they used. The caressing meditative rhythm, like the movement of hands touching an old clock or an old violin, carries much of the emotion here:

I see the hands of the generations
      That owned each shiny familiar thing
In play on its knobs and indentations,
      And with its ancient fashioning
            Still dallying:

Hands behind hands, growing paler and paler,
      As in a mirror a candle-flame
Shows images of itself, each frailer
      As it recedes ...
                  ('Old Furniture', CP, p. 456)

In another poem an old house boasts to a new house of 'the Presences from aforetime that I hold', and predicts that though 'a new house has no sense of the have-beens', still a time will come when the dwellers in the new house will 'print on thee their presences as on me':

      Where such inbe,
      A dwelling's character
   Takes theirs, and a vague semblancy
To them in all its limbs, and light, and atmosphere.
            ('The Two Houses', CP, pp. 563–5)

These presences are not subjective inventions. The people who played on the instruments, or used the old furniture, or lived in the old house have instilled their lives into the physical objects they have used, so transforming them that the objects remain permeated with their presence and can liberate them in afteryears, like an aroma freed from a sealed vase. This theme, so Proustian in idea and treatment, echoes through Hardy's poems. For him, as for Proust, an event which includes strong emotional involvement with a scene is not just the subjective shadowing of inner feelings against a neutral background. The background lends its part to the feelings and embodies them, in an inextricable merger of inner and outer. While the event was going on feeling and gesture were objectified in the scene.

This theme is important evidence for Hardy's instinctive rejection of a firm division of mind and world. Just as there is no such thing as a completely detached consciousness for him, so there are no detached feelings, feelings which are purely subjective. The emotions people feel, the actions and gestures they perform, transfigure the scenes around them, even though they do not intend this. The scene remains pervaded by the emotion, stores it up, and may release it long after to those who are sensitive to such intangible presences. So in 'The Strange House' Hardy imagines two people living in his own house at Max Gate in the year 2000. Though the new couple do not know that he and his wife have lived there a hundred years earlier, the more sensitive of the new dwellers is disturbed by their presence and finds difficulty in living an independent life in a house which has old dreams 'imprinted ... on its walls' (CP, p. 550). The same theme appears in 'The Re-enactment' (CP, pp. 339–42). A love scene so permeates a room and has so 'enghosted' its walls that it is not only periodically repeated there, but keeps new lovers from fulfilling their love within the same house, for the 'intenser drama' of the old love 'fill[s] the air' and '[leaves] no room for later passion anywhere' (CP, p. 342).

The accumulation of history in the physical world is not an objective fact which people who come afterward can behold from the outside with dispassionate impunity. The past embodied in the physical scene has a coercive power. It creates a complex cultural environment made of the persistence of the past generations. This can impose itself on the people of the present and determine their lives, sometimes without their knowledge. Casterbridge, with its Roman amphitheatre and its Roman skeletons in every garden and field, is an example of the tangible presence of history which Hardy so often finds in his Wessex. Dwellers in Casterbridge are 'quite unmoved' by these 'hoary shapes'. 'They had lived so long ago, their time was so unlike the present, their hopes and motives were so widely removed from ours, that between them and the living there seemed to stretch a gulf too wide for even a spirit to pass.'[2] Nevertheless, in spite of their insensitivity to influences from the past, the citizens of Casterbridge are so much aware of the sinister events which have taken place over the centuries in the amphitheatre, events which have deposited themselves layer by layer there, that they use the spot only for 'appointments of a furtive kind' and never for love meetings (MC, p. 81). Even now, events which long ago took place in the amphitheatre have so impregnated the scene that they are periodically re-enacted there in a repetition like that in certain folk beliefs or like that in Yeats's 'Crazy Jane on God' and *The Words Upon the Window-Pane*: 'at certain moments in the summer time, in broad daylight, persons sitting with a book or dozing in the arena had, on lifting their eyes, beheld the slopes lined with a gazing legion of Hadrian's soldiery as if watching the gladiatorial combat; and had heard the roar of their excited voices' (MC, p. 82). When Henchard meets his estranged wife in the amphitheatre what takes place between them adds itself to the long sequence of such events, and it is as if their interview takes some of its sombre fatefulness from its placing.

The references to Job, to Faust, to King Lear, and to Saul which run through *The Mayor of Casterbridge* function in the same way.[3] The narrator makes these references, not Henchard himself, until the end of his life. Their cumulative effect is to suggest that Henchard, without at first being aware of it, is in his life repeating certain archetypal patterns of tragic experience which have echoed through the centuries incarnating themselves now in this person, now in that. Henchard is not living his life freely, but is determined in his actions by the irresistible force of universal patterns of recurrence. The strength of these lies partly in the fact that until the end of his life he is ignorant of them. This theme is reinforced by the way Henchard in his own life repeats compulsively the same movements of approach toward another person followed by rejection of him. Character may be Fate, according to the aphorism from Novalis which is quoted in *The Mayor* (MC, p. 131),[4] but Henchard's character seems fateful in that it forces him to relate himself to other people in a way which will make his life a variation on that of Cain, Saul, Job, Oedipus, Samson, or Lear. *The Mayor of Casterbridge* may be defined as a demonstration of the impossibility of escaping from the past. Though Henchard tries to free himself, his own past actions, as well as the universal patterns he unwittingly incarnates, come back to destroy him.

This notion of the fatefulness of character is reinforced by the fact that so many of Hardy's protagonists have already inextricably involved themselves in determining situations when the reader first encounters them. Like many of William Faulkner's characters, Joe Christmas, for example, or Bayard Sartoris, his heroes and heroines have often made fateful commitments or choices, or had fateful experiences, long before the first scene of the story. The action of the novel is in a sense the working out of a destiny which has long since been fixed. At the beginning of *The Return of the Native*, for example, Diggory Venn has long been in love with Thomasin, though rejected by her, and Eustacia's first liaison with Wildeve is already a thing of the past. Only the return of Clym Yeobright is needed to establish a tangle of thwarted desires, each character loving someone but not being loved in return. At the beginning of

The Woodlanders, to recall another example, Marty South is already in love with Giles Winterborne, though his marriage to Grace Melbury is already planned, and Fitzpiers' affair with Mrs Charmond is already past. The same sort of crisscross of four mismatched lovers as in *The Return of the Native* is already latent in the situation. The scene of the wife-selling in *The Mayor of Casterbridge* is in effect a direct presentation of what becomes Henchard's fatefully determining past, since it is followed by a gap of eighteen years and a new beginning in the story which presupposes the wife-selling as a distant and yet ominous background. Even when the reader first encounters Henchard his marriage to Susan and his ensuing disgust with her, the first such sequence in his life of which the reader is told, has already happened. Hardy's novels rarely begin with their true beginnings, but open in the midst of the action, with the characters already entangled in situations which hold their futures in predetermined suspension.
[...]

II

Certain temporal structures are characteristic of the love affairs which take place in ... magically charged milieus. Within the space created by the act of falling in love each love relationship moves onward through time, driven by its own energies, for nothing, in Hardy's intuition of human existence, remains static. Every human relationship keeps changing until it ends. This movement takes typical forms which recur from novel to novel.

If the spatial form of the novels is constituted by the polarisation of objects according to tensions across the distances which separate the main characters, their temporal form, as it is watched retrospectively by the narrator, is created by the movement of the characters toward one another or away from one another within a world which has been impregnated with emotions. The novels focus with great intensity on the minutiae of these movements, following them step by step and moment by moment as each successive phase embodies itself in circumambient objects. This country dance of approach and withdrawal is often symbolised by the literal dances which occur so frequently in Hardy's world, for example, the dance where Angel and Tess first see one another, or the rustic festivities where Eustacia and Wildeve secretly meet and dance together by moonlight: 'Eustacia floated round and round on Wildeve's arm, her face rapt and statuesque ... The dance had come like an irresistible attack upon whatever sense of social order there was in their minds, to drive them back into old paths which were now doubly irregular.'[5]

The circulation of mutually fascinated characters around one another, in a graceful dance of crossings and exchanges, generates the temporal structure of each of the novels. In concentrating so exclusively on this movement, these novels are excellent proof that a work of fiction has a predominantly temporal existence. Fiction is a temporal art in part because its fundamental theme, the development of interpersonal relations, exists in the openness of the movement of one person toward the future fulfilment of himself by possession of another person.

Hardy's lovers, like most lovers, seek to obtain possession of the persons they desire. They want to approach closer and closer to the central figure who radiates a divine glow transfiguring the universe. To possess the beloved would be to coincide with what appears the spiritual centre of the world, to enjoy directly what is visible everywhere in reflected, mediated forms, and thereby to achieve self-fulfilment. His characters, however, are special in the slowness, the reticence, the surreptitious indirection, with which they move toward those they love.

Sometimes his lovers seem to suspect that love will disappear as soon as the barriers are down. They linger in their approach, holding off the other, dwelling on all those things which keep the object of love at a distance as well as giving indirect access to it. Other lovers aim vigorously at possession, but are kept from it by a succession of obstacles, some accidental, some put there by the persons they love. The more they are thwarted from consummating their love, the more violent their desire. Sometimes a whole lifetime may be spent in a state of frustrated fascination, a tantalising movement toward someone who always slips away or is removed behind another ambiguous veil, another windowed wall, or some other obstacle which is a means of communication as well as an impenetrable barrier.

Some lovers move in an alternation between the inflaming and cooling of desire. This variation appears wayward, proof of the intermittences of the heart, evidence of the way his characters are the victims of emotions which, like the wind, blow where they list, driving the men and women subject to them to love or to feel indifference unpredictably. In other cases the alternations between desire and indifference are directed not toward a single person, but toward a series of different persons. Such a lover moves from infatuation to distaste, is attracted anew by someone else, goes through the cycle again and then again. He moves in an ever renewed rhythm of desire and disgust in which he always turns to a new object of love as soon as he abandons the old. Such lovers love only when they do not possess what they desire, ceasing to love when they obtain what seemed to promise perpetual happiness.

Hardy shows great inventiveness in imagining in each of his stories a new version of this theme. Once the situation of desire has been established, often a tangled one involving a crisscross of mismatching loves, the form of each novel is determined by the development of these loves. The narrator, from his safe detachment, watches them through their various stages of proximity and distance, describing each stage with minute circumstantiality as the characters circle around one another in willing enslavement to some form of fascinated desire.

Henchard in *The Mayor of Casterbridge* is Hardy's fullest portrait of the man who knows 'no moderation in his requests and impulses' (MC, p. 88). He is driven by a passionate desire for full possession of some other person. This means that his life is a sequence of relationships in which he focuses first on one person and then on another, desiring each with unlimited vehemence when she seems to promise what he wants, turning from her just as abruptly when she fails to provide it. From Susan, to Lucetta, to Farfrae, to Elizabeth-Jane, Henchard moves in exasperated desire, striving to fill the 'emotional void' in himself, turning from Susan and Lucetta, one after the other, when they have yielded to him, desiring Lucetta anew when she becomes desirable to Farfrae, centring his whole life suddenly on Elizabeth-Jane after Susan's death only to discover at that very moment that she is not his daughter, so that a new barrier is created as if by magic between them, turning against Farfrae in an attempt to destroy the rival who is the mediator of his loving, determining for him without his awareness which women will be desirable to him, turning back again at last to Elizabeth-Jane and desiring her with burning possessive jealousy when Farfrae comes again between him and what he wants to take her too from him.

The Mayor of Casterbridge is a nightmare of frustrated desire. It is structured around episodes which provide repeated opportunities for formulations of the law of love in Hardy's world. '[W]hen I was rich', says Henchard, 'I didn't need what I could have, and now I be poor I can't have what I need' (MC, p. 269). If he has something he does not want it. When it is unavailable his desire is inflamed. Elizabeth-Jane suffers the same incongruity of desire and possession: 'Continually it had happened that what she had desired had not been granted her, and that what had been granted her she had not desired' (MC, p. 205). When Lucetta was Henchard's mistress he felt nothing for her but 'a pitying warmth' which 'had been almost chilled out of him by reflection', but as soon as she begins turning toward Farfrae and so becomes 'qualified with a slight inaccessibility' she becomes 'the very being to make him satisfied with life' (MC, p. 201). Her marriage to Farfrae makes him desire her all the more: 'During the whole period of his acquaintance with Lucetta he had never wished to claim her as his own so desperately as he now regretted her loss' (MC, p. 264). The same pattern is repeated later with Elizabeth-Jane. 'Shorn one by one of all other interests', says the narrator of Henchard, 'his life seemed centring on the personality of the stepdaughter whose presence but recently he could not endure' (MC, p. 333). This new movement of desire, like the others, produces the circumstances which will frustrate it, in this case the return of Newson, Elizabeth-Jane's real father, and the courtship of Elizabeth-Jane by Farfrae after Lucetta's death. The 'sudden prospect of [Elizabeth-Jane's] loss' causes him 'to speak mad lies like a child', and his affection for her grows 'more jealously strong with each new hazard to which his claim to her [is] exposed' (MC, p. 338, 339). The narrator speaks towards the end of the novel for Henchard's indistinct awareness of the pattern of his life: 'Susan, Farfrae, Lucetta, Elizabeth – all had gone from him, one after one, either by his fault or by his misfortune' (MC, p. 341).

It is both his fault and his misfortune, or rather it is neither. It is a law of life in Hardy's world that if someone by nature seeks complete possession of another person he is doomed to be disappointed over and over, either by his failure to obtain the woman he loves or by his discovery that he does not have what he wants when he possesses her. Character is indeed fate, and *The Mayor of Casterbridge* is the story of 'the life and death of a man of character', as the subtitle says. Henchard is destroyed neither by an external fate nor by a malign deity, but by 'the shade from his own soul upthrown', as the quotation from Shelley's *The Revolt of Islam* specifies (MC, p. 376). The context of the phrase from Shelley sheds much light on Hardy's conception of Henchard. The passage comes in the eighth canto of *The Revolt of Islam*. The heroine, having been captured by some sailors, explains to them that the conception of God has arisen by projection from evil qualities in man:

> What is that Power? Some moon-struck sophist stood
> Watching the shade from his own soul upthrown
> Fill Heaven and darken Earth, and in such mood
> The Form he saw and worshipped was his own,
> His likeness in the world's vast mirror shown ...
> (ll. 3244–8)[6]

Just as in Shelley's view God is not an independently existing Power who governs heaven and earth, but is the reification of tyrannical tendencies in man's mind, so Henchard is not, as he sometimes thinks, the victim of a malign power imposing suffering on him: 'The movements of his mind seemed to tend to the thought that some power was working against him' (MC, p. 219). Henchard's fate is determined not by a 'power' external to himself, but by his own character. This has projected itself on the world around him, creating necessarily the conditions which will produce repetitions of the same pattern of failure in his relations to other people. His fate-producing character is not a psychological mechanism, not some unconscious drive to self-punishment. He is rather one of Hardy's most dramatic demonstrations of a condition of existence in his universe. However vehemently Henchard approaches another person, the shadow cast between them by his own soul will remain as an impenetrable obstacle, his consciousness forbidding union with any of the people he loves.

From J. Hillis Miller, *Thomas Hardy: Distance and Desire* (Cambridge, MA, 1970), pp. 96–102, 144–50.

NOTES

[J. Hillis Miller's discussion is broadly phenomenological in orientation, combining this approach with analysis of character psychology. The first extract addresses the fateful aspect of Michael Henchard's character, while seeing the development of the character as a result of the return of past forces and experiences which are archetypal in nature. The second extract, again concentrating on Henchard in relation to those around him, relates temporal structure to desire, and thus connects the theme of eternal recurrence to the individual's compulsion to repeat in form if not in content his acts and errors. Ed.]

1. Thomas Hardy, 'Haunting Fingers: A Phantasy in a Museum of Musical Instruments', *The Collected Poems* (1930) (London, 1952), pp. 559–60. [All further references to the poems are cited parenthetically by title and the abbreviation CP. – Ed.]

2. Thomas Hardy, *The Mayor of Casterbridge* (New York and London, 1920), p. 80. [All further references to the novel are cited parenthetically as MC. – Ed.]

3. See Julian Moynihan, '*The Mayor of Casterbridge* and the Old Testament's First Book of Samuel: A Study of Some Literary Relationships', *PMLA*, 71 (1956), 118–30.

4. Hardy's source here is apparently George Eliot's somewhat modified version in *The Mill on the Floss* of Novalis' text. In *Heinrich von Ofterdingen* Novalis says, 'Ich einsehe, dass Schicksal und Gemüt Namen eines Begriffes sind'. This becomes in *The Mill*, '"Character", says Novalis, in one of his questionable aphorisms – "character is destiny"'. See Gordon S. Haight's note in the Riverside Edition of *The Mill on the Floss* (Boston, 1961), p. 351, and W. E. Yuill, '"Character is Fate": A Note on Thomas Hardy, George Eliot, and Novalis', *Modern Language Review* (1962), 401–2.

5. Thomas Hardy, *The Return of the Native* (New York and London, 1920), pp. 310–11.

6. Percy Bysshe Shelley, *The Complete Poetical Works*, ed. Thomas Hutchinson (London, 1960), p. 117.

2

The Mayor of Casterbridge

BRUCE JOHNSON

Hardy does not again engage the problem of relating tragedy with a return to natural and even rustic identity of the sort seen in *The Return of the Native* until what Michael Millgate calls his period of 'recession' is over and the minor novels of 1880–82 have been published. Of these three (*The Trumpet Major* 1880; *A Laodicean*, 1881; and *Two on a Tower*, 1882), *A Laodicean* is fundamentally interesting for its relation to Matthew Arnold's definition of modernism as 'imaginative reason' and for its intense if awkward concern with the problem of relating the present to the past. Hardy in 1885 was settling in at Max Gate, discovering Roman burials in the very foundation diggings for his new house, relating himself once more to his ancient birthplace of Dorchester, and in general associating the correspondence of man with Nature (the 'return' in some sense) with the various aspects of mind or consciousness (imagination, reason, will, senses, and so on) that might be involved in any such return. Arnold says in a passage from the essay 'Pagan and Medieval Religious Sentiment':

> The poetry of later paganism lived by the senses and understanding; the poetry of mediaeval Christianity lived by the heart and imagination. But the main element of the modern spirit's life is neither the senses and understanding, nor the heart and imagination; it is the imaginative reason.[1]

The comment is typically symmetrical and committed to a rather unexamined faculty psychology which Hardy intuitively undercuts by having Paula Power in *A Laodicean* refer to it as the view of a 'finished writer'. Yet the phrase is important to his own manner of relating present to past in the novel and even more so in *Jude the Obscure*, where the isolation of 'reason' in Sue Bridehead becomes the paradigm of modernism.

In short, Hardy moves from the question of what constitutes a tragic figure in *The Return of the Native* to nearly the same issue in *The Mayor of Casterbridge*, but always by placing the problems of tragedy in the context of the return, of the correspondence of man to Nature. The two issues were apparently inseparable in his imagination, a fact that has not been sufficiently emphasised by those who regard him as an accomplished tragedian. Although all tragic figures seem inevitably to invoke questions of man's relation to Nature, and that because tragedy must be played against some coherent cosmic scheme of value, no one links tragedy with man's frustrated rediscovery of the true correspondence so insistently as Hardy. In *The Woodlanders* (1887), a similar scenario is played out for Grace Melbury and her frustrated love for the earth god Giles Winterborne. It may well be that for a writer who had never had any theological sense of a cosmic scheme of value, Christian or otherwise, the ancient folk sense that if Nature cohered in ways beyond man's describing, it nonetheless cohered, was both cosmic enough and value enough. If Hardy was able to create a genuinely tragic figure, it perhaps had to be against this natural background – against this problem of the correspondence. And most likely it had also to be in terms of whatever psychological or psychic faculties were paramount in the modern sensibility – were available in contrast to an ancient rustic sensibility that had created its great monuments to the achieved symbiosis in, say, Mai-Dun (Maiden Castle) or Stonehenge.

These are the imaginative categories with which Hardy approaches *The Mayor of Casterbridge*. Most readers agree that with Henchard, Hardy comes closer to creating genuine tragic stature than with Clym or Eustacia, and that with Jude we have tipped over into recognisably modern pathos rather than tragedy. But it may be more nearly correct to say that the very idea of tragedy finally seems to Hardy one of those nets that neither the ancient builders of Stonehenge nor Tess herself would have cast in the first place. Surely after *The Mayor of Casterbridge* not all his reading in Greek drama can save tragedy for the modern world.

Nevertheless, the ontological inspiration that guides this novel may best be described not as a further exploration of Hardy's sense of the tragic hero but as a willingness to probe one kind of being in terms of another kind – not simply synaesthesia or even the mixed categories of metaphysical poetry, but a peculiar experimentalism that, by the end of chapter four, has the reader accepting not only 'loaves ... as flat as toads' (made with Henchard's 'growed wheat') but the designation of those loaves as 'unprincipled bread': 'I've been a wife, and I've been a mother, and I never see such unprincipled bread in Casterbridge as this before.' This is the first characteristic of the 'new' Henchard that Susan and Elizabeth-Jane encounter on their entry into Casterbridge. And yet it is not unlike the capacity of the old Henchard to unprinciple things, to deny them something of their essence and substitute something of the informing principle of another kind of being. The wife auction has been just such an activity.

It is the 'crime' that takes him out of the natural life in the fields and puts him into commercial society. Earlier he had worn 'leggings yellow as marigolds, corduroys immaculate as new flax, and a neckerchief like a flower garden'. After the wife auction, he enters a world that can make him mayor but can never erase what D. H. Lawrence called the 'true correspondence between the material cosmos and the human soul'.[2] As John Paterson suggests ... Hardy, like his follower D. H. Lawrence, sought to expand the significance of his characters beyond 'the functions of their merely social values and conditions ... and to make them participants in some larger non-human drama'.[3] The very metaphoric texture of Hardy's prose will often suggest not that some human feature, physical or psychological, is 'like' some aspect of Nature (as in John Paterson's example of Tess's 'peony mouth' or in nearly every metaphor we have examined thus far) but that some larger ontology comprehends both. Hardy intends to expand our understanding of human nature by suggesting that the mainstream of the Victorian novel (with its key image of the web, man in society affecting and affected by the slightest movement of any strand) has led us to forget ancient connections with the non-human world.

Thus, the wife auction stands at a symbolic moment in Henchard's life, when he is willing to apply a commercial trope to matters between him and his wife (and between him and his self-image) that are not of that order of being, that are ontologically inappropriate, as, for example, other kinds of violence or even desertion would not have been. The auction signals the triumph of social and commercial signification over the more primitive, even atavistic sources of Henchard's being. Using the commercial trope to carry his feelings, whatever they may be, plunges Henchard out of his native element and into a commercial and social world where the talents of Farfrae will eventually, and with no malice, wear him down and finish him off. His life suggests the danger of allowing a man's social significance to be effectively severed from his non-human significance, from the source of his energy in natural forces that are not to be gambled upon in commercial speculation.

To begin the novel with such confusion of ontologies unsettles the 'nature', the secure essence, of other things throughout the story. It is almost as though the wife auction in some atavistic way had been blasphemy against the principle that such essences had better not be confused lest all Nature be set askew, decentred so that even names no longer seem to go to the heart of things and begin to lead a vagrant life of their own. To call the bread 'unprincipled' is far more than a rustic description intimating that Henchard is unprincipled for having sold the bakers and millers sprouted wheat, or the millers unprincipled for claiming they did not know it had sprouted, or all unprincipled for colluding in the deception (the most unprincipled thing of all). Bread, called symbolic of the transition from Nature to culture by men as different as Claude Lévi-Strauss and Thoreau, has thus been unprincipled as surely as Henchard's wife auction had earlier struck at marriage. We may well remember Thoreau's satire of those who would call yeast the essence of bread and his successive elimination of ingredients in search of a more genuine candidate for the role. Like Hardy, Thoreau was a great seeker of essences; not to know them was, after all, to miss Thoreau's own version of the 'true correspondence between the material cosmos and the human soul'.

The incident with the bread, the wife auction and, later, such incidents as Henchard's gambling on the weather are all exquisitely structured to suggest just such confusion. Somehow Susan's initially naïve and 'meek' belief in the 'binding force' or the 'transaction' strikes us as morally justified and really no mixing of ontologies at all. Henchard's subsequent pledge to stop drinking for as long as he has already lived (twenty-one years) emphasises only that his capacity for unprincipling his own life has little to do with his drinking. Liquor may have precipitated the crisis, but within him works the ancient antagonist of the pastoral otium, ambition itself, the aspiring mind. We are once again very much in the presence of Hardy's pastoral *Gestalten*, asking the ancient questions, reexamining the nature of otium, suspecting that it may consist in knowing what things are in their essence and particularly what common being man may share with the 'material world'.

That Hardy is particularly anxious to see man as anything but a unique mode of being we see upon Henchard's leaving the scene of the crime. Surely there was a part of Hardy that would have relished treating marriage as a mere contract, at least insofar as society forced other emotional and moral aspects of the relationship to conform painfully with that commercial mould. In his fascination with the wife auction (his poring over antique instances of it in country records), it is as though Hardy were saying to society: all right, you covertly regard marriage as a contract and commercial expediency while sanctifying that commercialism as though it were a spiritual thing sanctified by God. Let us bring its commercialism out in the open and, through the hyperbole of the auction, push it to a logical conclusion, or at least to a *reductio ad absurdum*. You will not make its legal and commercial aspect serve its psychological and moral reality, as wise men would; instead, as with Jude, you will allow the legal forms to victimise the psychological reality. So be it. If it is really commercial, let us externalise that essence and epitomise it in the auction. If it is spiritual, let us have no more of this covert commercialism.

The wife auction as a symbol is nicely arranged for the ontological exploration of a social institution as much as it is a complex revelation of Henchard's passing from the roughly georgic and pastoral world to the world of mayors and towns and business. Many of Hardy's symbols are precisely of this borderline variety, poised so that both author and reader may look off into two ontologically different sorts of country.

This mixing of categories is to be seen, then, as a means of gingerly probing the being of things – and certainly as a healthy and creative activity for the author. Within Henchard, however, and without the conscious manipulation that the author can manage for himself, such unprincipling can be tragic. Something of its process may be in the nature of art, but it is a dangerous element in a man's life if he is no artist, and possibly even if he is. When Henchard walks out of the tent, Hardy notes that 'the difference between the peacefulness of inferior nature and the wilful hostilities of mankind was very apparent at this place'. Yet he immediately remembers that mankind might 'some night be innocently sleeping when these quiet objects were raging loud' and includes Henchard's violence and Nature's under the comprehensive ontology of 'all terrestrial conditions', which are 'intermittent'.

That Henchard's hostility has been 'wilful' is not sufficient to exclude it from this category. Man's will is no ultimate determinant of ontology for Hardy, and Hardy's motive in this philosophic rumination (really an act of considerable daring) is no less expansive for his view of human nature than, for instance, seeing the sun in Elizabeth-Jane's loosely combed hair as though it were in some mode the same as the sunlight penetrating a hazel copse. There is nothing mystical in either of these perceptions; they are, rather, eloquent proof of Hardy's taste for the immanent reality of both the visual moment in the hazel copse and of a nearly unnameable quality in Elizabeth-Jane. The connection may depend on the most delicate perception of modes of being, but it is not transcendent in any Emersonian or Platonic sense. In some entirely legitimate sense of the word, it is more nearly empirical. As Hardy has said in a note, 'In spite of myself I cannot help noticing countenances and tempers in objects of scenery, e.g., trees, hills, houses'.[4]

While it is not true that the whole plot of The Mayor of Casterbridge consists of the consequences of this auction come back to haunt him, still the novel unfolds a sequence of paradoxes built upon the ontological symbol. The man whom Henchard loves, Farfrae, becomes his commercial rival largely because Henchard, having plunged into the commercial world, will not recognise that it is nonetheless outside his nature. While Henchard deals with a handshake and a 'Ye shall hae't', Farfrae writes out contracts and balances books; his talent for romance never impinges on his equal talent for orderly business. He sings nostalgic songs about a Scotland he never particularly wants to see again. He weighs alternatives and is expert in taking into account the feelings of others without really responding to those feelings. In short, he is totally untragic and has been made so in contrast to the self-defeating paradox of Henchard. Farfrae is an uncanny portrait of what might be called, in comparison with the Industrial Revolution, the Managerial Revolution.

Henchard's tragic qualities have been variously described, ranging from a subtle 'self-destructive' wish and melancholy need to strip people of their dignity, to a taste for liquor and a simple bad temper that plunges ahead without any long-range sense of consequences. If the wife auction, however, is a clue to the qualities in him that are tragic, we shall need to understand the paradoxes it produces in the subsequent action of the novel. Susan becomes a true wife to a man whose legal wife she can never be. She returns to a Henchard whose legal wife she is but with feelings and a child that in every sense belong to Newson. The auction creates a situation where there can be no further correspondence between social form and emotional content. Henchard, like some of Joseph Conrad's characters, has committed a 'crime' which has jolted things out of their customary significations and made us wonder, indeed, whether even names have anything intrinsic to do with what they are supposed to designate in the social and material world.

Especially Elizabeth-Jane sees the world in this seminal disorder as she sits the death watch beside her mother's bed. She is, after all, the victim of so many of these dislocations and dissociations. She hears

> The timepiece in the bedroom ticking frantically against the clock on the stairs [two orderly measures of time and 'reality' disagreeing stubbornly with one another]; ticking harder and harder till it seemed to clang like a gong; and all this while the subtle-souled girl asking herself why she was born, why sitting in a room, and blinking at the candle; why things around her had taken the shape they wore in preference to every other possible shape. Why they stared at her so helplessly, as if waiting for the touch of some wand that should release them from terrestrial constraint; what that chaos called consciousness which spun in her at this moment like a top, tended to, and began in. Her eyes fell together; she was awake, yet she was asleep.[5]

As Susan dies, she attempts to designate every detail of her funeral (down to the pennies on her dead eyes), to thrust Elizabeth-Jane into Farfrae's care, and in general to control all the details of existence that Elizabeth-Jane feels are about to spin out of their named and accustomed categories.

Yet the world, especially as it seems to exist after Henchard's crime, will not tolerate such management, any more than Elizabeth-Jane's name or the weather at harvest time will. Confronting Elizabeth-Jane with his desire to change and thereby manage her name, Henchard says, "Twas I that chose your name, my daughter; your mother wanted it Susan. There, don't forget 'twas I gave you your name!' But if in Hardy's world names are manipulated, essences cannot be, and Henchard has invited the wrath of the nonexistent gods in his bit of hubris.

Elizabeth-Jane, anxious to stop the ontological spinning mentioned earlier, says, 'If it is my name I must have it, mustn't I', and

Henchard, anxious to disguise the role of his own will in the matter says, 'Well, well; usage is everything in these matters'. Of course no sooner is the notice to the newspapers dictated than Henchard goes upstairs to find evidence of her name and discovers Susan's letter saying that Elizabeth-Jane is Newson's child. When, after an anguished walk that night, he returns to his newly named daughter, who is no daughter, ironically he finds an Elizabeth-Jane who from this moment on calls him father and nearly becomes his emotional child. This kind of irony concerning the identity of things and people is fundamental to *The Mayor of Casterbridge*.

Henchard creates his own fate by denying 'the true correspondence between the material cosmos and the human soul', by cutting himself off from a genius for such symbiosis in the sense of not recognising the wellspring of his true temperamental power. But he nonetheless dies having disappeared as though 'he had sunk into the earth', on the borders of the Ishmaelite Egdon Heath and among the tumuli of the earliest tribes, tombs which look like the breasts of 'Diana Multimammia fully extended there'. In his death the connection is reaffirmed. Farfrae may interpose harvesting and planting machines between the primordial sower and reaper and their connection with the very soil they turn, but Farfrae has nothing to lose in the way of that true correspondence: his temperament is modulated by rational considerations that Great Mother knows nothing of. She is tempestuous or tranquil in the passionate manner of a Greek god. And in Henchard, Hardy has phenomenologically caught this quality; it is the key to both his stature – as it is Lear's – and his fall. Although Henchard is nevertheless defined symbolically with a return to the multiple breasts of the earth, Hardy is obviously not yet finished with the hero who represents that great struggle between the demands of Farfraeite modern culture and society and those of the true correspondence.

From Bruce Johnson, *True Correspondence: A Phenomenology of Thomas Hardy's Novels* (Tallahassee, FL, 1983), pp. 76–83.

NOTES

[Bruce Johnson's extract stresses the relation of tragedy and the tragic flaw of Henchard's character to the theme of eternal recurrence. For Johnson, this is worked out through the ontological consideration of one 'kind of being in terms of another kind'. Henchard misunderstands the nature of his being in relation to others and the relation in which he stands to the world, and thus 'falls' as a result of his inability to comprehend what Johnson, borrowing a phrase from D. H. Lawrence, terms being's true correspondence. Ed.]

1. Matthew Arnold, *Lectures and Essays in Criticism*, ed. R. H. Super (Ann Arbor, MI, 1962), p. 230. Quoted by Hardy in his *Literary Notes*, 1: note 1018.

2. D. H. Lawrence, *Phoenix: The Posthumous Papers of D. H. Lawrence* (1961), 2 vols, ed. E. D. McDonald (London, 1968), vol. 2, p. 227.

3. John Paterson, 'Lawrence's Vital Source: Nature and Character in Thomas Hardy', in *Nature and the Victorian Imagination*, ed. U. C. Knoepflmacher and G. B. Tennyson (Berkeley, CA, 1977), p. 462.

4. This and other such comments are scattered throughout Florence Emily Hardy, *The Early Life of Thomas Hardy* (London, 1928) and *The Later Years of Thomas Hardy* (London, 1930), e.g., 'October 2. Looked at the thorn bushes by Rushy Pond [on an exposed part of the heath]. In their wrath with the gales their forms resemble men's in like mood'.

5. Thomas Hardy, *The Life and Death of the Mayor of Casterbridge: A Story of a Man of Character*, Wessex Edition (London, 1912), vol. v.

3

Fictitious Families

TESS O'TOOLE

Hardy's narrative poem 'Her Death and After'[1] hinges on a fictive intervention which leads to the restructuring of family ties. The poem's speaker raises his former lover's daughter as his own, pretending that the child's mother has made a death-bed confession identifying him rather than her husband as the father. The biological father's indifference to the child after his remarriage and the adoptive father's devotion to the daughter of his lost love combine to make the made-up family configuration more viable than the natural one. This father and daughter constitute one of the many fictitious families that populate Hardy's world, in which 'standard' family relations seem outnumbered by those that are in some way irregular.

Hardy's plots provide ample demonstration of the various senses in which families can be 'made up'. Most commonly, family alliances can be constructed or reconfigured through acts of marriage or adoption. They can also be fabricated, through, for example, a fraudulent transaction such as an illegal marriage or a lie about paternity. If procreation and fiction writing both constitute acts of making, the fictitious family and the fictional text have as common ground the act of pretence.

The metaphors through which our culture customarily represents the relationship between genealogy and fiction render the literary act a reflection of biological procreation. This tradition is underscored by Edward Said's meditation on the word 'author' as naming 'a person who originates or gives existence to something, a begetter, beginner, father or ancestor ...'.[2] Thus we speak, for example, of the prolific novelist such as Trollope or Balzac as a god or a father who populates his fictional world with the offspring of his fertile imagination. Hardy's treatment of genealogy reverses the characteristic direction of the metaphor, for he more commonly renders genetic process as an imitation of textual process. Thus ancestors in Hardy's world generate 'reprints', 'up to date editions', or 'debased copies' of themselves. It is the kinship he perceives between genealogy and fiction that causes Hardy to choose family history as the subject of his fiction with such regularity. The multi-generational patterns that inform the plots of novels like *Tess of the d'Urbervilles* and *The Well-Beloved* are only the most conspicuous instances of Hardy's engagement with genealogy. It is also manifested in his minute descriptions of genetic resemblances, which tend to emerge intermittently and at critical moments in the lives of his characters, and in the role played by illegitimacy or cases of confused paternity in so many of his plots.

The familiar metaphors equating genealogy and fiction most commonly link genealogical process to control and order, an association often played out in Victorian plots. In a novel like *Oliver Twist* or *Daniel Deronda*, genealogical origin authorises character and demystifies event.[3] But in Hardy's fiction, genealogy is habitually linked with ambiguity, and genealogical origin raises as many questions as it answers; in his case the relationship between genealogy and fiction is arguably more complicated than it is in the work of any other Victorian author. The particular types of genealogical events that Hardy repeatedly incorporates into his plots are characterised by their intersection with fictions of various sorts – lies, fraud, fantasy, or narrative interventions (such as the legends circulated about the d'Urbervilles or the gossip circulated about Jude Fawley's ancestors).

The involvement of the imagination in physical heredity itself is suggested by the narrative poem 'San Sebastian',[4] which concerns a peculiar case of genetic resemblance. The speaker in the poem is a retired army sergeant who habitually strays on Ivel Way to avoid the 'spectre' that haunts his home. The ghost is his daughter, a beautiful girl of seventeen whose eyes are identical to those of a young Spanish woman whom he raped decades before after a successful campaign in the Napoleonic wars. The sergeant muses to a friend: 'Maybe we shape our offspring's guise / From fancy, or we know not what / And that no deep impression dies, / – For the mother of my child is not / The mother of her eyes.' With his reference to two mothers, the sergeant identifies contrasting genealogies for his daughter based on alternate definitions of parentage, one biological and legal, the other supernatural and speculative.

As a 'spectre', the genetic product is at once the reincarnation of a figure from the past and an image that has been raised by a guilty party's imagination – 'I copied those eyes for my punishment in begetting the girl you see.' The sergeant's interpretation suggests the power of the imagination to intervene in heredity. But that intervention does not lessen the authenticity of the genetic imprint. While the imagination has played a role in its generation, it is also the locus of truth, for the critical, suppressed moment in the sergeant's biography, which is otherwise 'hid from men', manifests itself in that feature of his daughter's.

While 'Her Death and After' concerns a deliberate deception about paternity, 'San Sebastian' calls into question biological heredity altogether. The two poems suggest alternate ways in which 'legitimate' family relations can be superseded, a recurring preoccupation in Hardy's writing. It is not simply for their melodramatic function that cases of illegitimacy, fraudulent marriages, secret relationships, and the like are so common in Hardy's fictional world. Individually and in their almost overwhelming aggregate, they suggest the instability to which family structure is subject. This instability emanates from the competing claims of the body and the imagination in the forging of family relationships. In this chapter I will be concerned with the staging of this competition in genetic and marital relationships, as well as with the deliberate rescripting of family relations that it facilitates.

'BURIED GENEALOGICAL FACTS': *THE MAYOR OF CASTERBRIDGE*

Structured as it is around the career of a single, self-made protagonist, *The Mayor of Casterbridge* may seem an unlikely novel with which to begin a discussion of family history in Hardy. It is, however, an attempt to reconfigure family relations that sets its plot in motion; the opening episode of the novel, in which Henchard sells his wife and baby daughter to a sailor passing through town, portrays a dramatic dissolution of family structure, a willed unmaking of the marital and paternal ties forged by law and by biological procreation. This rupture in the family is succeeded by a narrative rupture, a prolonged ellipsis in the narrator's account of Henchard's life history. While Henchard's career starts over immediately after he sheds his family, the narrative thread is picked up at a point almost twenty years on, when his family resurfaces. The return of Susan leads to an attempted reconstruction of the family so abruptly sundered years before, as Henchard decides to remarry her and, in the guise of stepfather, to resume his paternal role over his supposed daughter. Family relations, then, are integral to the narrative pattern, while the relations themselves are inflected by various fictions.

Henchard's initiating act puts into motion a set of frauds concerning spousal and filial identifications. His wife, who will pass as 'Mrs Newson', is legally 'Mrs Henchard', and the baby who will pass as the sailor's daughter is biologically Henchard's. But these relatively straightforward frauds are succeeded by unexpected complications and ironies. The daughter named Elizabeth-Jane with whom Susan returns is not the same one with whom she left. While it is the townspeople's belief that Elizabeth-Jane is an adoptive daughter to the mayor which appears erroneous to the reader, in fact it is the reader's assumption that her identity as 'Elizabeth-Jane Newson' is an adoptive one that proves to be wrong. Susan genuinely believes that the financial transaction had legally remade her into Newson's wife, until she is informed much later of the letter of the law on that subject, while Henchard's paternal affection for Elizabeth-Jane grows until he discovers Susan's letter informing him of her daughter's paternity. His eventual puzzled recognition that sanguinal claims and the claims of human affection need not coincide, that this Elizabeth-Jane can adequately fill the role of his daughter, attests to the supersession of biological relationships by imaginatively created ones. In the cases of both Susan's status as wife to Newson and Elizabeth-Jane's as daughter to Henchard, a notion of family based on lived relations is juxtaposed to a legal, documented one. Acts of writing can also be used to rescript family relations, however; it is Susan's nomination of her second daughter in the same terms used for the first, an act prompted by her desire to revive the dead daughter, that in fact allows Elizabeth-Jane ultimately to take the place of her half-sister. Thus the two notions of 'forge' – to counterfeit or to make – can merge into one another.

Like the speaker in 'Her Death and After', Susan promotes a lie about paternity in order to protect a vulnerable daughter, allowing Henchard to draw the expected inference about Elizabeth-Jane's identity. Susan's deception is paralleled by the narrator's; he withholds one central piece of information when Susan is reintroduced with a daughter in tow. We read the scene through one that preceded it, assuming that the young girl with Susan is Henchard's daughter. The narrator encourages us to make this assumption, by pointing to a connection between the duo observed in Chapter 3 and the trio observed in Chapter 1: '[W]here the Henchard family of three had once walked along, two persons not unconnected with that family walked now'.[5] If Elizabeth-Jane's name is a red herring, her biological identity can be read upon her person, however; in this chapter occurs the first of two striking descriptions of Elizabeth-Jane in terms of genetic patterns. This one speaks only of her resemblance to her mother, and thus functions as a subtle clue that this Elizabeth-Jane is not Henchard's daughter – very subtle, because the emphasis on her resemblance to a young Susan seems warranted by the fact that it is her mother next to whom we view her. Just as the opening scene dramatised the notion of exchange or transfer in the context of marital relations, so this description emphasises the practice of transfer in parent–child relations:

> A glance was sufficient to inform the eye that this was Susan Henchard's grown up daughter. While life's middle summer had set its hardening mark on the mother's face, her former spring-like specialities were transferred so dexterously by Time to the second figure, her child, that the absence of certain facts within her mother's knowledge from the girl's mind would have seemed for the moment, to one reflecting on these facts, to be a curious imperfection in Nature's powers of continuity.
>
> (p. 86)

The description concerns itself less with genetic context and more with genetic process. Genetic material has been transferred from one generation to the next (just as affections and a name have been transferred from one child to another). Curiously, in its insistence on the notion of transfer, it invokes the dominant activity in the market town of Casterbridge. The genetic product thus reflects a central motif in this novel, which repeatedly illustrates the principles of exchange and substitution. Just as qualities previously located in Henchard can be found in Farfrae when he in turn occupies the position of outsider, so Elizabeth-Jane takes on the features that previously inhabited her mother.

A different kind of substitution comes to the fore, however, when Henchard learns that Susan has passed Newson's daughter off as his, rendering, her in his eyes a counterfeit product. The revelation of her paternity leads to a second, equally striking description of Elizabeth-Jane in genetic terms. In this passage in Chapter 19, a counterpart to the description cited above, we find a reflection of the other most important aspect of the Casterbridge setting, which as well as being a market town is also a former Roman settlement. The bones of old Romans are thus buried in the soil of Casterbridge; the town 'conceal[s] dead men' (p. 140). The same appears to be true of Elizabeth-Jane's countenance when Henchard examines it as she sleeps. Henchard's 'reading' of her face is mediated by his reading of another text which alters his visual perceptions, Susan's letter revealing her daughter's true paternity. In the earlier description of Elizabeth-Jane's genetic features freshness was the keynote; the faded mother's former youthful qualities were magically revived in her daughter. Now, in striking contrast, the genetic product appears not as an example of rejuvenation but as a crypt inhabited by the relics of those long dead; as in other places in Hardy's writing, the notion of the genetic legatee as a kind of ghost or spectre is suggested:

> In sleep there come to the surface buried genealogical facts, ancestral curves, dead men's traits, which the mobility of daytime animation screens and overwhelms. In the present statuesque repose of the young girl's countenance Richard Newson's was unmistakably reflected.
>
> (pp. 196–7)

The earlier description, with its emphasis on exchange, linked the genetic product to present day Casterbridge; the second one, with its archaeological orientation, links her to the Casterbridge of the past. Bodies and landscapes are often described analogously in Hardy, both serving as canvases on which the traces of history are recorded; the relationship between Elizabeth-Jane's face and the soil of Casterbridge provides a particularly vivid example.

The archaeological motif in this description of Elizabeth-Jane reflects a deeper structure of the narrative. Because of the rupture I alluded to earlier between the opening episode of the wife-sale and the rest of the story, we can almost say that the plot has an archaeological structure; the initiating act in which Henchard sheds his family functions as the buried past, the base on which and over which his subsequent career is built, and which will inevitably be uncovered in the end, just as the bones of the Romans' soldiers are unearthed. The wife-sale is the hidden skeleton in Henchard's closet, corresponding to the skeletons buried in Casterbridge's soil and those buried in Elizabeth-Jane's countenance, whose re-emergence is both inevitable and startling.

But just as the genetic product can be conceived alternately as a burial ground or as a site of rejuvenation, so too, alongside this deterministic plot that dictates the exposure of Henchard's crime and his punishment is an ultimately unrealised shadow plot; Elizabeth-Jane, whose identity as Henchard's 'daughter' initially relied on an act of pretence, might effectively take the place of his lost child. For the flexibility of family relations can work positively as well as negatively. If they can be disrupted by fraud, so can they be remade through the ties forged by the imagination and the affections.

Hardy was quick to point out the historical precedent for the episode of the wife-sale. What seems so implausible as to be only imaginable turns out to have a referent in the extra-fictional world. And just as Hardy often insisted on the precedents in reality that lay behind some of the most extraordinary of fictive events, so do the 'fictitious' relationships in his stories often end up with as great a claim to truth as those with a biological or legal reality. Hardy's plots are full of instances in which fictions intervene in genealogical patterns, interventions which encompass both deliberate deceptions and a more radical questioning of the notion of 'legitimate' family relations. *The Mayor of Casterbridge* contains many elements that recur in Hardy's treatments of genealogy: descriptions of the genetic product as a text read and interpreted by others, an attention to the ambiguities that plague definitions of both marital and parent–child relations, a sense of the fluid boundaries that separate acts of deception and acts of making in the construction of family units.

From Tess O'Toole, *Genealogy and Fiction in Hardy: Family Lineage and Narrative Lines* (Basingstoke, 1997), pp. 17–23.

NOTES

[Tess O'Toole's focus throughout her study is Hardy's interest in family histories and narratives, fictions of paternity, and, in the case of Michael Henchard, the narratives which are generated as a result of lies, omissions and miscomprehension. Ed.]

1. Thomas Hardy, *The Complete Poetical Works of Thomas Hardy*, ed. James Gibson (New York, 1976), p. 27.

2. Edward Said, *Beginnings: Intention and Method* (New York, 1975), p. 83.

3. In 'The Decomposition of the Elephants: Double-Reading in *Daniel Deronda*' (in *PMLA*, 93 [1978], 215–27; rpt. in K. M. Newton [ed.] *George Eliot* [London, 1991], pp. 198–217), Cynthia Chase convincingly demonstrates that the narrative ordering of Eliot's novel deconstructs its own genealogical logic, figuring Daniel's origin as the past effect of a present cause rather than the past cause of a present effect. Nevertheless, the novel ostensibly attributes explanatory power to genetic origin, since the revelation of Daniel's family history makes his encounter with the Cohens seem fated as well as fortuitous.

4. Hardy, *The Complete Poetical Works* (1976), p. 21.

5. Thomas Hardy, *The Mayor of Casterbridge*, ed. Martin Seymour-Smith (London, 1985), p. 86. [All further references to the novel are cited parenthetically in the essay – Ed.]

4

The Mayor of Casterbridge: The Fate of Michael Henchard's Character

SIMON GATRELL

In editions read today the title-page of the novel always identified as *The Mayor of Casterbridge* in fact reads *The Life and Death of the Mayor of Casterbridge: A Story of a Man of Character*. This is a complex announcement almost every substantive element of which rewards inspection, but it is perhaps more appropriate to begin further back historically, for, as with other novels, Hardy only gradually came to this fully-fledged description of his fiction. The earliest version of the title, written at the head of the holograph manuscript and used for both English and American serialisations in 1886, was simply *The Mayor of Casterbridge*. There are also two intermediate versions to consider. When Hardy revised the text of the novel for the English first edition towards the end of 1886, he decided to provide a more elaborate title: *The Mayor of Casterbridge: The Life and Death of a Man of Character*. Contemporary reviewers found material in this statement on which they could base a critical discussion of the novel, and in one of those characteristic responses to the fooleries of critics to which Hardy found himself throughout his life only too prone, he reduced this version when the novel was first reprinted in 1887 in one volume to *The Mayor of Casterbridge: A Story of a Man of Character*. It remained thus for Osgood, MacIlvaine's collected edition, and Hardy only reintroduced the 'Life and Death' element, in the form we now know it, in 1902 when Macmillan printed a new title-page for their issue of an impression of the Osgood plates.

To return, then, to the earliest, simplest title. The first question it provokes is why *The Mayor of Casterbridge*, not *Michael Henchard*? Why is Henchard's function more important than his name? The force of this question is intensified when it is remembered that he is mayor for less than half of the novel. A partial reason for the choice is probably to be found in one aspect of the novel's supporting structure of reference and allusion – classical and medieval theories of tragedy (almost purely Aristotelian, as Dale Kramer points out),[1] which demand that the tragic hero shall be a man of high social status, for whom the wheel of fortune will turn downwards. One of the novel's major topics is the nature and function of the town of Casterbridge (as the early title also suggests), and the mayor of the town is its first citizen under the crown. Although in England appointment or election to an important but temporary office does not for the most part entitle the holder to use the title for the rest of his or her life, nevertheless to have been mayor provides sufficient social status for the operation of the rules of tragedy in Henchard's rapid and inexorable decline from that status and what it implies.

Conformation with the conventions of tragedy is, however, superficial justification for Hardy's apparent concentration on Henchard's office; the name mayor means more to Henchard than it would to most others entitled to use it. To explore a little further it is useful first to go back eight years to *The Return of the Native*, Hardy's first attempt at an overtly tragic novel. The chapter entitled 'Queen of Night', the seventh of the first book, is the narrator's major attempt at defining Eustacia Vye, the tragic centre of the novel. Like the whole novel (and *The Mayor of Casterbridge*)[2] the chapter is a chaos of references and allusions, but the tendency of the whole is expressed in the first paragraph:

> Eustacia Vye was the raw material of a divinity. On Olympus she would have done well with a little preparation. She had the passions and instincts which make a model goddess, that is, those which make not quite a model woman. Had it been possible for the earth and mankind to be entirely in her grasp for a while, had she handled the distaff, the spindle, and the shears at her own free will, few in the world would have noticed the change of government. There would have been the same inequality of lot, the same heaping up of favours here, of contumely there, the same generosity before justice, the same

perpetual dilemmas, the same captious alternation of caresses and blows as we endure now.

(p. 63)

By raising this image of Eustacia ruling the world. Hardy deliberately draws attention to his insight that it is in part frustration at her lack of power in any area of life save the sexual, at her lack even of the possibility of ever obtaining such power, which drives Eustacia to the actions that lead ultimately to her death. Hardy intensifies this frustration by placing her in an environment where even her sexual energy and authority have an extremely limited range of potential subjects to subdue and control.[3]

In some interesting ways *The Mayor of Casterbridge* can be seen as a sequel to *The Return of the Native*, and in the current context it may profitably be suggested that if, in the preceding quotation, feminine nouns and pronouns were changed to masculine, and 'Eustacia Vye' to 'Michael Henchard', the passage would (in isolation) remain effective. The essential difference between the two characters is that, being a man, Henchard has the freedom and the opportunity, as he certainly has the desire, to attain power, to achieve a certain amount of control over a small section of earth and mankind. On the other hand, when we first see him he faces, in his class, another disabling obstacle (while he believes he has a second in his wife and child). The young Michael Henchard, like Eustacia Vye, is deeply ambitious, but Hardy chooses not to show the process by which, having shed one supposed impediment at Weydon, he manages to transcend the other in Casterbridge and reach his limited but real as well as symbolic power as Mayor. The narrator tells us that it is his great energy that has subdued others, made him rich, and persuaded the ruling class of Casterbridge that they would do well to let him, rough as he is, run their Town Council. We may, on reflection, not feel that such an explanation is fully adequate, but the fact that we are habituated to calling the novel *The Mayor* substantially helps Hardy persuade the reader to credit his brief account. It is almost as if we are persuaded to believe that the office was Michael Henchard's birthright.

It is not only his crossing of social barriers and his rise to power which are handled cursorily, but also his wielding of power. We are presented with no real evidence about what difference it made to any aspect of Casterbridge that Henchard was mayor. In part we accept that it is Henchard's wealth that represents his real power, and that his mayoralty is a sign of his power rather than an addition to it; but it is also true that Hardy is much more interested in the personal than in the political or social uses of power. It is further true that if the desire for the power that wealth and office can bring were all that motivated Henchard, if to be Mayor of Casterbridge sufficed him, then however tragic his fall, Hardy would scarcely be interested in him.

When Henchard has finally told Elizabeth-Jane that she is his daughter the narrator comments:

> He was the kind of man to whom some human object for pouring out his heart upon – were it emotive or were it choleric – was almost a necessity. The craving of his heart for the re-establishment of this tenderest human tie had been great during his wife's lifetime, and now he had submitted to its mastery without reluctance and without fear.
>
> (p. 125)

At this stage in the novel the desire to love is as strong in Henchard as the desire for power; and there is a further connection with *The Return of the Native*. In the same chapter as that already quoted from, 'Queen of Night', the narrator announces concerning Eustacia Vye: 'To be loved to madness – such was her great desire' (p. 66). We can adapt this announcement also to Henchard thus: 'To be permitted to love to madness – such was one of his two great desires.'

Vye's method of ruling others is through their passionate enslavement to her, it is her only available way to power; seen thus simply, she is what many contemporary readers of the novel would have called a bad woman. Henchard wants to subdue others through his passionate devotion to them. The fragment from p. 125 quoted above refers to Elizabeth-Jane, but it could apply equally to Farfrae earlier in the novel. Henchard's relationship with Farfrae is complicated, however, by his other desire. While Henchard still retains his office and his wealth, his desire for the power they bring remains strong, but (once an appropriate object appears in the person of Farfrae) his latent and perhaps not quite so strong desire to be allowed to love comes into conflict with his desire for power. It is not inevitable that it should do so: Farfrae might have been a woman (though Henchard's rather remote affair with Lucetta is all the evidence we have that he can be moved to love a woman as he loves Farfrae), in which case love need have been no obstacle to the maintenance of Henchard's power; he might have been a doctor who cured him of some obscure illness instead of curing his wheat, in which case, similarly, there need have been no opposition between Henchard's twin desires. But as circumstances (or the novelist) would have it, Farfrae's arable knowledge and his economical efficiency, his very qualifications for the position of manager, bring about a conflict in Henchard between his desire to maintain his status, and his desire to love Farfrae.

When the crisis comes, when it is apparent that Farfrae's authority in business carries more weight with the farming community than Henchard's, when Henchard perceives himself in danger of being 'honeycombed clean out of all the character and standing that he's built up these eighteen year' (p. 107), the narrator carefully points out that it would be possible for Henchard to compromise by getting Farfrae to marry Elizabeth-Jane, and (by implication) for him to retire gracefully from active business, providing the cash to finance his son-in-law's success. The firm would still be Henchard and Farfrae, and he might mellow into a Casterbridge landmark. But Henchard cannot voluntarily mingle and thus diminish his two desires; they will remain incompatible and in conflict so long as the obstacle to one is the object of the other.

From this crisis in the narrative the sequence of Henchard's attempts to love is rapid. Abandoning Farfrae as an object of love he turns to Elizabeth-Jane, only to find that she is not his daughter, and that the kiss of her cheek 'he had prefigured for weeks with a thrill of pleasure' tasted of dust and ashes. Abandoning Elizabeth-Jane he turns to Lucetta, only to find that she has turned to Farfrae. In his bid to retain the power of wealth and status he drives to economic and social ruin. The graphic emblem of his defeat is the replacement of his own name by Farfrae's on the sign above his old headquarters, but Farfrae has not only taken over Henchard's business, he has also married the woman Henchard intended to marry, and has pretty well bought all that Henchard possessed. When Farfrae becomes mayor the reversal is complete, though Henchard's desire for power is not yet fully quenched.

Abandoned by Lucetta he turns inward and to drink. His first act, though, under the renewed influence of alcohol is to force the church choir to sing the commination psalm at Farfrae; such hate is only the obverse of his love. Farfrae now treats him patronisingly as an object for charity, unable to recognise him as the same man who befriended him at the beginning of his time in Casterbridge; this patronage provokes Henchard to competition once again, first to test (at the royal visit) how far his once secure power still resides with him and then (after his social powerlessness is made evident even to him) to demonstrate that his physical strength will provide him with another kind of power over Farfrae. But beneath this hostility to Farfrae is the abiding love.

He wrestles Farfrae, and has him at his mercy. Farfrae says he should take his life: 'Ye've wished to long enough.' Henchard's reply, as their eyes meet, their bodies in a close violent embrace, is (bitterly) 'O Farfrae – that's not true ... . God is my witness that no man ever loved another as I did thee at one time ... . And now – though I came here to kill 'ee, I cannot hurt thee! Go and give me in charge – do what you will – I care nothing for what comes of me!' (p. 273). The sequel makes it clear that the desire to be allowed to love Farfrae is by no means yet dissipated: after Farfrae goes Henchard was so thoroughly subdued 'that he remained on the sacks in a crouching attitude, unusual for a man, and for such a man. Its womanliness sat tragically on the figure of so stern a piece of virility' (p. 274).

Why is the posture of submission womanly? Perhaps because it is conventionally the role of the woman to play the weaker part, to long for reconciliation, for reinstatement of regard, of affection, to want to sue for the return of love. Henchard murmurs to himself: 'He thought highly of me once ... . Now he'll hate me and despise me for ever', and the narrator continues: 'He became possessed by an overpowering wish to see Farfrae again that night, and by some desperate pleading to attempt the well-nigh impossible task of winning pardon for his late mad attack.' When Henchard does find him he says: 'Oh, Farfrae, don't mistrust me – I am a wretched man, but my heart is true to you still!' (p. 286). Henchard the bull-like man, the man of strong appetites, powerful desires, apparently thoroughly masculine, overturns the conventional expectations of the novel's Victorian readership; his passion is in submission rather than domination; he wishes to give love, to adore, rather than to be adored. Like Eustacia Vye, he is in erotic terms a character subversive of the norms of the dominant culture.[4]

Farfrae, the representative of that culture in the novel, doesn't believe him, probably cannot comprehend him. He has insufficient imaginative sympathy to understand the complex of desires in Henchard, he cannot respond to the richness and power of a phrase like 'my heart is true to you still' in the mouth of a man.

The episode has finally buried Henchard's desire for power, and he finally ceases to be mayor. His desire to love is all that remains, and Elizabeth-Jane is now the only possible object for that desire. Under pressure from overpowering need, in a characteristically impulsive moment, he tells Newson that his daughter is dead. From that moment of radical deception he is loving on borrowed time.

He sees Elizabeth-Jane and Farfrae often together: he hates the possibility of their union, he cannot accept that such a marriage would be good for her and for him any more now than he could when he and Farfrae first began competing commercially. The narrator says that uncompromising powerful impulsive desire is 'the idiosyncrasy of Henchard's which had ruled his courses from the beginning, and had mainly made him what he was. Time had been when such instinctive opposition would have taken shape in action' (p. 304), but now the 'netted lion' schools himself in restraint as he tries to hang on to Elizabeth-Jane. Henchard is to the community of Casterbridge dangerous like a wild animal; thus the network of allusions connecting him with the bull that threatens Lucetta and Elizabeth-Jane, and the references to his 'tigerish affection' (p. 91), and (after his defeat) to himself as a 'netted' and 'fangless' lion (pp. 303, 309). So long as his energy and strength can be harnessed safely for the good of the community it is prepared to give him the right he craves to assume power as mayor and to use for its benefit that energy and strength. Casterbridge is, however, relieved when, through Henchard's misjudged application of those energies in his commercial competition with Farfrae, it can deprive the barely controllable individual of power. And now he suppresses his instincts and desires in subjection to the perceived will of the beloved.

Later on the same page the narrator comments further on Henchard's subjection: 'The *solicitus timor* of his love – the dependence upon Elizabeth's regard into which he had declined (or, in another sense, to which he had advanced), denaturalised him.' It is a decline because though he needs desperately to be allowed to show human affection, he has up to now never submitted his own will or need or desire to any object of his affection, has never sought to alter his nature in order to retain affection; it is an advance because his life (and those of others) might have been less painful if he had tried earlier to alter his nature, and now at the last gasp he is beginning to see that there are communal needs and rights which in ordinary human intercourse, let alone loving relationships, require respect. In his bare need, perhaps for the first time in his life, the desire to be loved is equal in him with the desire to love.

Once we develop from the narrator's hint these alternative views of Henchard's dependence on Elizabeth-Jane, we are also forced to consider our response to the transformation that he has effected. Do we regret the Henchard who was proud, fiery, driven by imperious desires, uncaring of consequences, ruthlessly honest, but destructive of himself and others around him if they could not stand up to him, or escape? Or do we feel it is right, or a cause for gladness, that he is humbled, socialised, taught to respect and consider the lives and needs of the community if he would gain his own ends, that he becomes devious, indirect, but potentially a productive member of the social organism, a proper relation for the proper Elizabeth-Jane?

It is not an easy opposition to resolve, and it is clearly possible to hold both views at the same time, as perhaps Hardy did. In the event the question is not sustained for long, for the final object of Henchard's desire to love is removed from him by the return of Newson, and all possibility of his socialisation ends; all that remains is death.

His last words are in his will, which ends:

> & that no man remember me.
> To this I put my name.
>
> Michael Henchard.

For most of his life Michael Henchard's ambitious and passionate nature has sought the power of wealth and status – to make a name in the world. The name he ultimately achieves is Mayor of the town of Casterbridge. This name, to be known thus throughout the region, provides him at last with a space for his ambition to fill; but as he enjoys it, he finds it is not enough. It is deeply ironic, if not tragic, that his pursuit of the well-beloved reduces him at last to his bare name and an attendant, though futile, injunction that the name itself be allowed to subside into oblivion. Despite Henchard's will it is certain that Casterbridge will remember him; to have been Mayor is to have left several indelible marks in the records of the town.

So far I have only explored the first element of Hardy's early title, but it is also important that Henchard and Farfrae are mayors of *Casterbridge*. There is, though, already an extensive critical discussion of Casterbridge, to which I do not wish to add very much.[5]

Though the narrator spends a substantial number of words evoking the town and its inhabitants for us, the impression we derive from his account is by no means homogeneous. The narrator of any Hardy novel is a complex organism, and in this instance he speaks with (at least) three separate accents. The physical detail of the town derives from the Dorchester experienced by the schoolboy Thomas Hardy, walking in every day from Bockhampton in the 1840s and 50s, very much in the same way as Egdon Heath in *The Return of the Native* is the recreation of the vision of the same boy who played on Puddletown Heath in the days before he went to school – the distortions of observable reality are of the same kind in either case.

Analysis of Casterbridge is sometimes in the voice of that boy grown up and living in the town, intimately re-experiencing it, and sometimes in the voice of the cosmopolitan author from the metropole, revisiting the home town from which he has risen, patronising it by building a *pied-à-terre* on its outskirts.

Casterbridge is sometimes seen as an extension of the countryside. The functions of the town are thoroughly ruralised, and '[b]ees and butterflies in the cornfields at the top of the town who desired to get to the meads at the bottom ... flew straight down the High Street without any consciousness that they were traversing strange latitudes' (p. 58). It is the countryside concentrated, as if it were a group of rural parishes compressed into a narrower space, 'shepherds in an intramural squeeze' as the narrator describes the inhabitants of the suburb of Durnover (p. 92); the professional class that makes up the Town Council are the equivalent of the landed gentry, the village craftsmen represented by the shopkeepers (who sell agriculturally useful goods) and tradesmen (who deal in agricultural produce and perform agricultural services), the peasantry by the patrons of Peter's Finger. But there are distinctions as well as similarities.

Architecturally and historically the antiquity of Casterbridge as an urban community is carefully established, its close clutter of shops and dwellings and public buildings physically opposes the scattered countryside, sharply divided from the surrounding fields by the dark square of avenues that encloses it. Though all activity in the town is designed to serve the ends of the farmer and the surrounding rural parishes – markets, fairs, bulls and butterflies – yet still the gathering below the bow window of the Kings Arms hotel, carrying unsatisfactory loaves of bread, shouting through the window at the mayor, has a distinctly urban feel to it. For all its agricultural interdependence, Casterbridge is the home of essentially urban people. The professionals – doctors, lawyers, teachers – need the base of population to flourish. The bustle of life observed by the idle rich (Lucetta) is very different from the prospect from a manor-house window; at the other end of the social spectrum the dwellers of Mixen Lane – a fragment of the town notably outside the neat enclosing framework of hedges – are recognisably slum-dwellers.[6]

It is also true, however, that Casterbridge is contrasted with what we might think of as cities; it is not enough simply to consider town and country oppositions in Hardy. Casterbridge is urban without doubt, but it has a kind of intermediate existence which contrasts radically with metropoles; the context of comparison is partly size, partly economic function, and partly human behaviour:

> The yeomen, farmers, dairymen, and townsfolk, who came to trans-act business in these ancient streets, spoke in other ways than by articulation. Not to hear the words of your interlocutor in metropol-itan centres is to know nothing of his meaning. Here the face, the arms, the hat, the stick, the body throughout spoke equally with the tongue.
>
> (pp. 61–2)

The responses and interactions that Hardy describes are essentially rural, having nothing of characteristic metropolitan inwardness. It is a matter of expressiveness, of energy, vitality, of living your meaning, which in cities has become overlaid with the middle-class restraints of polite custom and behaviour, or the working-class restraints of secrecy and indirection. Henchard attempts a similar process when he tries to enforce standard speech on Elizabeth-Jane – the upper-middle class of the rural town aping the middle-class of the metropole. The narrator makes the direct functional comparis-on of rural with manufacturing towns. The latter 'are as foreign bodies set down, like boulders on a plain, in a green world with which they have nothing in common' (p. 62), a description that parallels the earlier description of Casterbridge: 'it stood as an indistinct mass behind a dense stockade of limes and chestnuts, set in the midst of miles of rotund down and concave field.' The essent-ial urban similarity is in the 'mathematical line' (p. 29) separating town and country; the essential difference is the harmony in which the town of Casterbridge lives with its surrounding fields and downs, the symbiosis between the two.

It is a further complicating element in the reader's experience of Casterbridge that the narrator, or at least one of the narrative voices, that of the metropolitan sophisticate, is predictably patronising about the place, talking of 'the venerable contrivances and confusions which delighted the eye by their quaintness, and in a measure reasonableness, in this rare old market town …' (p. 62)

It is thus hard to pin down in a single definition Hardy's imaginative recreation of Dorchester, and perhaps its ambiguity is essential: both urban and rural, more urban than rural, yet so far from what most readers in 1886 as well as the present would immediately represent to themselves as urban, that it seems at once rural again. Henchard is the least urbane of men, and only in such a shiftingly envisioned place could he plausibly be mayor.

Casterbridge, however, and its inhabitants are quite sufficiently urban to provide in concentrated form material for a sharp insight into economic oppression, a community at war with itself, the first that Hardy consciously offers in his novels. While Henchard resides over a banquet at the best hotel, at which guests were 'sniffing and grunting over their plates like sows nuzzling for acorns' (p. 35), the poor in the streets finger inedible bread. The same night Christopher Coney says to Farfrae 'we be bruckle folk here – the best o' us hardly honest sometimes what with hard winters, and so many mouths to fill, and Goda'mighty sending his little taties so terrible small to fill 'em with' (p. 53), and in the morning Henchard urges the Scotsman to 'a solid staunch tuck-in' on pigeon-pie and home-brewed ale, at which his plate is heaped 'to a prodigal fulness'. With characteristic irony Hardy notes that in Peter's Finger ex-poachers and ex-gamekeepers, equally victims of arbitrary rural class-power, swap stories of their bloody fights conducted over the rights of a few men to keep food away from those who need it. The condition of life, seen from the perspective of Mixen Lane, is one of perpetual economic struggle or collapse, and from this essentially urban point of view the novel might further be read as a tale of class revenge.

'I do like to see the trimming pulled off such Christmas candles' (p. 267). Thus Nance Mockridge on Lucetta at the high-point of her life – wealthy, married to the Mayor of Casterbridge, in the public eye at a civic ceremony as the first lady of the town and all the surrounding countryside. The skimmity-ride, anticipation of which stimulates Nance's remark, is Jopp's personal revenge on Lucetta for not helping him to a place, but for Nance Mockridge and others like her it represents the levelling of Lucetta to Mixen Lane, the vivid demonstration to the Casterbridge world and to Lucetta herself that she is no different from the white-aproned women in the doorways of the Lane. It is an unintentional product of the event that it reduces Lucetta further, to the ultimate condition of all humanity; and the revelation the ride embodies ensures that (unlike Henchard, the man with whom she is coupled in the ride) she is rapidly forgotten by all after her death, and particularly by her husband.

The revenge of Mrs Goodenough the furmity-seller is equally powerful and, directed against the function and the man at the centre of the novel, has wider ramifications. The immediate situation – Henchard the ex-mayor, the magistrate, sitting in the court's 'big chair', still retaining position, authority, the appearance of wealth, Mrs Goodenough standing before him, seedy, vulgar, penniless – offers so strong a contrast, that when she reveals Henchard's wife-selling and proclaims that he is morally unfit to judge her, the reader, who has always known of the wife-sale, still feels a sense of shock at the revelation. This is perhaps the central moment of the novel, the moment when the tragic hero is confronted with the consequences of his own moral flaw, the moment when the mayor understands that his power and his name will disappear. It is appropriate that it comes for the furmity-seller as a triumphant moment of class-revenge, but it is also appropriate in that Mrs Goodenough, more sharply than other characters, perceives the equality of all human beings in their weaknesses. As she talks to Susan of past days, she says:

> nobody could go, without having a dish of Mrs Goodenough's furmity. I knew the clergy's taste, the dandy-gent's taste; I knew the town's taste, the country's taste, I even knew the taste of the coarse shameless females.

> (p. 24)

Her litany of customers spans in a concentrated form the range of society; none was exempt from her own illicit trade, all are rendered alike in her account, the vicar with the prostitute.[7]

This reconnection of Mrs Goodenough and Michael Henchard contains, on reflection, more than the revenge of the underclass on the ruling class. The furmity-seller is Henchard's nemesis, but she is also his replicator in several ways.

Neither is a native of the area. The grain-based food she sells is not altogether what it seems, it has a hidden agenda, which

Henchard's 'perverseness' finds out swiftly; the grain we hear Mayor Henchard has sold was similarly not what it seemed – the bread from his growed wheat is held to be 'unprincipled', as one might say the laced furmity is 'unprincipled'. When Susan returns to Weydon eighteen years after her sale to Newson, she finds Mrs Goodenough 'an old woman haggard, wrinkled, and almost in rags ... once thriving, cleanly, white-aproned and chinking with money – now tentless, dirty, owning no tables and benches' (p. 23). The reader is offered no account of her decline, but her 'steeped' aspect in court at Casterbridge a year later, and the drunk and disorderly charge brought against her there, suggest that a partial cause at least might have been the too ready consumption of her profits. On the other hand the secret of her illicit dealing was bound to be found out at some time by someone in authority, by undercover excise officers, for example. The deleterious influence of alcohol and secrets on Henchard's career is evident.

Mrs Goodenough has a different, though hardly reliable, explanation of why she has come down in the world: 'Lord's my life – the world's no memory; straightforward dealings don't bring profit – 'tis the sly and the underhand that get on in these times' (pp. 23–4). The irony of this account is matched by the irony of Henchard and Jopp's manifestly improbable suggestion that Farfrae uses witchcraft to succeed in business, a suggestion followed swiftly by Henchard's visit to Conjuror Fall (pp. 184–6).

The furmity-seller, when interrogated by Susan at Weydon, faithfully recovers from her memory Henchard's instruction of seventeen years before to tell any woman who asked for him that he had gone to Casterbridge, when there was no inducement for her to do so, save common humanity.[8] It is similarly one of the deeply saving graces of Henchard that, amidst the multitude of wrong things he does, there is the startling and instinctive doing of the morally right thing.

Thus, when Mrs Goodenough and Henchard are brought face to face again in the court at Dorchester, Hardy has carefully prepared the reader to accept, almost before she announces it, equality between mayor and prisoner (in more than their common humanity), and further prepared the reader for Henchard's rapid disintegration. In part perhaps Hardy's motive for reintroducing her is the basic strategy which suggests that two similar careers establish a higher degree of mimetic verisimilitude than one, that the replication indicates a truth about the human condition; but in fact such replication can be taken much further in analysis of the novel.

None of the major characters in the novel is a native of Casterbridge or even of South Wessex. Save for a vague unstressed interlude while Dr Chalkfield is mayor, the chief citizens of the town are foreigners, and their wives are foreigners. All enter the novel with barely enough money to survive upon, and all at some time achieve or marry wealth and power. From the current point of view in the novel we may say that Lucetta was brought down by class-warfare, as was Henchard, and (possibly) the furmity-woman. All of which leads to the question: Is there any reason to think that Farfrae will not be similarly reduced? Does the fiercely repetitive nature of the plot more or less force us to the conclusion that Farfrae too will be driven to a fall by the underclass of Casterbridge, and Elizabeth-Jane with him? Well, I would like to postpone considering this question until later, since there are other issues raised by the extended title of the novel that have first to be taken into account.

For the first edition of the novel, it will be remembered, Hardy augmented the title to read: *The Major of Casterbridge: the Life and Death of a Man of Character*, adding two further elements that provoke discussion. There is a fairly straightforward though superficial reason available for the introduction of 'Life and Death'. The stress in the earlier simpler title on the office rather than the in-dividual left the way open for perverse readings of the novel that would give as much consideration to Farfrae as to Henchard, or even more perverse, that might argue that Farfrae, the surviving mayor at the end of the novel, is the true centre of the narrative. I have no wish to explore these possibilities, though it is easy enough to imagine how an argument might be framed, setting aside in the process only the whole tonal structure of the novel. It was perhaps in part to dissociate himself from any such possible reading that Hardy developed the more elaborate title, pinning the name Mayor firmly to the name Michael Henchard.

The effect of introducing the phrase 'Life and Death' goes, however, beyond that proposed in such an explanation. It raises two questions: first, if Hardy wishes thus to stress Henchard's life in the novel, why are twenty years of his brief maturity passed over; and second, what in the novel suggests that Henchard's death should be held thus in balance with his life?

An answer to the first question can be reached by reconsidering Henchard as mayor from a slightly different point of view. When Susan and Elizabeth-Jane see him through the window of the King's Arms, Henchard has reached a crucial moment in the development of his life. Aged forty, he has fulfilled the prediction he made of himself to the company in Mrs Goodenough's tent at Weydon: 'I'd challenge England to beat me in the fodder business; and if I were a free man again I'd be worth a thousand pound before I'd done o't' (p. 10).[9] He is wealthy; and more, he is the first citizen of his chosen town. The progress of his life for the last nineteen years is summarised by his success, and Solomon Longways provides the essentials for the reader (and Elizabeth-Jane); first that he is lonely, and then that he is

> the powerfullest member of the town-council, and quite a principal man in the country round besides. Never a big dealing in wheat, barley, oats, hay, roots, and such-like but Henchard's got a hand in it. Ay, and he'll go into other things, too; and that's where he makes his mistake. He worked his way up from nothing when 'a came here; and now he's a pillar of the town. Not but what he's been shaken a little to-year about this bad corn he has supplied in his contracts.
>
> (p. 37)

Farfrae, passing the hotel, hears Henchard defy anyone to make the bad corn good again, and cannot resist entering Henchard's life.

Henchard has achieved all the material goals his imagination can suggest to him, and he knows they are not enough; he is alone, 'stately and vertical, silently thinking' (p. 40), while his fellow diners melt into drunken bonhomie. The whole of his life since rejecting Susan, even including his misty affair with Lucetta in Jersey, has been merely a preparation for the moment in which he meets Farfrae and conceives a passionate love at first sight for him. The personal has re-entered his life, and his crisis begins, the conflict between his twin desires the course of which has already been sketched. Hardy implies, perhaps, in his expanded title, that Henchard's significant life, which was suspended when he failed to find Susan and Elizabeth-Jane, resumed only when he drew Farfrae into it.

The result is the inexorable and distinctly rapid process towards death, more than one death. He dies as a man of wealth and power, as mayor, long before he dies bodily. Once he is bankrupted and all that he possessed is auctioned, 'there was quite a sympathetic reaction in the town, which till then for some time past had done nothing but condemn him' (p. 220). Henchard's life as a public man is ended, framed for the townsfolk to examine. 'Now that Henchard's whole career was pictured distinctly to his neighbours, and they could see how admirably he had used his one talent of energy to create a position of affluence out of absolutely nothing – which was really all he could show when he came to the town as a journeyman hay-trusser with his wimble and knife in his basket – they wondered, and regretted his fall' (like the chorus in a classical tragedy). He seeks bodily death through suicide, but is metaphorically and painfully reborn for a brief life as a man for whom love is all-in-all; but the object of his love is withdrawn, and finally naked of desires, even of the desire for nourishment, taking all responsibility for all his actions into himself, he wastes away, and dies indeed.

This death is as strong evidence as one could wish to show how Hardy strained at the boundaries of realist fiction. The closest parallel is with Heathcliff, though the agent of Henchard's death is no spirit once human, but, perhaps, 'the coming universal wish not to live' (*Jude the Obsure*, p. 355). The death at an early age, through self-neglect and mental self-torture, of Louis Trevelyan (in Trollope's *He Knew He Was Right* [1869]) is a good example of how a fully realist novelist handles a similar situation. Henchard dies when he does because that is when he must die, because the imaginative logic of the narrative demands it; we only do not question his death, because we know it is right.

And then, finally, there is in the title the phrase that has remained crucial for very many interpreters of the novel: 'a man of character'. My attempt to understand what such a description of Henchard implies turns on a passage from John Stuart Mill's *On Liberty*. There is a certain amount of external evidence that Hardy knew the piece well, for he wrote on 20 May 1906 to *The Times* (the occasion was the centenary of Mill's birth) of his hearing Mill speak in 1865, identifying him as 'the author of the treatise *On Liberty* (which we students of that date knew almost by heart)'.[10] In these days we are not so familiar with *On Liberty*, and in order to establish the connection between Hardy's creation and Mill's analysis, substantial quotation from this third chapter, *Of Individuality*, is not redundant, if read with Henchard's character in mind.

Mill is concerned to show that contemporary society is mistakenly distrustful of extraordinary individuals who have unique talents in various directions; in these lines he discusses the significance of the person who possesses powerful desires and impulses:

> To a certain extent it is admitted, that our understanding should be our own: but there is not the same willingness to admit that our desires and impulses should be our own likewise; or that to possess impulses of our own, and of any strength, is anything but a peril and a snare. Yet desires and impulses are as much a part of a perfect human being, as beliefs and restraints: and strong impulses are only perilous when not properly balanced; when one set of aims and inclinations is developed into strength, while others, which ought to coexist with them, remain weak and inactive. It is not because men's desires are strong that they act ill; it is because their consciences are weak. There is no natural connexion between strong impulses and a weak conscience. The natural connexion is the other way. To say that one person's desires and feelings are stronger and more various than those of another, is merely to say that he has more of the raw material of human nature, and is therefore capable, perhaps of more evil, but certainly of more good.

The man of strong desires and impulses, Mill says, is potentially a greatly good man, so long as there is a balance in him between his desires and impulses and his conscience. This is a way of formulating the essence of much tragedy, for we may suppose that it is rare for any individual to hold within them this essential balance. More often, like most of Shakespeare's tragic figures, the intensity of desire and the power of its impulsive expression is at crucial moments uncontrolled by the conscience acting through the will. And so it is with Henchard. Amongst them the narrator and the other characters draw frequent attention to Henchard's deeply impulsive nature, put in service of his powerful ambition and his underlying desire to love. At the same time events demonstrate that at crucial moments in his life his conscience proves inadequate to the task of controlling his impulses. At first it seems like some diminishment of this condemnation that when he sells his wife, when he directs the commination psalm at Farfrae, when he interrupts the royal visit to Casterbridge, when he all but kills Farfrae in the hay-loft, he does so under the influence of alcohol, the effect of which is to put his conscience to sleep. But this is only the postponement of responsibility, for he deliberately drinks in order to dull his conscience, in order to allow his impulses to have free rein. And to make clear what Henchard is capable of, his final destructive impulsive act, when he tells Newson that his daughter is dead, is performed when he is perfectly sober.

Nevertheless readers have always recognised that Henchard has a greater potential, a fuller humanity than anyone else in the novel. It is in part his tragedy that his potential is not fulfilled. The identification of Mill's account with Henchard is reinforced in the continuation of the paragraph from *On Liberty*:

> Strong impulses are but another name for energy. Energy may be turned to bad uses; but more good may always be made of an energetic nature, than of an indolent and impassive one. Those who have most natural feeling, are always those whose cultivated feelings may be made the strongest. The same strong susceptibilities which make the personal impulses vivid and powerful, are also the source from whence are generated the most passionate love of virtue, and the sternest self-control. It is through the cultivation of these, that society both does its duty and protects its interests: not by rejecting the stuff of which heroes are made, because it knows not how to make them.

It is Henchard's extraordinary energy which allows him to surmount the prejudices of the ruling society of Casterbridge and compels them to elect him mayor, and, as Mill reiterates the supremacy of the energetic nature when combined with 'the most passionate love of virtue, and the sternest self-control', we recognise again the potential within Henchard that is essentially unfulfilled.[11]

Immediately Mill defines what he means by 'character', and here is the source for the final element in Hardy's title:

> A person whose desires and impulses are his own – are the expression of his own nature, as it has been developed and modified by his own culture – is said to have a character. One whose desires and impulses are not his own, has no character, no more than a steam-engine has a character. If, in addition to being his own, his impulses are strong, and are under the government of a strong will, he has an energetic character.

The remainder of the passage from *On Liberty* that I wish to quote turns from the definition of the potential Carlylean hero to a brief account of why contemporary society finds it hard to accept such individuals:

> Whoever thinks that individuality of desires and impulses should not be encouraged to unfold itself, must maintain that society has no need of strong natures – is not the better for containing many persons who have much character – and that a high general average of energy is not desirable.

In some early states of society, these forces might be, and were, too much ahead of the power which society then possessed of disciplining and controlling them. There has been a time when the element of spontaneity and individuality was in excess, and the social principle had a hard struggle with it. The difficulty then was, to induce men of strong bodies or minds to pay obedience to any rules which required them to control their impulses. To overcome this difficulty, law and discipline, like the Popes struggling against the Emperors, asserted a power over the whole man, claiming to control his life in order to control his character – which society had not found any other sufficient means of binding. But society has now fairly got the better of individuality; and the danger which threatens human nature is not the excess, but the deficiency, of personal impulses and preferences.

Thus, if we follow Mill, we can say that Henchard is a man of energetic character, but one dangerous to society because the strength of his impulse to power and of his desire to love is at crucial moments in his life not matched by the strength of his conscience operating through his will to prevent such impulses and desires infringing on the rights of others. Mill recognises that society is wrong (and ultimately deprives itself of potential for growth) to outlaw people of individual energy (and in fact the town council of Casterbridge does not initially do so with Henchard, but rather harnesses his energy – without however caring particularly for the individual who possesses it).

At the same time, however, Mill accepts that society has a right to protect itself when the operation of such energy limits the potential of others for growth. 'This means of development which the individual loses by being prevented from gratifying his inclinations to the injury of others, are chiefly obtained at the expense of the development of other people.' This point raises serious questions for the reader of *The Mayor of Casterbridge*; Farfrae and his wife Elizabeth-Jane are the most prominent and the most punctiliously proper representatives of society in the novel, and they reject Henchard, abandon him, outlaw him, and ultimately condemn him to death.[12] Following Mill, they are right to do so, for even if he has expiated the crime of selling his wife, he has sinned again in telling Newson his daughter is dead. However it seems clear from the hostility the narrator displays towards Farfrae at the end of the novel, and the coolness that seems the keynote of Elizabeth-Jane's nature, that Hardy and his narrator do not intend the reader to take Mill's position. There is no equivocation about Henchard's act of denial –

it is wrong; but the narrator ensures that the reader understands why the impulse to lie is so powerful for Henchard in a way neither of his judges does. Farfrae is incapable of distinguishing the man from the function, seeing him only as a day-labourer – he judges largely by the surface, and when he sees something deeper, he says: 'with a man of passions such as his there is no safeguard for conduct' (p. 242), forcing us to judge between passions and conduct, warmth and cold, anarchy and disruptiveness and moral conformity to conventions of behaviour – the range or the limits of human potential. Elizabeth-Jane is sympathetic, kind, loving even, but she has so little passionateness herself that it is impossible for her to comprehend her step-father. Even Newson, who is not bothered by the 'trick' once he has become reunited with his daughter, and treats the matter as a practical joke, is wrong in this instance.[13] It is no joke, but rather the desperate instinctive grasping of a passionate man for his last chance of happiness in a society that has little sympathy or understanding for the passionate and the energetic.

If we are inclined to forgive or even to approve Henchard's lie to Newson, then we are parting company with Mill, and becoming ourselves revolutionaries against Victorian society. This is Hardy's ultimate critique – or maybe his amplification – of Mill's ideas on a man of character. A social theorist cannot deal in individual cases, and Hardy's application of Mill's ideas reveals Hardy's fundamental discontent with a society that can abandon a man such as Henchard to death. But we cannot rest content with such a conclusion, for at the same time Hardy shows that the strength and energy that drives Henchard to success drives him equally rapidly to defeat, and the working out of this sequence suggests that Victorian society is not unique in penalising powerful energies and desires, that the nature of human existence anywhere in the world and at any time ensures that the controlled and the equable alone prosper.

This is a familiar proposition in Hardy criticism. Though the success of the mediocre is seldom found in so naked a form as it is in *The Mayor of Casterbridge* – perhaps Gabriel Oak's triumph in *Far From the Madding Crowd* is the only comparably powerful statement of the idea – from Sergeant Troy to Jude Fawley and Sue Bridehead Hardy's novels offer a series of individuals who try in some way to fight social convention and the nature of human existence, and are destroyed in the conflict.

The Life and Death of the Mayor of Casterbridge: A Story of a Man of Character is permeated with confusing and conflicting accounts of why things happen in the world the way they do. If Henchard is 'a man of character', then the place to begin an investigation of these accounts would seem to be with the notion that character is fate, even though the context in which the issue is raised in its definitive form concerns Farfrae rather than Henchard:

> Whether it was that his northern energy was an overmastering force among the easy-going Wessex worthies, or whether it was sheer luck, the fact remained that whatever he touched he prospered in. ... But most probably luck had little to do with it. Character is Fate, said Novalis, and Farfrae's character was just the reverse of Henchard's.
>
> (p. 115)

There is little doubt that this is one of the theses the novel tends to validate. When (to refer to an example that also relates to Farfrae) Lucetta says 'Donald's genius would have enabled him to get a footing anywhere, without anybody's help!' (p. 266) we accept that she is right, despite the narrator's subsequent doubts; we have no trouble in imagining him (had he turned Henchard's original offer down) the mayor of some Canadian grain-belt town. His character would ensure a similar fate.

There are, however, certain unsettling features within this apparently authoritative passage. For instance, it is not unreasonable for the narrator to stress Farfrae's 'northern energy' as the character trait responsible for his success, but he then confuses the issue by saying that Farfrae was in character precisely Henchard's opposite. This is confusing since the reader cannot help but recall the narrator's previous assertion that it was Henchard's exceptional energy which had brought *him* success. How acute, we are led to ask, is the narrator as a judge of character? Another troubling detail is that most commentators suggest (intertextually) that Hardy's allusion to Novalis's idea cannot be read without reference to George Eliot's prior use of it in *The Mill on the Floss*, where Eliot's narrator calls the notion that character is destiny one of Novalis's 'questionable aphorisms' (Book VI, Ch. 6), and proceeds to suggest that circumstance is equally powerful in shaping our ends.

Up to a point, however, it is demonstrable that the natures of the major figures in the novel shape their own lives and those of others. But the greatest problem at the heart of the proposition that character is fate is its apparent exclusivity; it tends to limit to one the range of meanings of the name 'fate', a limitation which is strongly at odds with other formulations in the novel, and with the form of the narrative itself. On the one hand there is the notion of a personal fate – what happens to a person; on the other, there is abstract fate – a force that causes things to happen to all people. Novalis seems to have had the personal sense in mind: our future is what it is because we are the people we are. Ultimately his neat aphorism has insufficient potential for the analysis conducted by the narrative voices (or by the characters themselves), and there is a plethora of references in the novel to concepts like Providence, fortune and destiny, which exclude human agency altogether.

It is inevitable in any approximately realistic interpretation of Victorian society that some characters should attribute events to divine intervention. When Farfrae finally gives in to Henchard's impulsive, compulsive desire for him to stay in Casterbridge and become his manager it is because he is convinced that their encounter is 'Providence! Should anyone go against it?' (pp. 64–5). There is a conventional Christian overtone to the word 'Providence'; and his religious (if not Christian) understanding of causation is made clear in a parallel phrasing at a similar moment of decision (his acceptance of the mayoralty of Casterbridge). Farfrae says to Lucetta (who had hoped they would leave Casterbridge): 'See now how it's ourselves that are ruled by the powers above us! We plan this, but we do that ...' (p. 243). The question is, how far do we accept Farfrae's approach to life, here or elsewhere?

That Hardy was attempting in the novel to draw a distinction between a religious understanding of a causative force and a secular one is suggested by two further passages from the novel: on p. 179 the narrator, considering the consequences for Lucetta and Elizabeth-Jane of the newly-fledged attraction between the former and Farfrae, says of Lucetta that she 'with native lightness of heart took kindly to what fate offered', and of Elizabeth-Jane that she 'wondered what unwished for thing Heaven might send her in place of [Farfrae]'. The tenuously religious Lucetta receives contentedly the chances that neutral 'fate' presents her with, but the deeply religious Elizabeth-Jane ponders on the agency of the explicitly Christian 'Heaven'.

A similar distinction is perceptible in a paragraph on p. 88 when the narrator says of Elizabeth-Jane that she retained a 'fear of the coulter of destiny despite fair promise', while reporting in the same

paragraph that she says to herself (in interior monologue) that she
will not be gay because it 'would be tempting Providence to hurl
mother and me down, and afflict us again as he used to do'.
Though 'he' is not capitalised, Elizabeth-Jane's identification of
Providence with God seems to be implied, while the narrator uses
the neutral 'destiny'.

Farfrae and his wife Elizabeth-Jane are the only characters to
attribute agency to 'Providence' or 'Heaven', and though they do
not invoke God directly this may well only be because they consider it unlucky or ungenteel or vaguely blasphemous so to do. By
the end of the novel they have become representatives for the reader
of all dominant social norms, and one of these, one indeed of the
most important, is an observance of religious conventions. There
seems to be some doubt, then, about a divine version of the causality of events.

Henchard himself is contradictory in this area as in many: he is
the only major character to invoke God by name; he is a churchwar-
den; and yet there is no sense at all of him as a man who sets any
store by Christianity or Christian observance.[14] For a brief time after
he is saved from killing himself by the appearance of his effigy at the
place he had chosen for his suicide, he wonders if his preservation is
miraculous. The narrator comments: 'The sense of the supernatural
was strong in this unhappy man, and he turned away as one might
have done in the actual presence of an appalling miracle' (p. 297).
Even when he sees that there is a natural explanation for the appearance of his image in the pool, he says 'Who is such a reprobate as I!
And yet it seems that even I be in Somebody's hand!' (p. 299). It is
just possible to imagine at this moment that Henchard has at last
seen the light, will become born again, and thus finally integrated
into society. On the next page, however, the narrator comments: 'the
emotional conviction that he was in Somebody's hand began to die
out of Henchard as time slowly removed into distance the event
which had given that feeling birth', and at once we recognise how
characteristic it is (character being [personal] fate) that his belief in a
beneficent divine providence should be purely transitory.

When Henchard decides to forswear strong drink, he does it
before God, in a church, head on a Bible; but he does so not out of
religious conviction, but because the imagery and associations of
the place and objects and ritual are appropriately solemn and portentous, and suit his current frame of mind. The narrator of
Larkin's 'Church-Going' shares some of these apprehensions.

Henchard is impulsive, and his capacity for feeling is very great; for the most part he is unconcerned with supernatural agency, but at moments when emotions of some description are intensely roused in him, he turns outside himself. When, for instance, he discovers that Elizabeth-Jane is not his child the narrator analyses his response:

> His lip twitched, and he seemed to compress his frame, as if to bear better. His usual habit was not to consider whether destiny were hard upon him or not – the shape of his ideas in cases of affliction being simply a moody 'I am to suffer I perceive', – 'This much scourging, then, is for me.' But now through his passionate head there stormed this thought – that the blasting disclosure was what he deserved. ... Henchard, like all his kind, was superstitious, and he could not help thinking that the concatenation of events this evening had produced was the scheme of some sinister intelligence bent upon punishing him. Yet they had developed naturally.
>
> (pp. 126–7)

In this passage, as in the 'character is fate' passage, there is evidence of radical ambiguity. The narrator's account is that because the pain Henchard feels is sharper than usual, sharper than he can easily contain, he turns outside himself, speculating that the force ordering events in the world, neutral destiny in this instance (the existence of which he has apparently always implicitly accepted), has for once judged him, and personally intervened with a punishment to match the crime of wife-selling. The narrator, however, dismisses Henchard's 'sinister intelligence' as the over-wrought emotionalism of an unintellectual and superstitious man, and points out the traceable sequence of cause and effect that had brought him to this moment. George Eliot would have been proud of her disciple, and the reader is encouraged to feel thoroughly superior to Henchard. But there are (at least) two narrative voices speaking to us in the novel on this issue, voices that might be characterised as 'rationalist/realist' – the voice just attended to, that finds a logical antecedent cause in the past of human action for every present event – and 'determinist/immanent will' – the voice that uses in many places 'destiny', 'fate' and other such words to indicate a force that makes things happen quite independent of human agency.

Consider, for example, the following: 'Ever since the evening of his wife's arrival with her daughter there had been something in the air which had changed his luck. That dinner at the King's Arms with his friends had been Henchard's Austerlitz: he had had his successes since, but his course had not been upward' (p. 135). Only twenty pages earlier the (a) narrator had denied that luck had anything to do with Farfrae's success.[15]

Or again this, where the (a) narrator says that access to music might have rendered Henchard less comfortless in his despair, 'for with Henchard music was of regal power ... . But hard fate had ordained that he should be unable to call up this Divine spirit in his need' (p. 296). It isn't altogether clear why music should be unavailable to him; even if he can't play himself, there is music in Mixen Lane or he can go to hear church-music. But the point is that this narrator specifically invokes 'hard fate' whose ordinance has prevented the man from gaining relief. How is this different from Henchard's 'sinister intelligence'?

Or lastly, this: 'Poor Elizabeth-Jane, little thinking what her malignant star had done to blast the budding attentions she had won from Donald Farfrae, was glad to hear ...' (p. 166). There is a perfectly adequate sequence of cause and effect in the previous chapters to account for the growth of attraction between Lucetta and Farfrae, and yet we are told here that such a rational explanation is illusory, and that Elizabeth-Jane's personal 'malignant star' had in fact caused it all.

Since the narrative voice is fundamentally contradictory, not anyway a homogeneous thing, the reader is left free to choose one or all of these methods of accounting for the way things turn out. When Elizabeth-Jane watches by her mother's death-bed we are shown 'the subtle-souled girl asking herself why she was born, why sitting in a room, and blinking at the candle; why things around her had taken the shape they wore in preference to every other possible shape; why they stared at her so helplessly, as if waiting for the touch of some wand that should release them from terrestrial constraint; what that chaos called consciousness, which spun in her at this moment like a top, tended to, and began in' (p. 119).

There is no answer, and the narrator's silence in face of these direct questions is perhaps the most eloquent commentary of all on the issue. But there is the temptation for the critic of the novel to draw back one step further towards the creative fount, and consider the role of the Thomas Hardy who is the inscriber of the chaotic consciousness/es that 'guide' the reader through the fiction. In this novel the veil of realism over the fiction is stretched very thin in some places, particularly those that have to do with the way things happen. It might be said with some justice that it is T. Hardy novelist who is fate. It is he who ensures that for Henchard and for others at the moment of intensest hope there comes crashing destruction of hope. This instrumentality of the author is closely tied up with another aspect of causality, a view that might be expressed by 'secrets are fate'.

It is possible to argue that the really disabling element in life is to have secrets; that much of the evil that occurs in this novel, and in others by Hardy – *Tess of the d'Urbervilles*, or *The Return of the Native* for instance – occurs because secrets have not been told (thus leading one to take a dim view of the ending of *Under the Greenwood Tree*).

> Had the incident [Henchard's selling his wife] been well-known of old and always, it might by this time have grown to be lightly regarded, as the rather tall wild oat, but well-nigh the single one, of a young man with whom the steady and mature (if somewhat headstrong) burgher of to-day had scarcely a point in common. But the act having lain as dead and buried ever since, the interspace of years was unperceived; and the black spot of his youth wore the aspect of a recent crime.
>
> (p. 218)

At any moment in Henchard's career in Casterbridge the revelation of this secret would have been a setback, but coming as it does at the time of his greatest financial difficulty, it prevents the possible extension of his credit through the influence of his good name, and rapidly accelerates proceedings against him for bankruptcy.

If Lucetta's secret liaison with Henchard had always been known, then there would have been no skimmity-ride, and she would not have died (though also she might not have married Farfrae). Henchard warns Lucetta that Farfrae 'is sure to find out something of the matter, sooner or later', offering advice that he cannot follow himself.

The discovery of Susan's secret would have hurt Henchard at any time; but it is so grotesquely painful as to be deliberate, not just as a fictional device for effect, but as a direct statement from the novelist about the nature of existence, that immediately after opening of himself 'without reluctance and without fear' to Elizabeth-Jane as his daughter, Henchard opens a letter which reduces all the anticipation, love, hope to a ruin of ashes. He finds she is not his daughter.

Henchard keeps to himself his knowledge of Newson's return. The narrator notes of Henchard that 'a great change had come over him with regard to [Elizabeth-Jane], and he was developing the dream of a future lit by her filial presence, as though that way alone could happiness lie' (p. 290). In the next sentence Newson returns to destroy the dream – as the narrator memorably says, 'Henchard's face and eyes seemed to die.' Secrets, Hardy says throughout his fiction, are destructive; but here as elsewhere it is not the fact of the secret's revelation that is so striking – if Newson is alive, then there is every reason why he should exert himself to find Susan and his daughter; it is the timing of the revelation at the moment calculated to cause the deepest anguish that reveals nakedly the malice of the author. Here, one might say, is Henchard's 'sinister intelligence'. Hardy simply destroys the illusion of mimesis, removes his novel from the conventions of Victorian realism, and announces that the novelist is fate.

Study of his work, particularly of the last novels, *The Dynasts* and the poetry, suggests though that there is for Hardy a deeper realism involved in his manipulation, in that he is thus only reject-ing the ill-managed plan of causation in the world. What does it ultimately matter who or what is responsible for what happens; Elizabeth-Jane's questions need no answer; it is the pain or the pleasure that results which is important.

As the man of character leaves Casterbridge as fully bereft of all things as when he had arrived there, the narrator summarises for us his thoughts:

> He experienced not only the bitterness of a man who finds, in looking back on an ambitious course, that what he has sacrificed in sentiment was worth as much as what he has gained in substance; but the superadded bitterness of seeing his very recantation nullified. He had been sorry for all this long ago; but his attempts to replace ambition by love had been as fully foiled as his ambition itself. His wronged wife had foiled them by a fraud so grandly simple as to be almost a virtue.
>
> It was an odd sequence that out of this tampering with the social law [presumably the same social law that the narrator of *Tess* says Tess has been made to break] came that flower of nature Elizabeth. Part of his wish to wash his hands of life arose from his perception of its contrarious inconsistencies – of nature's jaunty readiness to support unorthodox social principles.
>
> (p. 319)

The first paragraph neatly catches the essence of Henchard's life; but the second is rather strange. It suggests that Henchard wants to die in part because the social law is not always supported by nature. But when has Henchard ever felt that conformity with society's orthodoxy was the only virtue in life? Perhaps what the narrator intends here is to say that Henchard shares the basic human wish to have life predictable, to have appropriate effect follow the cause; when it doesn't, when we seem sport for the gods (or nature), then life isn't worth living?

On the next page there is a further portentous narratorial commentary:

> Externally there was nothing to hinder his making another start on the upward slope, and by his new lights achieving higher things than his soul in its half-formed state had been able to accomplish. But the ingenious machinery contrived by the gods for reducing human possibilities of amelioration to a minimum – which arranges that wisdom to do shall come *pari passu* with the departure of zest for doing – stood in the way of all that. He had no wish to make an arena, a second time, of a world that had become a mere painted scene to him.
>
> (p. 320)

This passage bears a family resemblance to that at the end of *Tess of the d'Urbervilles* in which the narrator talks of the President of the Immortals at play with Tess, and it is relatively easy to set aside the mechanical machinery of the gods as proceeding from the frustrations of a cynical narrative voice. If the gods really rule the world, then any claim that character is fate is nonsense, and life and free-will an illusion. But by this time we know, despite the tone, that the voice making this statement represents only one aspect of authority in the novel, which is so fragmented as to be no authority at all.

There are other questions raised by the passage. What, for instance, are Henchard's new lights? Self-restraint; humility; socialisation? And what 'higher' things might he be able to accomplish? Presumably higher in a moral sense, more directly beneficial to his fellow humans? And are we to believe that the series of events recounted in the novel has proved the world a vale of soul-making for Henchard? Apparently so, but this account seems to describe quite another man from the one we see trussing hay and wishing for death. The image of Henchard's past life conducted in an arena, full of conflicts with wild beasts and gladiators, taking up the whole Roman background to the narrative, is more appropriate.

The Mayor died a long while ago in the Casterbridge arena; Michael Henchard dies in a hut in the heart of Egdon Heath, the natural environment above all untamable by man. Like Eustacia Vye he dies because there is no longer any reason he can see to live, or because Hardy can see no reason for him to live; because ambition has dissipated and love comes to ashes and there is nothing else. Unaccommodated man is destroyed by vacancy within and by the elements without.

The last word in the novel is with Elizabeth-Jane:

> Her experience had been of the kind to teach her, rightly or wrongly, that the doubtful honour of a brief transit through a sorry world hardly called for effusiveness ... her strong sense that neither she nor any human being deserved less than was given, did not blind her to the fact that there were others receiving less who had deserved much more.

> (p. 334)

The question raised by this summary is who or what gives to humans less or more? If character is fate, then Elizabeth-Jane's understanding is sharply awry. It is most likely that she would credit the Anglican Providence with agency, but the narrator who is interpreting her thoughts would more probably have some neutral concept like the Immanent Will in mind. The reader is at liberty to feel that Hardy has so manipulated the lives of his characters that to go beyond the idea that the writer is destiny serves no purpose.

From Simon Gatrell, *Thomas Hardy and the Proper Study of Mankind* (Basingstoke, 1993), pp. 68–96.

NOTES

[Simon Gatrell's study begins with a consideration of the complexities of Thomas Hardy's titles as a means for comprehending how rich and ambiguous Hardy's writing is. He examines thoroughly all aspects of the novels, from the construction of characters and their roles in narratives to questions of narrative voice. The narrative voice in *The Mayor of Casterbridge* proves a particularly complex form, made up of several voices. Placing Henchard at the centre of his study, Gatrell reads the construction of this character through a dialogue between the novel and John Stuart Mill's *On Liberty*. Ed.]

1. In Dale Kramer, *Thomas Hardy: The Forms of Tragedy* (Detroit, 1975), ch. 4.

2. Thomas Hardy, *The Return of the Native*, ed. Simon Gatrell (Oxford, 1998); *The Mayor of Casterbridge*, ed. Dale Kramer (Oxford, 1987). [All page references to the novels are found parenthetically in the essay – Ed.]

3. Two of the three novels that Hardy wrote after *The Return of the Native* – *A Laodicean* and *Two on a Tower* – also contain studies of women whose lives are also conditioned by their lack of access to power in a male-dominated environment, despite the fact that one is fundamentally ironic, and though Lady Viviette Constantine loves and is loved in return, male authority determines her subsequent unhappiness and death.

4. Elaine Showalter's fine essay 'The Unmanning of the Mayor of Casterbridge' reaches a similar conclusion by a different route. The essay is in *Critical Approaches to the Fiction of Thomas Hardy*, ed. Dale Kramer (London and Basingstoke, 1978), pp. 99–115.

5. See, for instance, the first chapter of David Enstice's *Thomas Hardy: Landscapes of the Mind* (London and Basingstoke, 1979) with its reliance on A. Lindsay Clegg's *A History of Dorchester, Dorset* (London, 1972), and almost every substantial commentator on the novel.

6. Another aspect of the urban nature of Casterbridge is the rapidity with which gossip spreads through the community: 'By this time the marriage that had taken place was known throughout Casterbridge; had been discussed noisily on kerbstones, confidentially behind counters, and jovially at the Three Mariners' (p. 217). The actions of prominent people in the town are speedily and intimately discussed by the workfolk and out-of-workfolk of the town. Similarly, at the beginning of the next chapter: 'The retort of the furmity-woman before the magistrates had spread; and in twenty-four hours there was not a person in Casterbridge who remained unacquainted with the story of Henchard's mad freak at Weydon-Priors Fair, long years before' (p. 218). Gossip is one of the many potential agencies of events that the novel empowers, as for instance when inaccurate gossip about Farfrae's intentions with regard to purchasing a seed shop for the bankrupt Henchard creates enmity in the ex-mayor where none was intended (p. 241).

7. The incident is a triumph of a different sort for Henchard, too, in that he does not use his authority to attempt to crush the woman, but at once accepts the inherent validity of her claim.

8. It is then a reasonably harsh criticism of Susan and of conventional morality when the narrator adds: 'Mrs Newson would have rewarded the old woman as far as her small means afforded, had she

not discreetly borne it in mind that it was by this unscrupulous person's liquor her husband had been degraded' (p. 25). Elizabeth-Jane's concern for respectability, the anxiety of saving herself and her mother from categorisation by observers as 'the lowest' must share this criticism.

9. This speech echoes Thomas Leaf's unintentionally comic story at the end of *Under the Greenwood Tree*, in which a man is supposed to make a thousand pounds through a kind of natural multiplication. Henchard actually does it, though we have no details about how he does it. His achievement might also lead a reader to imagine that the tendency of this novel is to attack the institution of marriage.

10. Florence Emily Hardy, *The Life and Work of Thomas Hardy*, ed. Michael Millgate (London and Athens, GA, 1985), p. 355.

11. There is a strong flavour of Blake underpinning the idea of energy in both Mill and Hardy: 'Energy is the only life, and is from the Body; and Reason is the bound or outward circumference of Energy. Energy is Eternal Delight. Those who restrain desire, do so because theirs is weak enough to be restrained; and the restrainer or reason usurps its place & governs the unwilling. And being restrain'd, it by degrees becomes passive, till it is only the shadow of desire' (from *The Marriage of Heaven and Hell*). Energy, defined in the OED as 'vigour of action, utterance, etc. Hence as a personal quality: The capacity and habit of strenuous exertion', has its earliest record in Coleridge 1809–10; but the word was in the air at the end of the eighteenth century as descriptive of painting and so on.

12. The narrator comments that 'Any suspicion of impropriety was to Elizabeth-Jane like a red rag to a bull. Her craving for correctness of procedure was, indeed, almost vicious' (p. 216). With regard to Farfrae a good example of his adherence to social conventions is on p. 307, where Henchard thinks how he could alienate 'the correct' Farfrae from Elizabeth-Jane by revealing her bastardy to him.

13. The novel defines 'practical jokes' as something rather more sinister and dangerous than I am used to considering them; there is also a considerable number of them. As well as telling a man his daughter is dead when she is alive, threatening to sell your wife is a joke (though actually doing it is not) (p. 14); making a man ride to work half-naked is a joke (p. 150); a bull charging two women intends a practical joke rather than murder (p. 207), and the same is true of Henchard wrestling Farfrae (pp. 235, 239); Henchard's reading aloud of Lucetta's love-letters is a joke (p. 251, and Lucetta herself calls it 'horse-play' p. 249); some people think the skimmity ride 'too rough a joke', and for Jopp 'it was not a joke, but a retaliation' (p. 268). This extensive list might provide the basis for a study of playfulness in Hardy.

14. There are thirteen places in the novel where God is named, and
    Henchard is responsible for ten of them (the others are Christopher
    Coney, Joyce and the landlady of Peter's Finger). From the oath he
    swears before God in the church near Weydon Henchard uses the
    name freely, telling Farfrae to 'pray to God' that he may never suffer
    fits of desperate gloom (p. 78), saying to himself that God knows
    whether Lucetta will be contented to be put off with a cheque now
    Susan has returned (p. 81), using the exclamation 'Good God' twice to
    introduce chastisements of Elizabeth-Jane's Dorset speech and humble
    actions. As he looks forward to the day when his oath will be fulfilled,
    he says 'then I mean to enjoy myself, please God'. When he has
    Farfrae's life in his hands, and the Scotsman tells him to take it as he
    has long wished to, he replies 'that's not true! ... God is my witness
    that no man ever loved another as I did thee...'

    Apart from his oath-swearing, we never see Henchard in church
    (though as a churchwarden presumably he must go), and it is hard to
    imagine him there. The narrator repeatedly stresses Henchard's super-
    stitious nature, and it would be possible to say that his frequent refer-
    ence to God is an instinctive superstitious attempt to ward off evil
    consequences rather than a deeply held belief in the Christian God's
    power in the world. A different reading might suggest that Henchard is
    more open to the supernatural, more naturally religious, than any
    other character in the novel. As usual the ambiguity leaves us free to
    choose, to construct our own meaning.

15. The Napoleonic allusion also directs one's thoughts immediately to
    The Dynasts and the Immanent Will.

5

The Mayor of Casterbridge: The Bounds of Propriety

MARJORIE GARSON

The common impression that *The Mayor of Casterbridge* is the most controlled and shapely of Hardy's novels depends upon the reader's recognition of the conventions of classical and Shakespearian tragedy.[1] Henchard, who completely dominates the narrative, is brought down by a fatal flaw which is also the source of his greatness; the plot, depending as it does on the ill-timed disclosure of various secrets which were bound to come to light eventually, is a careful structure of plausible coincidences, and – with its relentless demonstration that 'Character is Fate'[2] – a perennially useful topic for examination questions.[3] The minor characters, rightly called 'choric' in this novel, are kept under firm control, intervening only to signal important transitions in the main narrative, and so are the female characters: although the way the plot unfolds suggests that a man cannot get away from women, the focus is kept firmly on the two principal men, Farfrae gaining what Henchard loses in a way which is as schematic as the contrast between them. The text incorporates a number of parallels to *Lear* and concludes with a resonant tribute both to the oldest who hath borne most and to the young Elizabeth-Jane who, though she will never see so much, will see it steadily and see it whole through the smoke-coloured glasses of a peculiarly Hardyan pessimism. It is to the tragic shape of the narrative that we must first respond, whether or not we finally locate the novel's meaning in, or in divergence from, that paradigm.

If this way of describing the novel's sense of generic decorum makes it sound somewhat pompous and schematic, it should be added that some of the shrewdest and funniest moments in *The Mayor of Casterbridge* depend upon the reader's, and sometimes the characters', sense of the boundaries between discourses. When we first meet Farfrae singing at the Three Mariners, the class antagonism he evokes from Christopher Coney is dramatised as a clash of genres, Coney taking the singer's lyrics about 'yer own country' (p. 60) as an expression of personal feeling, the 'literal' (p. 278) Farfrae interpreting Coney's 'grim broad way of talking' (p. 64) ('the best o' us hardly honest sometimes', p. 60) as sociological data ('None of ye has been stealing what didn't belong to him?', p. 60). And at the trial of the furmity woman, Stubberd's testimony, with its euphemistic Bs and Ds and its disrupted syntax, is an ironical contrast to Mrs Goodenough's own language. When she testifies against the mayor – 'Twenty years ago or thereabout I was selling of furmity in a tent at Weydon Fair' (p. 231) – her suddenly folk-loric idiom restores to his life-story the inexorable continuity missing in Stubberd's narrative about her own; and when she objects to Stubberd's testimony on the grounds that 'I was not capable enough to hear what I said, and what is said out of my hearing is not evidence' (p. 231), the joke – which turns on her blithely collapsing two speech-acts into one (her own words then and Stubberd's words now) while simultaneously splitting the subject into two (the 'I' who speaks and the 'I' who hears the speaking) – inverts and parodies legal discourse, with its unproblematic assumption of the identity of the subject and its obsessive focus on sequentiality. In *The Mayor of Casterbridge* the discourse of the 'minor' characters is often not merely a quaint contrast to that of the protagonists but a dialogical intervention in it.[4]

In other ways, too, this novel is unusually controlled. There is little of the melodrama which for some readers mars *Far from the Madding Crowd* and *Tess of the d'Urbervilles*; few of the purple patches – like the narrator's descriptions of Eustacia and Tess – which evoke a questionable kind of pathos; little of the grotesque, or of that startling somatic imagery with which this study has been concerned. Potentially inflammable material – pregnancy, illicit sexual relationships, illegitimacy, and even the possibility of homoerotic attraction – is dealt with in terms so delicate and ambiguous that the text has traditionally been judged particularly appropriate for teaching to high-school students.[5] Unable, in the context of

Victorian expectations, to do what Henchard urges Stubberd to do – 'Say the words out like a man' (p. 231) – Hardy handles the women's stories rather as Stubberd handles the furmity woman's or as Henchard handles Elizabeth-Jane's – with a discretion 'worthy of a better man' (p. 40), as the narrator rather oddly remarks.

Lucetta in particular is a potentially scandalous figure.[6] But although the text has its own ways of signalling that she is a 'false woman' (p. 243) who could be called 'something worse' (p. 244) – indeed it makes her suggest in her own words what the 'something worse' might be (the 'woman you meet in the street', p. 283) – she is for the most part decorously enough dealt with in a somewhat stylised way for which she herself provides the cue. Content to be defined by her clothing (she will *be* 'the cherry-coloured person' for the season, p. 191) and to stage herself in a series of calculated vignettes, she is characterised by Hardy in the same way, by means of slightly theatrical encounters and elegant costume. The skimmity-ride, which reduces her to a 'piece of silk and wax-work' (p. 297), might be read as either a fitting retribution for her triviality[7] or a parody of the method by which she has been constructed by the text.

Another way of putting this is to say that Lucetta has no body. Indeed all the bodies, male and female, in this text are cannily constructed, decorously self-contained, and carefully subordinated to their thematic function. Although Elizabeth-Jane and Henchard are presented as emotionally or spiritually 'deep' – she a 'dumb, deep-feeling, great-eyed creature' (p. 152) with 'an inner chamber of ideas' (p. 109), he filled with 'volcanic stuff beneath the rind' (p. 129) – there is little of the *somatic* depth and penetrability so characteristic of Hardy. The one body on which the eye lingers for a moment is Farfrae's – on 'his cheek ... so truly curved as to be part of a globe', on 'the lids and lashes which hid his bent eyes', on the 'velvet-pile or down ... on the skin at the back of his neck' (p. 50) – but it is a female eye and it stays on the surface. Indeed Farfrae, whether in his own natty clothing or 'in the costume of a wild Highlander' (p. 121), is all surface – shallow where Henchard is deep – and the two men are constructed as opposites in every way: Farfrae, 'slight in build' (p. 42), 'fair, fresh and slenderly handsome' (p. 180), something of a lady's man, Henchard, with his 'heavy frame, large features, and commanding voice' (p. 36), eminently male ('constructed upon too large a scale' to observe the minutiae of female behaviour, p. 209); Farfrae graceful and flexible,

Henchard inflexibly erect – 'stately and vertical' (p. 44); Farfrae double if not duplicitious – described in terms of 'second thoughts' (p. 42) and 'double strands' (p. 183): 'warm or cold, passionate or frigid', 'commercial and ... romantic' (p. 183) – Henchard emphatically unitary: straightforward and single-minded. The novel encodes Henchard as a real man by setting him against the smaller, younger, more ambiguous figure. This somewhat relentless schematisation is perhaps why Farfrae does not really seem to *inhabit* the body Elizabeth-Jane gazes at: the two men's bodies are so contrapuntally moralised that they have little erotic life of their own.

Surprisingly, the women's bodies are even more generalised than the men's: Susan 'the pale, chastened mother' (p. 104), 'a mere skellinton' (p. 96); 'subtle-souled' (p. 135) Elizabeth-Jane with her 'grey, thoughtful eyes' (p. 100); Lucetta a phenomenon of 'artistic perfection' (p. 153). There is a good deal of emphasis on clothing in this novel, but it is clothing as costume or as class notation rather than as second skin. There is no sense here of sexy texture, no rustling of silken skirts, no garments which define the boundaries of the body, no textile which takes on a life of its own. (Indeed, the one peculiarly Hardyan metaphor in the narrator's description of clothing – his assertion that Elizabeth-Jane's plumes are *not* Argus-eyed – deprives her precisely of the kind of erotic self-consciousness which makes his more compelling heroines so memorable.) The most vivid image of female flesh we are given, the glimpse of the young Susan's face in the opening chapter, penetrated by the afternoon sun 'which made transparencies of her eyelids and nostrils and set fire on her lips' (p. 2), precisely makes the point that her corporeal vitality depends upon what is outside herself. Although Lucetta is pregnant when she goes to meet Henchard in the Ring to beg the return of her letters, the narrator, intent though he is on emphasising the pathos of her appearance and its power over Henchard's feelings, alludes to this fact only in the most decorous and ambiguous of phrases.[8] Female bodies in *The Mayor of Casterbridge* neither expand to decentre the man's story nor open up to expose male fantasy of penetration and control. Their containment is an aspect of the novel's tragic decorum and one of the reasons that *The Mayor of Casterbridge* has no compelling female character.

If there is a deeply imagined body in this text, it is the body of Casterbridge itself, rightly given equal emphasis, in the title, with the central human character. There is some contradiction in the way this body is presented. A rectilinear shape ('like a chess-board on a green table-cloth', 'a place deposited in the block upon a corn-field', p. 105, 'a plot of garden ground [with] box-edging', p. 30) with a firmly delineated border ('square earthworks', p. 72, 'a square wall of trees', 'a rectangular frame of deep green', p. 30), Casterbridge has seemed to readers analogous to the figure of the mayor himself with his solid 'frame' (pp. 36, 238).[9] Yet the town is also characterised in more organic terms as a 'nerve-knot of the sur-rounding country life' (p. 70), and although 'Country and town met at a mathematical line' (p. 30) its frame is nevertheless penetrable by the richness of the countryside.[10]

Indeed, the central trope in this novel is the boundary which is stable and yet permeable – the body which retains its essential shape and yet merges with or is penetrated by other bodies.[11] An aural avatar of this idea is the series of clock-bells Elizabeth-Jane hears as she enters the town, each with its own particular tune but each overlapping the next, binding the town's hours each to each in charming technological obsolescence; and the single most memo-rable visual representation is what she sees her first morning in Casterbridge:

> When Elizabeth-Jane opened the hinged casement next morning the mellow air brought in the feel of imminent autumn almost as dis-tinctly as if she had been in the remotest hamlet. Casterbridge was the complement of the rural life around; not its urban opposite. Bees and butterflies in the cornfields at the top of the town, who desired to get to the meads at the bottom, took no circuitous course, but flew straight down High Street without any apparent consciousness that they were traversing strange latitudes. And in autumn airy spheres of thistledown floated into the same street, lodged upon the shop fronts, blew into drains; and innumerable tawny and yellow leaves skimmed along the pavement, and stole through people's doorways into their passages with a hesitating scratch on the floor, like the skirts of timid visitors.
>
> (p. 65)

Doors and windows tend to be open in this novel; here they let the country in. The town is eroticised: the bees and the seeds which penetrate it pollinate it, and whispering skirts rustle here only in the timid leaves. Passageways are also important: the two women have entered the town along a 'road dark as a tunnel' to find 'a sense of great snugness and comfort inside' (p. 31), and individual buildings in Casterbridge repeat on a smaller scale the same pattern of penetration via passageway and *copia* at the centre:

> The front doors of the private houses were mostly left open at this warm autumn time ... Hence, through the long, straight, entrance passages thus unclosed could be seen, as through tunnels, the mossy gardens at the back, glowing with nasturtiums, fuchsias, scarlet geraniums, 'bloody warriors', snapdragons, and dahlias, this floral blaze being backed by crusted grey stone-work remaining from a yet remoter Casterbridge than the venerable one visible in the street.
>
> (p. 68)

To look through these houses is to glimpse the past, and so is to dig into the earth: excavators in Casterbridge may come upon a Roman skeleton 'lying on his side, in an oval scoop in the chalk, like a chicken in its shell' (p. 80) – or a foetus in the womb. Indeed once the town's framework has been firmly established and we move inside it, the square or rectangle gives way to ovoid or rounded shapes as walls bulge into picturesque irregularity.[12] The same houses which were pierced to reveal their secret gardens become bodies, 'bow-legged and knock-kneed' (p. 68), which jut into the street. The Three Mariners, famous for its 'good stabling and ... good ale', is entered through a 'long, narrow, dimly-lit passage' (p. 46) but inside it is at once snug and bountiful: beer-making facilities obtrude into the rooms for guests and 'beams and rafters, partitions, passages, staircases, disused ovens, settles, and four-posters, [leave] comparatively small quarters for human beings' (p. 50). Henchard's own house, with a passage through which Elizabeth-Jane can see 'to the end of the garden – nearly a quarter of a mile off' (p. 71), is always entered in well-defined stages, 'through the tunnel-shaped passage into the garden, and thence by the back door towards the stores and granaries' (p. 87) which are 'packed' and 'bursting' (p. 71) with grain. The garden itself, 'silent, dewy, and full of perfume', can be reached from the yard through a 'private little door' (p. 88) – the same 'green door' (p. 312) which, when Henchard has become Farfrae's employee, shuts him out from what has become 'Farfrae's garden' and from Lucetta.

Architecture in Casterbridge, speaking 'cheerfully' of fertility, of social and economic integration, and 'of individual unrestraint as to boundaries' (p. 68), has indeed become eroticised. Henchard's house, which reflects and endorses him at the height of his power,[13] also epitomises the town itself, which is at once a city, a walled

garden, and – with its stable 'frame' and rich vital centre – a splendidly androgynous body. Because, like the Great Barn in *Far from
the Madding Crowd*, this body has a maternal aspect, it is para-
doxical but consistent that the countryside is felt as enriching the
town only as long as Henchard is *inside* Casterbridge. Whenever he
is drawn out from the centre – to value the wheat in Durnover, to
save the women from the bull on the road to Port-Bredy, to spy on
Farfrae courting Elizabeth-Jane on the Budmouth Road – he learns
something to his disadvantage; and on two occasions – when he
holds his doomed entertainments on the ancient earthwork and
when he consults Wide-Oh Fall about the weather – nature turns
violently against him. Indeed, this last journey – a 'crooked and
miry' way along a 'turnpike-road' which becomes successively 'a
lane ... a cart-track ... a bridle-path ... a foot-way overgrown with
brambles' (p. 212–23) to a cottage, 'which, with its garden, was
surrounded with a high, dense hedge' – is a kind of demonic parody
of the way into his own house. And when at the end of the novel he
is exposed on the heath, the land – explicitly a maternal body, with
the tumuli jutting 'roundly into the sky ... as though they were the
full breasts of Diana Multimammia supinely extended there'
(p. 381) – does not succour him and he dies of starvation.

Yet even as it expels him, the town endorses the man who represents what was best in it. Casterbridge, open to nature and just
touched by technology but not yet penetrated by the railway, is not
punctured, does not burst, sprawl, or dissolve. This, the text seems
to suggest, is the body which produced Michael Henchard, even
though he is born as a tragic hero precisely through his expulsion
from it. Casterbridge as an erotic presence displaces and diminishes
the individual female characters, all of whom contribute to
Henchard's exile at the end of the novel.

Casterbridge is more than a physical entity; it is also a social
organism. The notion of the border or boundary continues,
however, to be important in its conceptualisation. The various
social groups which make up the town 'touch' at the very borders
which mark them off.[14] Spatial boundaries often correspond to
social boundaries in this novel. There is a precise distinction
between the clientele of the Three Mariners and that of the King's
Arms, between those who sit at 'the lower end of the table' and
those who sit at the top, between those inside the building and
those outside, between 'the west end of a church' and 'the leading
spirits in the chancel' (p. 40); there is a clear if subtle difference

between the two bridges which mark at once 'the lower part of Casterbridge town' and 'the merging point of respectability and indigence' (p. 257), and between the two classes of alienated men who frequent them. 'Merging points' are important: the novel deals with points of contact between social groups and with moments of penetration.

Boundaries and their breaching help to construct the figure of Henchard in his social and economic as well as in his personal relationships. The mayor's relationship to the town is adumbrated in the episode which introduces him, when he is seen at the King's Arms sitting in that 'spacious bow-window' which 'projected into the street' (p. 35), exposed to the people on the pavement, who can enter the dialogue without entering the building.[15] The scene in fact punctually dramatises the very situation which will bring about his downfall – his accountability to the ordinary people of the town and yet his distance from them – as well as the quality in him which will make him vulnerable. Henchard is an expansive character who eventually expands too far. Continually blundering across borders he ought to have respected, he expands – like the bow window he sits in, like the bad bread he is responsible for, which runs all over the ovens – until he falls flat, goes 'so far afield' (p. 123) that he ends up on the heath. Yet the image of the mayor in the window, while ominous in the context of the plot, is also ideologically and generically reassuring, endorsing as it does the basic institutions of a nation whose ordinary people are used to making their voices heard while at the same time making an easily readable distinction between those anonymous voices and the larger individualised figure who is being framed for his central role in the tragedy.

The novel seems to depict as a particularly English strength the mingling of classes and the crossing of boundaries. All but one of the novel's main characters move on a horizontal axis, entering the town on foot and mingling with its people as they become established. Farfrae succeeds because he is willing to move from Scotland to England and America and because his affability and competence soon commend him to the local people; Elizabeth-Jane is idealised at the Three Mariners for her 'willingness to sacrifice her personal comfort and dignity to the common weal' (p. 49) and in Henchard's household for keeping the feelings of the servants in mind;[16] Henchard, on foot at the beginning and end of the novel, comes to grief when he loses contact with his customers and his fellow townsmen. Lucetta alone, with her 'ups and downs' (p. 187), is defined from the beginning on a vertical axis and in terms of her 'great elevation' (p. 309) above the community. Looking down from High-Place Hall on to a town square which serves as 'the regulation Open Place in spectacular dramas' (p. 190), she is an observer of rather than a participant in the theatre of the town. Inevitably, it is when she hears the two housemaids identifying her effigy – "tis dressed just as *she* was dressed when she sat in the front seat at the time the play-actors came to the Town Hall!' (p. 320) – and realises that she is not part of the audience but part of the play that she is brought low.[17] Pride will have a fall, as we know from the moment we hear the name of her mansion.

It is perhaps worth noting however that the metaphor cuts both ways. The very imagery of the theatre which satirises Lucetta as a mere observer also focuses attention upon her and on those who come to visit her. It is the people in the box seats who are after all the protagonists in the drama *we* are watching. While endorsing the life of the common person by implicitly criticising Lucetta for looking *down* on it, Hardy's fable at the same time unabashedly chooses as its central characters only individuals who are elevated by their uncommonness. Our sense of generic conventions reinforces the social distinctions which the narrative takes for granted even as it uses Lucetta and her mansion to moralise about them.

The novel handles criminality with a similar ambiguous tact. The group which destroys Lucetta is identified with a particular part of town, Mixen Lane – an area which, though quite distinct from Casterbridge proper, also has permeable boundaries. Though the clientele of Peter's Finger is quite different from the Three Mariners', 'the lowest fringe of the Mariners' party touched the crest of Peter's at points' (p. 296). Mixen lane itself has a mixed population – it is home not only to petty criminals but also to 'needy respectability' (p. 295) – and in Peter's Finger 'ex-poachers and ex-gamekeepers, whom squires had persecuted without a cause' (p. 296) consort amicably enough. Prostitutes standing in doorways invite border-crossing; Peter's Finger itself, with its unused front door and its well-used side door, functions as the town's back door, and much is made both of the river which separates it from the countryside and of the traditional process by which this border can be breached.

The Mixen-Lane mixin' is on the whole presented with sympathy and with humour. Yet the crossing of legal and social lines is cannily handled. While Hardy presents Mixen Lane's evasion of the police as a game and suggests that the solidarity of poacher and gamekeeper against an oppressive system has some legitimacy, at the same time he presents the pathos of 'needy respectability' precisely in terms of its being obliged to mix with genuinely low-life characters. The text suggests that the strength of English life is in the flexibility of its social borders, but its tolerance of Mixen Lane is made possible by the very borders, internal and external, which constitute it. Hardy can express a certain sympathy with the dispossessed within a fictional structure which keeps them firmly in their place.

The novel, then, has a powerful investment in the permeable boundary as a positive image. There is one passage, however, which violently reverses these established associations and also undercuts the essential verticality of Lucetta's home, High-Place Hall. This mansion is initially presented, with an almost Gothic intensity, as a border-point – a point at which the upper world and the underworld have met. Like Peter's Finger, the building has two doors and the back one is involved with criminal activity: it opens on to a sinister alley by which 'it had been possible to come unseen from all sorts of quarters in the town – the old play-house, the old bull-stake, the old cock-pit, the pool wherein nameless infants had been used to disappear' (p. 161). It is at this point that the *corps morcelé* reappears: the mask on the *key*stone of the door, traditionally stoned by Casterbridge boys, has become almost as 'ghastly' as Troy's gargoyle, with its 'comic leer' and its lips and jaws 'chipped off ... as if they had been eaten away by disease' (p. 161). Perhaps because of the previous reference to unwanted pregnancy, the macabre image of the mouth decayed and gaping suggests sexual horror, syphilitic degeneration, and the mask above the door becomes itself a kind of door (or key*hole*?), a terrifying aperture which devours and contaminates.

We might expect truly corrupt dealings to take place in that lane, but they do not (the only time the door is actually used is when Henchard goes through it to visit Lucetta, narrowly missing Elizabeth-Jane). Just for this reason, it becomes clear, if only in retrospect, that the house asks to be read as emblematic. But emblematic of what, precisely? There seem to be three alternatives, which depend upon three unstated analogies with other figures in the text. If we see the house with its two doors as like Peter's Finger, the analogy is between the corruption of wealth and the corruption of poverty. By having the mansion announce that

'Blood built it, and Wealth enjoys it' (p. 160), the text might seem to identify Lucetta with a social class whose economic exploitation and decadent pleasures have oppressed and even helped criminalise the underclass which destroys her.[18] (The language taints Lucetta not Mixen Lane, whose individual inhabitants are never involved in the vicious and depressing activities adumbrated here.) If on the other hand High-Place Hall is – as most readers assume and as the sexual imagery implies – like Lucetta herself, the mansion points to her duplicitous character and suppressed past, perhaps even to her 'ghastly' body, and hints at the kind of corruption Hardy cannot make explicit.[19] If, finally, Lucetta's house is – like Henchard's – seen as an epitome of the town of which it is a part, its ominous 'back door' is Mixen Lane itself, the *porta Esquilina* of Casterbridge.[20] These readings work in opposite directions: while the first two tend to imply that Lucetta deserves what she gets, the third casts a more sinister light on her victimisers than readers are accustomed to notice.

This last suggestion might be allowed to unfold. Unlike High-Place Hall's, Casterbridge's 'back door' does figure in the plot: it admits Newson, who not only intervenes to disastrous effect in Henchard's life but who also contributes to the skimmity-ride which kills the lady of High-Place Hall. Lucetta is a peculiarly disposable character,[21] discarded as easily as her effigy, which – unlike Henchard's – never turns up to haunt the story with a specular *frisson*. Perhaps because the skimmity-ride, as Henchard himself points out, kills her but saves his life, its organisers are dealt with complacently enough – their duping of the constables treated as essentially comic – and Newson's willingness to contribute to the fun seems merely an index of his rather thoughtless geniality.

Responding no doubt to the dominant tone of the narrative here, few readers take the criminality of the skimmity-ride very seriously, apparently assuming that Lucetta's miscarriage and death were not foreseen or intended by its organisers.[22] The impression is facilitated by Victorian decorum – the decorum which forbids specific or repeated references to Lucetta's pregnancy. A reader who cannot be very aware of her condition as the skimmity-ride is being planned can be counted on not to raise the question of whether the people in Peter's Finger would have been aware of it (but surely they would?). Politics of class displace politics of gender: foregrounding Lucetta's power as a wealthy person – as Nance and the group do as they discuss bringing her down – obscures her vulnerability as a pregnant woman – which Hardy cannot in any case have them discussing – and allows the danger and malice of what they are doing to be underplayed.

The text, then, although it allows a 'political' reading of Lucetta's fate, also contains an excess of meaning which complicates such a reading. By treating the Mixen-Lane machinations as social comedy and by metaphorically displacing the less endearing kinds of criminality from Mixen Lane on to Lucetta, Hardy loads the narrative against her in ways which seem motivated as much by misogyny as by sympathy with the underclass. Because Hardy is making the town into a positive body which will be used to endorse Henchard, and because he is willing to taint with deeply sinister associations the woman who prefers Farfrae to his protagonist, he constructs Casterbridge's doubleness as social flexibility and displaces that doubleness on to the duplicitous woman. Permeability can be constructed as creative and comic on condition that the too-penetrable, too-flexible woman be cast out. Lucetta miscarries and dies: the expansive potential of the female body is decorously displaced to testify to masculine magnanimity and to the organic vitality of the community which has killed her.

The survivors in the novel have – like Hardy himself – a canny sense of boundaries. While intuitively aware of borders, Farfrae is untroubled by them; he can move from Scotland to England, from song to calculation, from one idiom to another, in a way which keeps all his options open. Master of many discourses, he not only has a 'special look when meeting women' (p. 196) but also two distinct ways of talking: a simple, single, manly language with men and a coy, suggestive style with women – a pastiche of secondhand lyrics and sentiments. So firmly is this contrast established that Hardy can amusingly suggest a flash of real feeling in Farfrae simply by having him get his languages crossed – when during his first meeting with Lucetta he suddenly finds himself bursting into an unpremeditated paean to the joys of trading.

As Farfrae appropriates discourse, so too does he appropriate bodies. Farfrae *puts on* a role as he dons a Highland costume; he takes possession by getting inside – taking from Henchard his business, which Henchard insisted he enter, Lucetta, whom he impregnates, and his house, into the heart of which Henchard had originally conducted him. Emblematic of this facility is the image of Farfrae inside the agricultural machine – a grotesquely hybrid body, 'compound of hornet, grasshopper, and shrimp' (p. 191) – humming one of his Scottish songs. Like the figures in a Jonsonian antimasque, who metamorphose into emblems of their ruling passions, Farfrae easily assumes the body of the horse-drill – the wooden horse by which technology is being smuggled into Casterbridge? – and speaks for it. His incorporation into a technology which will obviate the old pieties ('the romance of the sower is gone for good', p. 194) points not only to his identification with the modern but also to his power to enter and withdraw from whatever machinery he puts in motion.

With Elizabeth-Jane Farfrae is equally lithe and elusive. He stays 'on the border' with her until the very end of the novel, archly humming and whistling at her, hinting at deeper intentions or at the disappointments of his first marriage, advancing and retreating in a way which causes her considerable pain.[23] Perhaps the most touching encounter between them is the one which raises the issue of touching, and has everything to do with the sense of bodily boundaries: their meeting in the granary, with its emblematic ironies and the 'extreme delicacy' (p. 108) of its imagery. Farfrae's closest approach to intimacy is the moment when he blows the dust and chaff off Elizabeth-Jane's clothing. The gesture is like a caress which moves over the surface of her body – though here it is her clothing which is of concern, and *as* clothing, not as a kind of second skin (he is afraid that rain will spoil the fabric). There is a charming decorum both in his solution, which suggests his sense both of the boundaries of her body and of the social boundaries he cannot cross, and in the solution of Hardy, who hints so deftly at what cannot be written. Indeed, the scene invites comparison with Oak's sheep-shearing and Troy's sword exercise, though such a comparison generates its own ironies: if Oak is all tender touch and Troy all blazing brand, Farfrae is all hot air.

There is a level of course on which he himself recognises this and the very recognition helps make him invulnerable. Although Farfrae owes much of his popularity to his singing and to the romantic Highland persona which the songs construct, he is quite willing to admit that his nostalgia lasts only as long as the songs. Farfrae's 'literalness' and 'simplicity' (pp. 114, 187) – the very frankness with which he owns up to what might be considered somewhat factitious emotions in this particular case – protect him from wider-ranging criticism.[24]

And they protect the text at the same time. For the way Farfrae characterises himself is merely an extension of the way the novel characterises him. As allusions to Sir Walter Scott remind us, Farfrae's famous two-stranded nature has a textual basis.[25] Generated as a 'character' not only in binary opposition to Henchard but in terms of a paradigm worked out in the Waverley novels, Farfrae, when he creates a persona from borrowed bits of speech and song, at once collaborates in and parodies his own construction. Hardy has delineated in Farfrae both the charm and the limitations of the 'literal' mind, and the instinctive shrewdness of its exploitive strategies. But if Farfrae is too 'literal' to scrutinise what he is doing, so perhaps is the text which has cannily constructed him for its own purposes.

One of these purposes is the simultaneous expression and disguise of homoerotic feeling.[26] There is a sense in which Farfrae's flirtation with Elizabeth-Jane at once doubles and blurs his relationship with her stepfather. Hardy manages, while making perfectly clear that the relationship between the two men means much more to Henchard than it does to Farfrae, to make us sympathise deeply with Henchard when Farfrae becomes indifferent to him. Because Farfrae cannot justly be accused of leading Henchard on, the text can demonstrate how the break between them proceeds from the hero's own nature, as a properly tragic plot should. But because we have seen him leading Elizabeth-Jane on, we are ready to *feel* with Henchard that Farfrae has indeed been a tease, even if we are unable to pinpoint precisely where his behaviour has been unreasonable.

The text represses this analogy, however; and it does it by encouraging the reader to take for granted an absolute distinction between male–male and male–female relationships. While Farfrae's relentless archness where Elizabeth-Jane is concerned might call into question the 'simplicity' he displays with Henchard, the text naturalises the discrepancy by consistently suggesting that, although women evoke double-talk, transactions between men can be simple and straightforward. Henchard feels a frank, spontaneous, truehearted affection for Farfrae – an affection we are not invited to question. Though it is possible to feel that there is an erotic dimension to Henchard's attraction for the younger man, Farfrae's failure to recognise the intensity of Henchard's emotion facilitates the repression of this dimension. Farfrae's unselfconsciousness keeps *Henchard* 'simple' and single, and the nature of his feeling for

Farfrae undefined and unexaminable. Lawrence in *Women in Love* will rewrite the wrestling match to release its erotic potential, but Hardy's text depends upon the reader not questioning Farfrae's 'natural' tendency to draw a firm line between male friendship and heterosexual flirtation.

Farfrae's facility in drawing lines comes increasingly to the fore at the end of the novel, when pity for Henchard's poignant situation is being demanded of the reader. Under these circumstances the narrator lets Farfrae speak for himself. When he lumps Henchard, as his employee, in with '"the rest of the men"' (p. 313); when, after Newson has taken Henchard's place as prospective father-in-law, he concludes that '"all is as it should be, and we will have no more deefficulties at all"' (p. 362); when during the final search for Henchard Farfrae demurs about going further because he does not want to stay out overnight and '"make a hole in a sovereign"' (p. 381) – Farfrae's words are given in direct discourse, and the narrator, who perhaps feels he can count on the reader's appalled sympathy for Henchard at this point, makes no comment on them.[27] On the other hand, when Farfrae, having shed wife and child so much more easily than Henchard was able to do, concludes that 'by the death of Lucetta he had exchanged a looming misery for a simple sorrow' (p. 348), the somewhat ambiguous handling of the free indirect discourse implies that the narrator endorses his judgement. Farfrae's compartmentalising is essential to the economy of the text. His 'simplicity' contains the erotic reverberations of male friendship; his equanimity as a widower keeps the fallen woman in her place. The novel needs the lines Farfrae draws to keep itself in line.

Repellent though Farfrae's canniness may appear to the reader at the end of the story, it evokes no objection from Farfrae's wife, who seems to have aligned herself unproblematically with his proprieties. Farfrae's and Elizabeth-Jane's common concern for the 'respectable' (pp. 43, 49), though it keeps them apart until all the bloom is off their romance, makes it inevitable that they should end up together. But whereas Farfrae's propriety is handled with restraint by the narrator, who leaves us, moved by affection for his victims, to draw our own conclusions, Elizabeth-Jane's is foregrounded in ways which are more ambiguous.

Readers, while not vitally interested in Elizabeth-Jane, tend to idealise and simplify her, responding to emphatic cues from the text. What is rarely commented on is that it is her terrible sense of

propriety which kills Henchard.[28] When Elizabeth-Jane primly announces to Newson that she really 'ought to forget him now'
(p. 364), when she addresses him with chilling propriety as
'Mr Henchard' (p. 376) and berates him for having 'cruelly' sent
'my warm-hearted real father' away 'with a wicked invention of my
death, which nearly broke his heart' (a 'wicked invention' of her
own), her ruthless prissiness breaks *his* heart in a way that would
seem difficult to ignore. Yet the narrator seems to ignore it and the
text almost forces us to ignore it too in the long run, because
Elizabeth-Jane is rehabilitated in the last pages to generate its philosophic ending. Our desire for generic decorum – our insistence that
character shall be coherent in a realistic novel – invites us to repress
or downplay evidence which seems contradictory. I propose to read
Elizabeth-Jane more sceptically as a construction of the text and to
look particularly at the gaps and discontinuities in the treatment of
her propriety.

On the whole the text seems to approve of Elizabeth-Jane's sense
of decorum, for it is in terms of this that her sensitivity, refinement,
and maturity are constantly defined. It is her almost paranoid sobriety, her very moderate estimate of life's possibilities, which is the
basis of her judgement of what is fitting, and that sobriety seems
usually to be presented as wisdom. Her humility, as well as her conviction that mental cultivation is more important than physical, make
her uncomfortable with showy clothing; her sense of the seriousness
of life makes her dislike jokes and indeed any kind of premature or
excessive celebration – even dancing at her own wedding. The coda
of the novel ('happiness was but the occasional episode in a general
drama of pain', p. 386) seems generated equally by Elizabeth-Jane
and by the narrator, who endorses, by expressing it in his own idiom,
the attitude he describes. It seems clear that some of her authorial
father's own attitude to life has gone into the construction of
Elizabeth-Jane and that she is to be seen as decidedly superior to the
ordinary woman precisely because of her greater seriousness of mind.

The treatment of Elizabeth-Jane's various excellences remains
however somewhat blurred and ambiguous. Take for example the
issue of her self-improvement – so vital an aspect of *Jude the
Obscure* and presumably so meaningful to Hardy himself. We keep
being told that she is improving her mind and that her main interest, when she achieves a degree of middle-class security, is to rectify
those inadequacies of education and culture of which she is so conscious. Henchard, when he visits her room after her departure, is

touched and impressed to find it full of 'books, sketches, maps, and little arrangements for tasteful effects' (p. 196). But it is hard to believe in those books she reads so 'omnivorously' (p. 149), hard to imagine them actually being consumed,[29] for these are books without *bodies*, without print or binding or titles. (Henchard's own token library, with its three titled volumes, is more fully realised.) It is hard, too, to believe that Elizabeth-Jane gains in wisdom and understanding as her education progresses, for she is already level-headed and wise and temperate when we first meet her. She is also well spoken. It is not the articulate young woman we meet in Chapter 2 but young Thomas Hardy who calls wild hyacinths greggles;[30] the only time Elizabeth-Jane uses dialect words is when Henchard chastises her for it, and the only way we know which specific words she learns to avoid is in the paragraph where the narrator tells us she used them no more.

We must believe, on the other hand, in her sartorial transformation. When Elizabeth-Jane first meets Farfrae, her 'plain dress' is in accord with her 'earnestness and soberness of mien' (p. 63) and he appreciates the harmony. When her adoption by Henchard has enabled her to improve her wardrobe, Elizabeth-Jane resolves not to 'blossom gaudily' and suddenly, feeling that to do so would be 'inconsistent with her past life' (p. 109). The narrator's florid characterisation of the attitude she does *not* take – 'she refrained from bursting out like a water-flower that spring, and clothing herself in puffings and knick-knacks, as most of the Casterbridge girls would have done in her circumstances' (p. 100) – is presumably to be read as praise of her moderation. But because each item she purchases demands something else to 'go with' it, to 'harmonise' (p. 109), she ends up remade from top to toe. The metamorphosis is oddly enough effected by the same principle of decorum which had kept her plainly dressed before. The fact that she is then said to be distressed by the discrepancy between her improved appearance and her unimproved intellect is (so to speak) window dressing. What has been dramatised is the change in her appearance, and if we are impressed by her it has to be at least in part by the same phenomenon which impresses the worldly observers of Casterbridge, if not for the same reason.

'We now see her in a black silk bonnet, velvet mantle or silk spencer, dark dress, and carrying a sunshade' (p. 101). The change in her wardrobe marks the change in her social status. The sunshade is to protect her skin, to keep it white. Pale skin is a mark of

beauty because it is a mark of social class, a sign which differentiates the middle class from the working woman. How we are to
read Elizabeth-Jane's attitude to such differentiation remains
undecidable.

Elizabeth-Jane will be blamed by her father for not drawing the
line clearly enough. Though from the time she is adopted by
Henchard she earnestly desires to fulfil his expectations and is
terrified of the possibility that 'her tastes were not good enough for
her position, and would bring her into disgrace' (p. 125), Elizabeth-
Jane keeps making mistakes, apparently because of her natural,
artless humility. Hardy enlists our sympathy for her in a series of
episodes which cast Henchard as the heavy father and Elizabeth-
Jane as his innocent victim. When he berates his stepdaughter for
dancing with Farfrae, using dialect words, failing to write lady's-
hand, and thanking the housemaid, Henchard is brutal, arbitrary,
and clearly wrong. But the longer the sequence goes on the more
questionable it becomes, and its climax – the scene when she carries
bread and cider to Nance Mockridge – undercuts the very pattern it
seems to complete.

By this time one might expect Elizabeth-Jane – so 'thoughtful'
(p. 100), 'reflective', and 'observant' (p. 196) – to think twice before
serving the servants: it is equally hard to believe, after four previous
warnings, either that she would believe such a gesture appropriate
or that she would do it if she did not. The way Nance is described –
standing, like the prostitutes in Mixen Lane, 'with her hands on her
hips, easefully looking at the preparations on her behalf' (p. 151) –
and the way she behaves complicate the situation. While Nance's
instinct to snap back at Henchard is understandable, her exposure
of Elizabeth – at best impulsive, at worst gratuitously spiteful – displays her as inferior in moral as well as in social qualities to the
mistress who serves her.[31] The more deeply we sympathise with
Elizabeth-Jane, the more strongly we register the misdirected malice
of Nance's retort.

Accordingly Elizabeth-Jane's implausible gesture marks the point
at which too much deference to the working classes becomes indecorous. Even while we recoil from the *manner* in which
Henchard attacks her and Nance, his *judgement* seems to be
confirmed by Nance's vengeful reflex, and his *motive* may evoke
our sympathy: his baffled rage can be read as a defence against the
affectionate pride he had begun to develop in her, a pride based
partly on his sense of her social superiority to himself. Hardy seems

to be implicated with Henchard in his attraction to the refinement of their 'daughter' and in the sense of her (specifically class-based) superiority to the working people from whom she has risen.

The anomalies here invite a rereading of the episode to which Nance refers – the scene in the Three Mariners where Elizabeth-Jane worked to help pay for their room. They might even remind us that the narrator's praise of her as willing 'to sacrifice her personal comfort and dignity to the common weal' (p. 49) is illogical. It is because she herself insists on being 'respectable' that she and her mother are in the Three Mariners in the first place; working for the room is not sacrificing her dignity but preserving it, and she is doing it for herself as much as for 'the common weal'. And her demeanour in the inn manifests quite a sharp awareness of class distinctions (she will serve in the private but not in the public rooms, she does not mind waiting on Farfrae because 'He's so respectable, and educated – far above the rest of 'em in the inn', p. 64). The attempt to read her as caught in a double bind – forced to offend against a tyrannical bourgeois standard of gentility in order to finance it – is actually undermined by the specious tribute, which blurs her motivation. What seems to be happening here is that the narrator himself has enough of a stake in the notion of respectability to feel that her gesture needs to be defended.

The issue of the sunshade compounds the ambiguities. The narrator's language attributes an almost moral dimension to Elizabeth-Jane in her care of her skin ('deeming spotlessness part of womanliness', p. 101). Spotlessness is an excellent thing in a woman just because it is anomalous. The prostitutes in Mixen Lane also keep themselves curiously pristine – a quality which is noteworthy precisely because it is an exception to the rule: 'A white apron is a suspicious vesture in situations where spotlessness is difficult' (p. 295). Like the prostitutes, the furmity woman, too, is distinguished by a 'white apron, which, as it threw an air of respectability over her as far as it extended, was made so wide as to reach nearly round her waist' (p. 5) and which even at her trial contrast 'visibly with the rest of her clothes' (p. 229). An apron throws an 'air of respectability' over a woman by concealing and displacing what the furmity woman exposes when she is caught committing a 'nuisance' (p. 230) in the gutter by the church.[32] Mrs Goodenough is the novel's witch – she is repeatedly described as a 'hag' (pp. 6, 23, 24) and a 'haggish creature' (p. 5) – and the narrator also describes Elizabeth-Jane, in her prescience, as a 'discerning silent witch'

(p. 197).[33] The very language which differentiates Elizabeth-Jane not only from the working woman but from the fallen women and the witch links her, as a woman, with them as well.

Indeed, although she is schematically contrasted to Lucetta and at key moments opposes her, Elizabeth-Jane becomes defined for us to some extent as Lucetta is defined, in terms of her clothing and her image in the mirror. Although Lucetta speaks of herself *as* clothing, the narrator actually tells us as much about Elizabeth-Jane's wardrobe as about hers. Lucetta is introduced as Elizabeth's 'wraith or double' (p. 153) and the women – both of whom have occasion to examine themselves in the glass and predict, ruefully, the coolness of male response to their physical charms – are constructed by and in mirrors. Lucetta's experience of the skimmity-ride is a specular epiphany: hearing the voices of 'scandal' in the excited conjectures of the housemaids, seeing herself as others see her ("'Tis me!'), and as her husband will see her from now on, she suddenly understands that her world is a hall of mirrors and the revelation kills her. But this violent event is foreshadowed not only by the scene in which Lucetta searches her glass for signs of ageing but also by the moment when Elizabeth-Jane looks at her carefully adorned self as she would be looked at by Farfrae and 'luminously' comprehends that her appearance is '"just enough to make him silly, and not enough to keep him so"' (p. 128). It is because Elizabeth-Jane is aware of the specular nature of the subject – more aware, perhaps, than any of Hardy's other characters – that she is so stoical and self-controlled; but she is ineluctably linked with Lucetta nevertheless, defined, like all of Hardy's women, by the male gaze which alone can fulfil her.

The two women are most sharply contrasted in their notions of propriety – notably at the moment when Lucetta, broaching the subject of her marriage to Farfrae, invites Elizabeth-Jane to condone a woman's breaking her engagement to a man she no longer loves. Elizabeth's judgement – 'there is only one course left to honesty. You must remain a single woman' (p. 248) – itself evokes explicit judgement. On the one hand the narrator draws attention to her rigidity, pointing out that her 'craving for correctness of procedure was … almost vicious' and that 'Any suspicion of impropriety was to Elizabeth-Jane like a red rag to a bull' (an interesting simile in context: to the bull which 'viciously' threatened Lucetta only pages earlier?). On the other hand he apparently agrees that Lucetta ought to have fulfilled her engagement to Henchard regardless of her changed feelings (he later takes care parenthetically to gloss her dying confession to her husband, the exact words of which we are never allowed to hear, p. 332). Indeed the narrator's very intervention here functions – despite its suggestive echo – as much to explain and excuse Elizabeth-Jane's rigour as to condemn it.

This should not be surprising, since Elizabeth-Jane always lines up with the Father – whoever he happens to be at the moment – and with the patriarchal order, and that order is always endorsed by the narrator as long as Henchard is the patriarch. It is important to remember the sequence here: that Lucetta's marriage was hastened by the furmity woman's revelation and that the interview between Elizabeth-Jane and Lucetta takes place shortly after both women have learned Henchard's secret. Elaine Showalter points out a curious gap in the text when she observes that Elizabeth is never shown confronting Henchard with his offence against her mother: Hardy, she says, seems to have forgotten to write the scene.[34] Apparently the knowledge that Henchard had lied to her in asserting that he and Susan 'thought each other dead – and – Newson became her husband' (p. 140) and that he had sold her mother and, she believes, her own infant self spurs Elizabeth-Jane not to confront Henchard, not to question her own paternity, not to mourn the stain which this publicity might cast upon her own reputation but instead to urge the Father's claim to Lucetta!

The omission noted by Showalter is not the only gap in Elizabeth's story. Consider the text's account of her 'vicious' propriety. The narrator attributes it in this episode to 'her early troubles with regard to her mother' (p. 248) – evidently the wife-sale (Elizabeth-Jane admits to Lucetta that Henchard 'did treat my mother badly once, it seems, in a moment of intoxication', p. 249). But when, six chapters earlier, Elizabeth-Jane laments to Lucetta in very similar language that her mother's separation from her father had cast 'shadows' (p. 195) upon her life, she cannot *there* be referring to the wife-sale. Is she troubled by her mother's supposed involuntary bigamy? But this is a 'shadow' of which the townspeople (and presumably Lucetta herself) could know nothing, and which Elizabeth-Jane – who had transferred her loyalty to her new 'father' with some initial reluctance but with no apparent sense of *shame* – is never shown to ponder. In any case, Elizabeth's anxiety about 'respectability' antedates all such revelations: it is one of the first things we hear about her at the beginning of the novel when she can know of no 'shadow' on her reputation. Henchard, with his nagging about social decorum, plays on the anxiety – it is an irony the text does not particularly draw attention to that he helps strengthen the very propriety which leads her to reject him – but he does not create it.

The text has forgotten a lot about the inner life of Elizabeth-Jane, whose rage for order is at once overdetermined and underexplained. It is as if what Hardy knows about her – the fact that she is illegitimate – has shaped her own responses. Since we have learned to know Elizabeth as the text knows her, in terms of its needs and priorities rather than her own, we may not even register the incongruity of her reaction when the truth about her parentage does emerge. Although Henchard had plausibly believed that he could damage Elizabeth-Jane in Farfrae's eyes by revealing that she was 'legally, nobody's child' (p. 354), neither she nor Farfrae seems particularly to take in the awful fact when it is finally disclosed. Instead of the complicated dismay she might be expected to feel about Newson's exploitation of her 'simple' (pp. 17, 83) mother (dismay complicated by the realisation that it is to this exploitation that she owes her existence[35] – instead of distress at her own illegitimacy (or does it not matter now that she has acquired a stable surname from her husband?) – Elizabeth-Jane sympathises with the 'real father' (p. 376) in *his* simplicity ('you were always so trusting, father; I've heard my mother say so hundreds of times', p. 365). The one issue which would adequately have motivated her vicious sense of propriety – her shame at her own illegitimacy – is repressed at the very moment when that propriety comes most damagingly into play.

The text's forgetfulness serves its fable well. For his tragic ending, Hardy needs to have Elizabeth-Jane reject Henchard gratuitously and choose Newson over him. By having her ignore the circumstances of her birth, he can make his fictional daughter speak for the Father-as-biological-progenitor and the principle of patriarchy, and he can have her at the same time create, by means of her very rejection, the Father-as-tragic-hero she will pay tribute to at the end of the novel.

The question of Elizabeth-Jane's paternity is of course a literary trick on the reader. It is not only Henchard but the reader who is fooled by the narrator's carefully ambiguous language into thinking that the lost daughter has been found. When we discover the sleight of hand, it is a little disconcerting, perhaps because of the ease with which a girl-child can be dropped out of the text – as into that 'pool wherein nameless infants had been used to disappear' (p. 161). As Showalter suggests, Henchard would not have sold a son so easily,[36] nor could Hardy so easily have replaced one son with another. Because to his readers paternity would matter so much more in the case of a son than in the case of a daughter, one point the novel is making – that 'real' fatherhood is spiritual and emotional rather than biological – would have been unacceptable.

The whole question of the claims of paternity is, however, full of problems. If there is pathos in the fact that, though Henchard himself has finally risen above questions of biological relationship, has learned to be a father in a 'deeper' sense, he must lose the child he finally deserves, it is a pathos which blurs the real issue. The question is always about who gets the woman – whether she is Susan, Lucetta, or Elizabeth-Jane – and the pathos is that Henchard always loses to a male rival. Newson's *merely* biological fatherhood is played down only in the interests of Henchard's essential fatherhood. The conflict remains male rivalry over a disputed woman, and changing the basis of the claim from biological to spiritual fatherhood merely mystifies the notion of patriarchal possession. Though the novel can be read as a critique of patriarchal notions of ownership, I would argue that what it really expresses is the anxiety that such ownership is not possible. What happens to Henchard when his daughter turns brutally against him expresses as much the fear of a woman's 'vicious' propriety as compunction over patriarchal presumptuousness.

The focus on the rival claims of Elizabeth-Jane's two fictional fathers also blurs the paternal role of her authorial father. In her philosophy and in her deference to the claims of propriety Elizabeth-Jane is Hardy's own child. The problem is not only that she has too many parts to play in this text but that the parts are contradictory. She is the novel's 'poor only heroine' (p. 356) whose romantic feelings for Farfrae evoke our sympathy, especially in the first part of the novel, which is largely told from her point of view. But she also has to function as Henchard's nemesis – the last of the 'infernal harpies' (p. 145) which snatch away his feast, the Delilah to his 'Samson shorn' (p. 373), the tamer of the 'netted' (p. 349) and 'fangless lion' (p. 357)[37] – and thus in the final pages has to do heartless things. Yet too much cannot be made of her cruelty here, since she is going to be used in the last paragraphs of the novel to reflect a view of life very like that which Thomas Hardy in his own person has expressed in other texts. If Henchard is Lear and Whittle the Fool, Elizabeth-Jane is alternately Regan, Edgar, and Cordelia. She is indeed nothing but an image in a mirror.

For all its tragic decorum, then, the ending of the novel is somewhat muddled, both because Hardy's impulse to create Elizabeth-Jane in his own image is at odds with the functions she has to serve in the plot and because the text's more liberal and generous social notions are at odds with Hardy's instinctive terror of the woman who castrates and kills. Female characterisation escapes the boundaries Hardy has drawn and deconstructs his carefully wrought parable. What the story illustrates is not so much that Henchard should have been a better father as that he should never have exposed himself to the power of a woman.

The novel indeed turns on the question of exposure. The text eroticises the notion of exposure which it borrows from *Lear*: its central terror is not so much guilt as shame. Lucetta is exposed before the town and before her husband and dies of it. Elizabeth-Jane's indecorous past is exposed by Nance Mockridge and her real paternity is exposed when Henchard, as she sleeps, is able to trace Newson's features which 'come to the surface' (p. 144) in her face. (We seem not meant to register the impropriety of his visit to her bedroom: the text focuses so firmly on the notion of establishing paternity that it does not notice its own exposure of the father.) Abel Whittle is exposed in the physical sense, and so is the furmity woman, when Stubberd shines his light on her as she urinates ('"Put away that dee lantern"', he reports she demands, p. 231). Henchard is exposed repeatedly – by Susan, who calls his bluff by going off with Newson in the first chapter and who, by first concealing and then revealing the truth about Elizabeth-Jane, dupes him into exposing his feelings in a way he will bitterly regret; by Mrs Goodenough, who sends Susan on to Casterbridge, reveals the wife-selling to the town, and asks Jopp about Lucetta's letters; by Lucetta, who marries Farfrae behind Henchard's back and leaves him exposed to his creditor Grower; by Newson, who reveals the lie which turns Elizabeth-Jane against Henchard; and finally by Elizabeth-Jane herself, whose repudiation of him exposes him literally to death on the heath.

Women are at the bottom of Henchard's exposure. Even a thoroughly good woman is likely to expose a man in complicated ways; even a thoroughly bad man – like Jopp, so transparently constructed as a plot device – is dangerous only when mixed up with women. Grossly mistreated as he has been by Henchard, Jopp does harm only when he gets involved in Lucetta's scheme to repossess her reckless correspondence, and when – improbably ignoring his implied threat of blackmail – she snubs him and piques his desire for revenge. And Newson's intentions, apparently, are quite innocent. Though his behaviour is perhaps somewhat crude and thoughtless, the ultimate result of his intervention could not reasonably have been predicted. How could Newson have guessed either that Henchard would care so much about Elizabeth-Jane or that Elizabeth-Jane would care so little about Henchard?

A real man does not expose people. Although Henchard regrets telling Farfrae 'the secret o' my life', it is made clear that he risked nothing in doing so: '"I had forgot it," said Farfrae simply' (p. 114). Henchard's desire to expose is examined more carefully but only to be denied. Twice he is shown wrestling with the temptation to avenge himself on the women who have hurt him by destroying their relationship with his rival – and conquering it. The moral struggle is foregrounded, the temptation is, quite precisely, dramatised ('he had quite intended to effect a grand catastrophe at the end of this drama', p. 284) and we register the moral victory.

Whenever he is not harassed beyond endurance, Henchard's chivalrous instinct is to protect women, however exasperating they may be. He marries Susan and does in fact succeed in protecting her (she is the only person with a 'past' who is not exposed during her lifetime) – even if his gesture of sending her back the five guineas, which 'tacitly ... said to her that he bought her back again' (p. 79), is somewhat problematic in a text which deals explicitly if coyly with prostitution. And he fully intends to do as much for Lucetta – 'the double of the first' (p. 289) – if only in the sense that he no loner feels great personal warmth for either of them. He embraces Elizabeth-Jane with real feeling, hoping and waiting to endow her with his name; he saves Lucetta and Elizabeth-Jane from the bull without a second thought; he is easily persuaded to abandon any thoughts of revenge against Lucetta ('his heart smote him for having attempted reprisals on one of a sex so weak', p. 288).

Unfortunately, however, he just cannot seem to cope with the 'finnikin details' (p. 87) of the written word. Because he opens Susan's letter, Elizabeth-Jane is exposed to his wrath and emotionally, if not literally, expelled from the household. Because he leaves the packet of Lucetta's incriminating correspondence in his dining-room safe, he risks Farfrae's access to it. Because he fails properly to seal the packet Jopp carries, Lucetta is exposed and destroyed. 'Constructed upon too large a scale' to attend to the 'minutiae' (p. 209) of print or women, Henchard suffers disproportionately for what must be taken as involuntary errors. Yet the figurative language associated with him is ambiguous. Is he the 'bull breaking fence' (p. 311) driven back by Farfrae during the royal visit? the bull tormented in 'the old bull-stake' (p. 161) to which Lucetta's back door gives access? Or is he – 'by nature something of a woman-hater' (p. 89) as he admits to Farfrae – the bull who hunts down and fatally gores the woman he rescued?

The one incident which implicates Henchard directly in the process of exposure seems at the same time to make the point that man-to-man encounters are simple and straightforward. Henchard insists on Abel Whittle's coming to work without his trousers on, and Whittle is distraught at the prospect of specifically sexual shame. Though he has people pulling through the window on his great toe, he dreads 'the women-folk ... looking out of their winders at my mortification' (p. 113). However, nothing of the sort takes place, and by the reader who takes the episode, in context, as another step in the deterioration of the friendship between Henchard and Farfrae, nothing of the sort is expected. What is going on here is apparently between Henchard and Farfrae, not between Henchard and Whittle, and it has to do with justice and with managerial tact not with sexual curiosity. In retaliation for ordering Whittle to expose himself, Henchard is immediately exposed by Farfrae, who countermands his order 'before them' all instead of waiting 'till we were alone' (p. 114). Disagreement between men is open and straightforward and leads quickly to poetic justice – Henchard is obliged on the spot 'to feel what wretches feel'; forgiveness between men is equally straightforward – on the heath, exposed to the elements, Henchard is sheltered by the very man he would have stripped. The text does not encourage us to meditate on the erotic implications of Whittle's projected exposure or to connect it to a curiosity about what a Scotsman wears under his kilt – not even when the motif is repeated, when the witch who exposes Henchard turns out to have been herself exposed by Stubberd's lantern. Our sense not only of social decorum but of generic decorum works against Henchard's exposure here: it encourages us to see the protagonist's blunder merely as an expression of his tragically flawed nature, Whittle's loyalty as a moving corroboration of Henchard's essential good-heartedness and integrity.

Integrity is the impression we are left with. Although the scene on the heath invites comparison with *King Lear*, there is a sense in which the ending of the novel denies the very exposure it seems to dramatise. Unlike Shakespeare's protagonist, Hardy's is not stripped bare, nor is he reduced to incoherence. Rather – given as many words in the last few pages of the novel as he mobilises at a stretch anywhere else – he is clothed to the end in tendentious rhetoric which asserts the very ego-integrity it pretends to deny.[38] Precisely because his ordeal *is* modelled so self-consciously on Lear's, we can never forget that, unlike Lear, Henchard is always, as he realises when he sees his effigy in the water, '"in Somebody's hand"' (p. 345) – in the hand of the author who insists at the end of his story on endowing him with a factitious unity and wholeness.

That moment when Henchard confronts '*himself* ... his counterpart, his actual double' (p. 342) is a telling contrast to the mirroring of the women. When Elizabeth and Lucetta look into a mirror, they see themselves through the eyes of man. When Henchard on the other hand looks (*more* narcissistically?) into the *water*, he sees himself as seen by Somebody else. This, the text suggests, is how the genders are constructed: he for Somebody only, she for Somebody in him. Lucetta's last cry expresses her utter dependence on her husband's regard: '"he will never love me any more – and O, it will kill me – kill me!"' (p. 321). But – despite the fact that her lament could serve, both with and without a change of pronoun, for Henchard himself – the way the protagonist's death is handled suggests that things are otherwise with a man.

The emotional effect of the novel's ending depends on its success in imposing various kinds of unity on Henchard and his story. The return of Abel Whittle links the middle of the tale to its end and testifies to the essential unity of Henchard's life and character. His long speech is a flashback which recuperates events not focalised by Elizabeth-Jane and re-establishes the flow of the narrative. The episode reaches its emotional climax with Henchard's will, which, as 'a piece of the same stuff that his whole life was made of' (pp. 384–5), stands as a testimony to his essential integrity.

But the 'piece' is a piece of paper – the will is, as Whittle says, 'writing' (p. 384) – and there are paradoxes in a written document which solicits oblivion.[39] Henchard's will is a self-contradictory project, endlessly deferring the extinction it invokes. The writer ineluctably refers to his dead self by means of pronouns like 'I' and 'my' which imply that the 'I' continues to exist: it is 'behind *me*' that mourners will or will not walk 'at my funeral', it is 'I' who will or will not be buried in consecrated ground, '*my* dead body' which will or will not be looked at. The language implies the immortality of the essential Henchard, the man who lives on in Hardy's words as well as in his own. Yet if the will is 'a piece of the same stuff that his whole life was made of', it becomes (as indeed it literally is) a page in a volume called *The Life and Death of the Mayor of Casterbridge* – the *Life* becomes text and '*my* dead body' an illusion. Mrs Goodenough, in making clear that the 'I' is always split and always an effect of language, has already exposed the fantasy which shapes Henchard's rhetoric.

The body is not in fact looked at. With proper tragic decorum, the protagonist dies off-stage:[40] we never get inside the hut and Henchard as a corporeal being vaporises into past tenses which testify to his permanent, essential qualities ('He was kind-like to mother', p. 383). Indeed, the illusion of Henchard's immortality seems to have infected the very tenses of the narrative voice, which, though it begins by distinguishing between the past and the past perfect ('What Henchard *had written* in the anguish of his dying *was respected* as far as practicable by Elizabeth-Jane') goes on to refer to 'her independent knowledge that the man who *wrote* them *meant* what he *said*' (p. 384) – as though the writing, the meaning, and the saying were all contemporaneous with the respecting. (The qualification – 'as far as practicable' – is a nice touch, deferring to the end to the claims of propriety: will the mayor's wife actually have her stepfather, the late mayor, buried in *un*consecrated ground?)

But whatever common-sense problems she presents, the text needs Elizabeth-Jane to perceive this writing, this meaning, this unity: it is her consciousness which generates the statement that his will is a piece of the same stuff as his whole life. Rehabilitated for the occasion and realigned with the *sententiae* of the narrative voice in the last two paragraphs of the novel, the woman who killed Henchard must be there to *know* him. But just because it is so conspicuous a piece of ventriloquism, Elizabeth-Jane's meditation deconstructs itself. Henchard is exposed not only by her rejection of him, which condemns him to death on the heath, but by her very tribute to him, which reinstalls the specularity it is constructed to repress.

A woman's death is different. When Susan and Lucetta die, not only do the other fictional characters quickly forget them (no need for a special request!) but, since their deaths lead directly to interesting plot developments, the reader forgets them too. As individuals they are nugatory; the rhetoric with which their dying is surrounded emphasises precisely the pathos of the representative and the continuity of life which goes on without them. Lucetta dies on the border – between bride and mother, between night and morning. As the sun rises and the birds stir, the housemaid comes to take the muffler off the door-knocker, 'Because they may knock as loud as they will; she will never hear it any more' (p. 333). There is more sense of Lucetta's inner life in these words than in all the scenes which 'characterise' her, but it is an inner life which is not at all individualised or morally shaped: simply sensation at its most random and ordinary.

Susan's death is also treated with great rhetorical power, though with little sense of her as an individual character. In death 'Mrs Henchard's dust mingled with the dust of women who lay ornamented with glass hair-pins and amber necklaces, and men who held in their mouths coins of Hadrian, Posthumus, and the Constantines' (p. 153). On the one hand this is a kind of dignity – on the other it is annihilation indeed (the point has already been made that the skeletons people find when they dig in Casterbridge do not even unnerve them, so remote do they seem from the present life of the town). Negligible as a personality, Susan nevertheless becomes the focus of some local attention when Mother Cuxsom reports her dying monologue and voices on her behalf the stylised lament so often quoted by Hardy's readers: 'And all her shining keys will be took from her, and her cupboards opened; and little things 'a didn't wish seen, anybody will see; and her wishes and ways will all be as nothing' (p. 138). Her eloquent words impose a slightly studied closure not only on her life but on the chapter and clearly signal that the novel is finished with Susan.[41]

Yet the figurative suggestions of the language speak not of closure but of opening up, of exposure. In her last words, Susan, like Henchard, describes the way she wants her burial to be handled. Like Henchard, too, she refers to her deceased self with the first-person pronoun:

> '"Yes," says she, "when I'm gone, and my last breath's blowed, look in the top drawer o' the chest in the back room by the window, and you'll find all my coffin clothes; a piece of flannel – that's to put

under me, and the little piece is to put under my head; and my new
stockings for my feet – they are folded alongside, and all my other
things. And there's four ounce pennies, the heaviest I could find, a-
tied up in bits of linen, for weights – two for my right eyes and two
for my left ..."'

(p. 137)

But unlike Henchard's, Susan's 'me' is a dead body in all its corporeality, a body whose eyelids have to be closed with some force
(with 'pennies, the heaviest I could find') until they stiffen, and her
concern with how it is to be handled is practical, concrete, house-
wifely. Susan envisages not the cemetery and the funeral service but
the house and the life which will go on in it after her death and she
makes no claims for the dead body but only for those who continue
to live in the house ('And open the windows as soon as I am carried
out, and make it as cheerful as you can for poor Elizabeth-Jane').

She does make one modest request on her own behalf – "'bury
the pennies, good souls, and don't ye go spending 'em'" – but her
will, unlike Henchard's, is ignored, and Coney spends the money at
the Three Mariners. The metaphorical language with which this act
is described ("''Twas a cannibal deed'") associates it not only with
digging up the body itself but also with digging *into* it. The women
are on the side of decorum – the men, truculently pragmatic, on the
side of 'life' ("'why should death rob life o' fourpence?'"). But
Solomon Longways, defending his crony ("'I wouldn't sell
skellintons'"), picks up the suggestion of penetration and exposure
and, even as he contrasts Coney's act with grave-robbery, helps
establish the parallel. Susan had requested that things be opened up
– the back room, the top drawer, the windows – but she will not be
able to arrest the process her death has initiated: her closets will be
opened by the servants, her body by the coffin-worm, and the
'things a' didn't want seen' (her underwear? her bones?) 'anybody
will see' – as coolly and promiscuously as they gaze at the Roman
skeletons exposed as the life of the town unfolds.

The final impropriety, the last dirty secret, is the extinction of the
subject. Sex and death are linked in the too-penetrable body of the
woman, the woman with a 'past', the woman with the skeleton in
her closet. Daughter or doll, witch or skeleton, prude or prostitute,
woman cannot after all endow a man with the integrity and stability
he desires. The intuitions about personal dissolution expressed in the
narrative of Susan's death deconstruct the fantasies of moral and
spiritual integrity expressed in the narrative of Henchard's. *The*

Mayor of Casterbridge is about exposure, and what is finally exposed is the text's own dream of phallic unity embodied in the tragic hero.

From Marjorie Garson, *Hardy's Fables of Integrity: Woman, Body, Text* (Oxford, 1991), pp. 94–130.

NOTES

[Marjorie Garson's study of Hardy is concerned with the construction of the self, with bodily and psychic identity. She pursues this reading through recourse to psychoanalytic discourse, especially Lacan's theorisation of the mirror-stage and the role this plays in the psychic constitution of the self. Also of interest to Garson is Lacan's consideration of Woman as Other, which engages her other principal theoretical paradigm, feminism. In elaborating her readings, Garson draws on Jacqueline Rose, Jane Gallop, Juliet Flower MacCannell, and Elizabeth Wright, among several feminist theorists who have discussed Lacan's applicability to a feminist criticism. In working from this dual focus, the critic gives detailed attention to the ambiguities of figural language, especially as this serves in the structural delineation of identity as a textual form. Ed.]

1. Those who discuss the novel in terms of tragedy include D. A. Dike, 'A Modern Oedipus: *The Mayor of Casterbridge*', *Essays in Criticism*, 2 (1952), 169–79; John Paterson, '*The Mayor of Casterbridge* as Tragedy', *Victorian Studies*, 3 (1959), 151–72, rpt. in Albert J. Guerard (ed.) *Hardy: A Collection of Critical Essays* (Englewood Clifs, NJ, 1963), pp. 91–112; Albert J. Guerard, *Thomas Hardy: The Novels and Stories* (Cambridge, MA, 1949); Michael Millgate, *Thomas Hardy: His Career as a Novelist* (London, 1971); Jean R. Brooks, *Thomas Hardy: The Poetic Structure* (London, 1971); Duane D. Edwards, '*The Mayor of Casterbridge* as Aeschylean Tragedy', *Studies in the Novel*, 4 (1972), 608–18; and Frederick R. Karl, '*The Mayor of Casterbridge*: A New Fiction Defined – 1960, 1975', *Modern Fiction Studies*, 21 (1975), 405–28. Lawrence J. Starzyk, 'Hardy's *The Mayor of Casterbridge*: The Antitraditional Basis of Tragedy', *Studies in the Novel*, 4 (1972), 592–607, and John Peck, 'Hardy and Joyce: A Basis for Comparison', *Ariel*, 12 (1981), 71–85, suggest that the conventional tragic paradigm is undercut; Irving Howe, *Thomas Hardy* (New York, 1967) and George Levine, 'Thomas Hardy's *The Mayor of Casterbridge*: Reversing the Real', in *The Realistic Imagination: English Fiction from Frankenstein to Lady Chatterley* (Chicago, IL, 1981), pp. 229–51 (rpt. in Harold Bloom [ed.], *Thomas Hardy's The Mayor of Casterbridge*, Modern Critical Interpretations [New

York, 1988], pp. 69–94), see Henchard rather as a romantic over-reacher. On what is repressed by the concept of 'the tragic', see George Wotton, *Thomas Hardy: Towards a Materialist Criticism* (Dublin and Totowa, NJ, 1985), pp. 63–5.

2. Thomas Hardy, *The Life and Death of the Mayor of Casterbridge: A Story of a Man of Character* (London, 1912), Wessex Edition, vol. v, 131. All subsequent quotations from the novel are from the same edition.

3. See Peter Widdowson, *Hardy in History: A Study in Literary Sociology* (London, 1989), pp. 89–92, and George Wotton, *Thomas Hardy: Towards a Materialist Criticism* (1985), pp. 201–7, on the way the educational establishment has produced the novels by means of examination questions and study guides.

4. See Wotton, *Thomas Hardy: Towards a Materialist Criticism* (1985), ch. 5, who cites Bakhtin; also p. 69 n. 27.

5. Along with *Far from the Madding Crowd* and *The Return of the Native*; see Peter Widdowson, *Hardy in History* (1989), pp. 80–2.

6. Her illicit affair with Henchard, avoided in the serial version of the text, was made clear in the book version; see Christine Winfield, 'The Manuscript of Hardy's *Mayor of Casterbridge*', *Papers of the Bibliographical Society of America*, 67 (1973), 37–58, 57–8 (rpt. in the Norton Critical Edition of *The Mayor of Casterbridge*, ed. James K. Robinson [New York, 1977], pp. 266–87).

7. See Penelope Vigar, *The Novels of Thomas Hardy: Illusion and Reality* (London, 1974), p. 163, and J. B. Bullen, *The Expressive Eye: Fiction and Perception in the Work of Thomas Hardy* (Oxford and New York, 1986), p. 149.

8. He mentions 'a natural reason for her slightly drawn look'. In the serial 'nature is displaced' by 'artifice ... the only practicable weapon left [Lucetta] as a woman': by the detailed description of the process by which, assisted by 'disfiguring ointments' from the druggist, she turns herself into a witch-like creature with 'a countenance withering, ageing, sickly'. See *Graphic*, 33 (1886), 421–2. The parallel passages are printed in Mary Ellen Chase, *Thomas Hardy from Serial to Novel* (New York, 1964), pp. 36–8.

9. See John Paterson, '*The Mayor of Casterbridge* as Tragedy' (1959), p. 163; Jean Brooks, *Thomas Hardy: The Poetic Structure* (1971), p. 205; Elaine Showalter, 'The Unmanning of the Mayor of Casterbridge' in Dale Kramer (ed.), *Critical Approaches to the Fiction of Thomas Hardy* (London, 1979: pp. 99–105), p. 107 (rpt. in Harold Bloom [ed.], *Thomas Hardy*, Modern Critical Views [New York, 1987], pp. 175–89; and Harold Bloom [ed.], *Thomas Hardy's The Mayor of Casterbridge* [1988], pp. 53–68).

10. Readers who have discussed the interconnection between town and country include Douglas Brown, *Thomas Hardy* (1954; rev. edn London, 1961), pp. 66–7; Jean R. Brooks, *Thomas Hardy: The Poetic Structure* (1971), pp. 205–7; D. H. Fussell, 'The Maladroit Delay: The Changing Times in Thomas Hardy's *The Mayor of Casterbridge*', *Critical Quarterly*, 21:3 (1979, 17–30, 21–2; J. B. Bullen, *The Expressive Eye* (1986), pp. 164–6. Andrew Enstice, *Thomas Hardy: Landscapes of the Mind* (London, 1979), pp. 12–34, demonstrates that Hardy makes Casterbridge more regular in shape, more unified, and more self-sufficient than the historic Dorchester. Bullen (1986), pp. 159–68, discusses the town and its architecture in terms of the nineteenth-century notion of 'an intimate connection between society and building style'.

11. Didier Anzieu's insights seem relevant; cf. *The Skin Ego: A Psychoanalytic Approach to the Self*, trans. Chris Turner (New Haven, CT, and London, 1989), p. 38, n. 28.

12. Andrew Enstice points out that Hardy's portrait of Casterbridge is not only selective – excluding Dorchester's Georgian facades and its modern buildings – but inconsistent in its own terms: 'the long gardens of all the major houses might ... seem strange in a town where the dwellings are "packed" together'; *Thomas Hardy: Landscapes of the Mind* (1979), p. 9.

13. Casagrande and Lock ('The Name "Henchard"', *Thomas Hardy Society Review*, 1 [1978], 115–18) have shown that Henchard gets his name from a Dorchester mansion the destruction of which Hardy regretted. Bullen in *The Expressive Eye* (1986), p. 159, finds Henchard's house 'an apt visual metaphor for his solid, old-fashioned principles'.

14. The various social groupings and the links between them have been discussed by Douglas Brown, *Thomas Hardy: The Mayor of Casterbridge* (London, 1962), pp. 56–7, and D. H. Fussell, 'The Maladroit Delay' (1979), 23–5.

15. Norman Page, *Thomas Hardy* (London and Boston, MA, 1977), p. 80, Jean R. Brooks, *Thomas Hardy: The Poetic Structure* (1971), p. 200, and John Goode, *Thomas Hardy: The Offensive Truth* (Oxford, 1988), p. 79, have discussed the way Henchard is framed in this scene. Michael Millgate, *Thomas Hardy: His Career as a Novelist* (1971), p. 223, calls attention to the intimations of class hostility here.

16. Elizabeth-Jane's association with the horizontal needs to be qualified; her tendency to look down on events has also been noticed (see Bullen, *The Expressive Eye* [1986], p. 158). The text's ambivalence about her social position – the tension between the 'horizontal' and the 'vertical' in her construction – will be dealt with later in this argument.

17. Jean R. Brooks, *Thomas Hardy: The Poetic Structure* (1971), p. 201, makes essentially this point. Michael Millgate, *Thomas Hardy: His Career as a Novelist* (1971) and Judith Bair, 'The Mayor of Casterbridge: "Some Grand Feat of Stagery"', *South Atlantic Bulletin*, 42:2 (1977), 11–22, discuss the theatricality of the novel as a whole; John Goode, *Thomas Hardy: The Offensive Truth* (1988), pp. 79–83, shows how Henchard's theatricality is ironised by Elizabeth-Jane's 'awareness'.

18. Brown, in *Thomas Hardy: The Mayor of Casterbridge* (1962), p. 31, emphasises the class associations of Lucetta's mansion.

19. See Paterson, 'The Mayor of Casterbridge as Tragedy' (1959), 164; Brooks, *Thomas Hardy: The Poetic Structure* (1971), p. 201; Penelope Vigar, *The Novels of Thomas Hardy: Illusion and Reality* (1974), p. 150; Juliet Grindle, 'Compulsion and Choice in *The Mayor of Casterbridge*, in Anne Smith (ed.), *The Novels of Thomas Hardy* (New York and London, 1979; pp. 91–106), p. 97; Bullen, *The Expressive Eye* (1986), pp. 160–6.

20. Michael Millgate, *Thomas Hardy: His Career as Novelist* (1971), p. 223, suggests this analogy. See Spenser, *The Faerie Queene*, II. ix. stanza 32, for a paradigmatic equation of the house, the city, and the human body.

21. At an early stage of composition Hardy had Henchard burn Lucetta's photograph: 'there's an end of her and here goes her picture. Burns it up flame creeps up face etc.' See Winfield, 'The Manuscript of Hardy's *Mayor of Casterbridge*' (1973), 37.

22. Readers who do take it seriously tend to deal with it in rather general terms as a reflection of class enmity: see Brown, *Thomas Hardy: The Mayor of Casterbridge* (1962), p. 57, and Laurence Lerner, *Thomas Hardy's The Mayor of Casterbridge* (London, 1975), pp. 77–8. Dale Kramer, *Thomas Hardy: The Forms of Tragedy* (Detroit, 1975), p. 175 n. 11, and Merryn Williams, *Thomas Hardy and Rural England* (London, 1972), p. 154, do point out that the skimmity-ride is conceived by its organisers specifically as an attack upon Lucetta rather than upon Farfrae. Williams is the only one to observe that Lucetta's punishment is quite out of proportion to her 'crime'.

23. Kramer, *Thomas Hardy: The Forms of Tragedy* (1975), pp. 70–80, analyses Farfrae's inadequacies in some detail, arguing that his character degenerates.

24. See Brown, *Thomas Hardy: The Mayor of Casterbridge* (1962), p. 27, who is thus disarmed.

25. See *The Mayor of Casterbridge*, pp. 69, 237, 296. Brown, *Thomas Hardy: The Mayor of Casterbridge* (1962), p. 44–8, who sees not Farfrae but Henchard as a typical Scott hero, identifies Farfrae rather

as 'the Canny Scot of tradition' (p. 16). Ralph W. V. Elliott, *Thomas Hardy's English* (Oxford, 1984), p. 40, suggests the music-hall Scot as a source for Farfrae.

26. See Kramer, *Thomas Hardy: The Forms of Tragedy* (1975), pp. 86–7, and Showalter, 'The Unmanning of the Mayor of Casterbridge' (1979), 106–7.

27. The narrator's irony about Farfrae's 'dear native country that he loved so well as never to have revisited it' (p. 373) and the detail about making a hole in a sovereign were added in late revision: see Chase, *Thomas Hardy from Serial to Novel* (1964), p. 52.

28. Ian Gregor's treatment of Elizabeth-Jane as a 'developed consciousness' (*The Great Web: The Form of Hardy's Major Fiction* [London, 1974], p. 125) is typical. Lerner, *Thomas Hardy's The Mayor of Casterbridge* (1975), p. 78, Brown, *Thomas Hardy: The Mayor of Casterbridge* (1962), p. 24, and Lance St John Butler, *Thomas Hardy* (Cambridge, 1978), p. 71, note her excessive interest in gentility, though Brown argues she outgrows it; Lars Hartveit, 'Thomas Hardy, *The Mayor of Casterbridge*: The Persuasive Function of Character', in *The Art of Persuasion: A Study of Six Novels* (Oslo, 1977) rationalises it in a some-what circular fashion. Henry Charles Duffin, *Thomas Hardy: A Study of the Wessex Novels, the Poems, and The Dynasts* (1919; 3rd edn with further revisions and additions Manchester, 1937; rpt. New York, 1962, 1964, 1967), p. 40, who realises that she is 'but an instrument' of the plot – 'the old bull is to be killed and she is the weapon chosen; no other could have served' – and Karl, 'A New Fiction Defined – 1960, 1975', (1975), 427, who suggests that Hardy's women tend to be 'furies or fates, temptresses, hostile creatures struggling to free themselves while entrapping males', confront her cruelty most directly. Goode, analysing the novel's two 'conflicting modes of narrative totalisation' (*Thomas Hardy: The Offensive Truth* [1988], p. 90), the masculine/theatrical and the feminine/analytical, sees 'respectability' as the limitedness of the latter. For me Goode's impressive argument is somewhat vitiated by his own binary oppositions which construct femininity as awareness and thus obscure the woman's body and the text's exploitation of it.

29. See Gregor, *The Great Web* (1974), p. 116, and Lerner, *Thomas Hardy's The Mayor of Casterbridge* (1975), p. 15.

30. Elliott, *Thomas Hardy's English* (1984), p. 31, cites the *The Life of Thomas Hardy* (London, 1962, 1982).

31. Robert Barne's illustration of this episode for the serial emphasises the class difference between Nance, boldly facing the reader and scratch-ing her elbows, and Elizabeth-Jane, daintily dressed, head deferentially bowed towards Henchard. See *Graphic*, 33 (1886), 241. [This illustra-tion is reproduced on p. 131 of the Penguin edition of the novel, ed. Keith Wilson – Ed.]

32. It also connotes the concealment of pregnancy: 'aprons-up' means pregnant (Eric Partridge, *A Dictionary of Slang and Unconventional English*, 8th edn, ed. Paul Beale [London, 1984], p. 24).

33. See also p. 98, n. 8.

34. Showalter, 'The Unmanning of the Mayor of Casterbridge' (1979), 109.

35. Goode, *Thomas Hardy: The Offensive Truth* (1988), pp. 92–3, who deals with the theme of joking, makes this point; on practical jokes in *The Mayor of Casterbridge*, see also Alexander Welsh, 'Realism as a Practical and Cosmic Joke', *Novel*, 9 (1975), 23–39, 26–7.

36. Selling a son, Showalter suggests in 'The Unmanning of the Mayor of Casterbridge', 'would be so drastic a violation of patriarchal culture that it would wrench the whole novel out of shape' (1979), 103.

37. The suggestions of castration are obvious. While I agree with Showalter (1979) that Henchard is unmanned, I see the way the text's attitude to unmanning is handled as decidedly more ambivalent than her argument would suggest.

38. Brown, *Thomas Hardy: The Mayor of Casterbridge* (1962), p. 62, and Lerner, *Thomas Hardy's The Mayor of Casterbridge* (1975), p. 68, suggest that we seem to hear his voice speaking.

39. See George Levine, 'Thomas Hardy's *The Mayor of Casterbridge*: Reversing the Real' (1981), 249: 'Henchard's last written words are the name he is asking to obliterate – and boldly imprinted ... It is as though Henchard has stumbled onto the modernist criticism that reminds us of the peculiar status of language.'

40. Butler, *Thomas Hardy* (1978), p. 72, suggests that the treatment of Henchard's death is 'a masterpiece of tragic reported action'.

41. See Philip Stevick, *The Chapter in Fiction: Theories of Narrative Division* (Syracuse, NY, 1970), pp. 43–5, 78–9, on the tension between finality and continuity in Hardy's chapter endings.

6

The Minimisation of Sexuality

ROBERT LANGBAUM

Exceptional in Hardy, the minimisation of sexuality is apparent in *The Mayor of Casterbridge* (1886) and in Hardy's last novel *The Well-Beloved* (1897). A few critics have recently noticed something special about Hardy's treatment of sexuality in *The Mayor of Casterbridge*. To take only two examples, J. Hillis Miller, in *Thomas Hardy: Distance and Desire* speaks of the book as 'a nightmare of frustrated desire', of sexual desire mixed with desire for possession (p. 148); while T. R. Wright, in *Hardy and the Erotic*, describes Henchard's relationship with Farfrae as 'never an avowedly homosexual relationship, but Henchard's manliness is clearly more complex than he cares to admit' (p. 78).[1] I would like to qualify these perceptions by noting a minimum of sexual feeling in the novel as a whole and almost an absence of it in the main character Henchard; so that talk of frustrated desire or homosexual desire is not entirely applicable. Ian Gregor describes *The Mayor* as 'one of the very few major novels ... where sexual relationships are not ... the dominant element'.[2] This turn away from sexuality in the novel as a whole is unusual in Hardy and may explain why D. H. Lawrence in his *Study of Hardy* says little about *The Mayor of Casterbridge*.

To be sure the idealists, Clym, Giles and Angel, seem low in sexual drive and Hardy's criticism of them seems to include a criticism of their low sexuality, even though the 'villains' – Wildeve, Fitzpiers and Alec – are better endowed sexually. But Henchard

presents a different case in that he is not an idealist, is even something of a 'villain', and has the energy and aggressiveness which
would lead us to expect a vigorous sexuality. Yet it is difficult to
believe on the evidence shown that Michael Henchard can ever
have been in love with his wife Susan, and we know that he fell
into a probably sexual relationship with Lucetta (explicitly sexual
in the manuscript[3]) not out of love or lust but out of gratitude to
her for having saved his life when he was ill in Jersey. In the novel
we see only his desire to escape these women. When later he decides
to marry Lucetta, a project interrupted by his need to remarry
Susan, his motive in both cases is pure moral obligation without
anticipation of sexual pleasure. (His pursuit of Lucetta becomes
more heated when he has to compete with Farfrae.) Henchard's
lack of sexual feeling throws the emphasis on his moral obligation
to these women, while the minimisation of sexuality in the novel as
a whole emphasises moral and public questions and indeed the
novel's tragic dimensions.

Susan figures on her reappearance as a ghost ('Mrs Henchard was
so pale that the boys called her "The Ghost"'), which she is in two
senses. She is the ghost of a past crime, the wife-sale, but she is also
ghostly in her lack of sexual vitality. 'He pressed on the preparations for his union, or rather reunion, with this pale creature',
feeling 'no amatory fire'.[4] But this pale creature is deceiving him
since she is remarrying only for the sake of her daughter whom she
passes off as the Elizabeth-Jane he gave away. Only after Susan's
death does he learn from a letter she leaves that his daughter died
and that this Elizabeth-Jane is Newson's daughter.

The wife-sale scene at the beginning sets the tone. Henchard's
mind is entirely on the economic drag of wife and daughter: '"if I
were a free man again I'd be worth a thousand pound before I'd
done o't"'(ch. I, p. 7). We see also his tragic flaw, his lack of moderation, in the explosive drunken action which he regrets the next
day, a pattern he will repeat even when not under the influence of
liquor. The wife-sale itself is not given the erotic colouring it might
have had. Newson's motive in purchasing Susan might be kindness
no less than sexual interest, as shown by his gentle considerateness.

Hardy's foreshortening of time, so that Susan's return with the
grown-up Elizabeth-Jane follows upon Henchard's penitential oath
the day after the wife-sale, shows that the consequences of the
crime begin immediately and will have no end. In revising, Hardy
made the wife-sale particularly outrageous by deleting precedents

for wife selling which Henchard cites in his defence.[5] The wife-sale cannot be laid entirely to impulse, for Michael has, says Susan, '"talked this nonsense in public places before"' (ch. I, p. 8). Clearly Henchard has chosen the pursuit of money and power over the pleasures of sexuality. His penitential oath to avoid alcohol for twenty-one years furthers his chosen pursuit, as does his abstinence from women with the exception of Lucetta. '"No wife could I hear of in all that time"', he tells Farfrae, '"and being by nature something of a woman-hater, I have found it no hardship to keep mostly at a distance from the sex"'(ch. XII, p. 60).

Henchard's asceticism proves useful for the accumulation of money and is notably a bourgeois characteristic, as described by Max Weber in his seminal work *The Protestant Ethic and the Spirit of Capitalism*.[6] Yet Henchard hardly seems bourgeois, what with his country mentality ('he had ... received the education of Achilles', that is, no education; ch. XII, p. 58), his rough, irregular ways of doing business and his feudal relation to his employees. 'We have little sense of the class to which Henchard has risen', says a socially oriented critic like John Goode.[7] Of the two, Donald Farfrae, who has a normal if tepid sex life, is the bourgeois. Perhaps we are seeing two phases of capitalism, the early heroic and the developed.

It is difficult to believe that a man so virile in body and in super-abundance of energy should show so little sexual interest. At the time of his fall, every one marvelled at 'how admirably he had used his one talent of energy to create a position of affluence out of absolutely nothing' (ch. XXXI, p. 169). His violently explosive behaviour might be attributed to sexual repression. But that Freudian concept does not seem to apply, largely because we are not given a sense of charged-up sexual energy and because Henchard's two soaring expressions of love, for Farfrae and Elizabeth-Jane, are not apparently directed toward physical gratification though they might have been portrayed that way. As Dale Kramer points out, neither readers nor other characters in the novel think of sexual implications when the forty-year old Henchard goes on living with the twenty-year old Elizabeth-Jane after discovering that she is not his daughter.[8]

Henchard's sudden passion for Farfrae, which is striking after his coolness toward women, suggests homosexuality on his side (Farfrae's response never exceeds cool affection). But their relation does not develop in a way that bears out this hypothesis; for it quickly turns into male power rivalry once Farfrae breaks out of Henchard's proprietorship. Another sign is that the wrestling match between them is not, like the match between Gerald and Birkin in *Women in Love*, given a homosexually erotic colour. For one thing they wrestle with their clothes on, whereas Gerald and Birkin strip naked. After an initial homo-erotic detail – Henchard 'gazed upon the lowered eyes of his fair and slim antagonist' – the details lead our thoughts away from eros toward power: 'the pair rocking and writhing like trees in a gale'. There is no complete body contact – 'this part of the struggle ended by his forcing Farfrae down on his knees by sheer pressure of one of his muscular arms' – until the Scotsman, to save himself from the precipice, 'for the first time locked himself to his adversary' (ch. XXXVIII, p. 209). The initiative is Farfrae's and the emphasis is on the danger to Farfrae's life. The fact that Henchard wrestles with one hand tied emphasises the test of physical power.

In Henchard the desire for power replaces sexuality; he seeks to possess completely the people he loves or is unable to distinguish the pleasure of love from the pleasure of proprietorship. Early in the novel Elizabeth-Jane observes 'Henchard's tigerish affection for the younger man, his constant liking to have Farfrae near him, now and then resulted in a tendency to domineer' (ch. XIV, p. 69). And in the period when Henchard thinks Elizabeth-Jane is his daughter, he provides her with money and clothing but seeks to dominate every aspect of her life, blowing up with fury when she slips into dialect.

In portraying Henchard's love of Farfrae, Hardy suggests if not homosexuality at least the inevitable homo-erotic element in male bonding. We read of Farfrae's slight stature compared to Henchard's bulk and of Henchard's prolonged 'holding [of] the young man's hand' as he tries to persuade him not to go to America: '"Come bide with me – and name your own terms. I'll agree to 'em willingly and 'ithout a word of gainsaying; for, hang it, Farfrae, I like thee well!"' Henchard's enthusiasm for Farfrae contains but also exceeds business considerations, for 'this man of strong impulses declared that his new friend should take up his abode in his house' (ch. IX, pp. 49–50) and they become inseparable though Farfrae declares that they ought to separate if he was to be valuable 'as a second pair of eyes' (ch. XIV, p. 69).

The example which best points toward homo-eroticism comes from Elizabeth-Jane's observation of them at a time when she is feeling the first stirrings of her own fragile sexuality in response to signs of Donald's admiration. She envies 'Friendship between man and man; what a rugged strength there was in it, as evinced by these two' (ch. XV, p. 74). Elizabeth-Jane keeps her eye on Farfrae as though she were competing with Henchard for his affection.

Homo-eroticism but also power hunger shows itself in Henchard's extravagantly irrational reaction when Farfrae steps out of the passive role assigned him to challenge Henchard's authority in the disciplining of Abel Whittle. By dismissing Farfrae Henchard encourages him to set up a rival firm, and in all the subsequent acts of rivalry, always initiated by Henchard, Farfrae wins. These self-destructive hostilities – self-destructiveness is the key to Henchard's character – are ways of remaining in contact with Farfrae, who continues to dominate Henchard's consciousness. This self-destructive way of remaining in contact reaches a climax through the body contact of the wrestling match, which follows the powerful scene in which Henchard is publicly humiliated by Farfrae, who is now Mayor of Casterbridge, before the Royal visitor. Henchard by appearing in his oldest clothes and trying to pre-empt the City Council's welcome is asking for such public humiliation. What matters is Farfrae's *physical* dislodgment of Henchard.

> He seized Henchard by the shoulder, dragged him back, and told him roughly to be off. Henchard's eyes met his, and Farfrae observed the fierce light in them despite his excitement and irritation. For a moment Henchard stood his ground rigidly; then by an unaccountable impulse gave way and retired.
>
> (ch. XXXVII, p. 204)

The test of body contact and will shows that the power relation between them has been reversed. The 'unaccountable impulse' will cause Henchard again to surrender after he has won the wrestling match.

Henchard seeks to restore the balance by asserting his superior physical strength in a wrestling match to the death. But we know from the start that he will not be able to kill Farfrae, for Farfrae enters the barn singing the song he sang when Henchard first met him. 'Nothing moved Henchard like an old melody. He sank bank. "No; I can't do it!" he gasped' (ch. XXXVIII, p. 208). Henchard's susceptibility to music, one of his endearing characteristics, signifies here his continuing love of Farfrae. He finally brings Farfrae to the point where he can say to him: '"Your life is in my hands."'

> 'Then take it, take it!' said Farfrae. 'Ye've wished to long enough!'
> Henchard looked down upon him in silence, and their eyes met. 'O Farfrae – that's not true!' he said bitterly. 'God is my witness that no man ever loved another as I did thee at one time... . And now – though I came here to kill 'ee, I cannot hurt thee!'
>
> (ch. XXXVIII, p. 210)

The cadences of that declaration suggest continuing love, '"My heart is true to you still"', he declares later, when Farfrae does not believe his warning of the danger to Lucetta (ch. XL, p. 219). His capacity to love Farfrae and Elizabeth-Jane, together with his susceptibility to music and his inability (after the initial blunder of the wife-sale) to carry through any ruthless design – all these virtues make Henchard, despite his blunders, a tragic hero rather than a villain who gets his just deserts.

Henchard's change after his self-defeat in the wrestling match is strikingly pictorialised. 'So thoroughly subdued was he that he remained ... in a crouching attitude, unusual for a man, and for such a man. Its *womanliness* sat tragically on the figure of so stern a piece of virility' (ch. XXXVIII, p. 210, my italics). 'Womanliness' presents a stunning reversal of Henchard's characterisation so far. Virility has been the main point of his characterisation (making remarkable, as I have said, his lack of sexual feeling). Susan, when she catches her first glimpse of him since their separation, sees signs of a temperament, which having cut all ties with women, has become thoroughly male, 'a temperament which would have no pity for weakness, but would be ready to yield ungrudging admiration to greatness and strength' (ch. V, p. 26). Dale Kramer argues that the gestures and language which might suggest Henchard's latent homosexuality actually reflect his worship of male power and his 'scornful opinion of women as weak'. But after suffering humiliation and defeat he 'transfers his affection from Farfrae to Elizabeth-Jane: "Above all things what he desired now was affection from anything that was good and pure"' (pp. 87–8). The fact that 'womanliness sat tragically' upon him suggests, given his values, a reduction of stature. Now, however, there has taken place within him an enrichment of values.

The novel traces a process of 'unmanning' that marks Henchard's decline, according to his values, but also the acquisition of feminine values which makes him capable of tragic sympathy with suffering. The word 'unmanned' is first used when in the Roman theatre he gives up his desire for revenge over Lucetta, agreeing to return her letters, because he is reminded 'of another ill-used woman [Susan] who had stood there'. But he harbours still 'his old feeling of supercilious pity for womankind in general' (ch. XXXV, p. 192) when actually he is deceived by Lucetta, who has dressed in a way to induce his pity, and by Susan, who not only made the wife-sale go through but keeps up her sleeve the revelation about Elizabeth-Jane (these in addition to the furmity-woman who directly causes his downfall). It is in his return to Elizabeth-Jane, whom he cast out after learning she was not his daughter, that his feminisation is complete, for 'he schooled himself to accept her will ... as absolute and unquestionable' (ch. XLII, p. 232).

In her brilliant feminist essay, 'The Unmanning of the Mayor of Casterbridge', Elaine Showalter writes:

> Henchard's efforts, first to deny and divorce his passional self, and ultimately to accept and educate it, involve him in a pilgrimage of 'unmanning' which is a movement towards both self-discovery and tragic vulnerability. It is in the analysis of this New Man, rather than in the evaluation of Hardy's New Women, that the case for Hardy's feminist sympathies may be argued.[9]

Hardy himself describes the change in Henchard more ambivalently: 'the dependence upon Elizabeth's regard into which he had declined (or, in another sense, to which he had advanced) – *denaturalised* him' (ch. XLII, p. 233, my italics). 'Denaturalised' suggests that Hardy does not abandon 'declined' for 'advanced', but maintains both possibilities.

I do not find in Hardy's text any sign that 'the effigy which Henchard sees floating' after the skimmity-ride is, as Showalter puts it, 'the symbolic shell of a discarded male self' (p. 112). Hardy does not use the word 'effigy', but makes Henchard perceive 'with a sense of horror that it was *himself*. Not a man somewhat resembling him, but one in all respects his counterpart, his actual double, was floating as if dead' (ch. XLI, p. 227). In this partly objective, partly subjective self-perception, Henchard's manliness would seem to remain intact. But I do agree with Showalter's argument that

> the nature and intensity of Henchard's need is [not] sexual. It is an absence of feeling which Henchard looks to others to supply... What

he wants is a 'greedy exclusiveness,' a title; and this feeling is stimulated by male competition.

(p. 106)

Thus, he shows himself to be the same old Henchard when, on an impulse triggered by his proprietary love for Elizabeth-Jane, he informs her father Newson, who comes looking for her, that she is dead. Worst of all and most fundamentally characteristic of him is the self-destructive impulse that makes him, after he sees in his telescope the face of Newson returning, announce to Elizabeth-Jane that he will leave Casterbridge. Wiping out all he has accomplished, dressing the way he began as a hay trusser, with a hay trusser's tools, he flees both Newson and the need to attend Elizabeth-Jane's wedding to Farfrae. Hardy speaks of Henchard's 'own *haughty* sense that his presence was no longer desired' (ch. XLIV, p. 245, my italics). His haughtiness and self-destructive decision are signs of the pride and impulsiveness which are his tragic flaws. A few pages later Hardy quotes Shelley's *Revolt of Islam* (canto VIII, st. vi: 1.2) to say that Henchard 'stood like a dark ruin, obscured by "the shade from his own soul upthrown"' (ch. XLIV, p. 249).

The irony is that Newson was not planning to interfere in the relation between Henchard and Elizabeth-Jane. Had Henchard rationally stayed on to face the consequences of Newson's return and Elizabeth-Jane's wedding, all would have gone well. But if Henchard were rational, he would not be a tragic hero – a character who, as Hardy sees here, *creates* like Eustacia his own tragedy. It was his destiny to break every tie of love, to will himself into a condition of loneliness and alienation. 'Susan, Farfrae, Lucetta, Elizabeth – all had gone from him', he reflects, 'one after one, either by his fault or by his misfortune' (ch. XLI, p. 226). By his fault, we are to understand, for it is truer of *Mayor* than of the other major novels that, in the remark of Novalis cited here, 'Character is Fate' (ch. XVII, p. 88). 'A Man of Character' in the novel's subtitle may refer to a man who has determined his own destiny despite the coincidences of the plot. In the Preface Hardy calls this story 'more particularly a study of one man's deeds and character' than any of his others (p. 1).

As he takes his lonely way out of Casterbridge, Henchard dramatises his plight self-consciously: '"I – Cain – go alone as I deserve – an outcast and a vagabond."' In contrast to Cain, who in Genesis 4: 13 says, '"My punishment is greater than I can bear"', Henchard says, '"But my punishment is *not* greater than I can bear!"' (ch. XLIII, p. 239). Now he understands the cause of his tragedy – he had let concern for money replace love (the love–money antithesis is largely the book's point). 'But his attempts to replace ambition by love had been as fully foiled as his ambition itself' (ch. XLIV, p. 243). Henchard begins to triumph over circumstances as he gains a glimpse of the whole scheme.

So we see how through self-punishment Henchard generates his own tragedy and, as with all Hardy's tragic heroes, Henchard's display of imaginative and emotional resources too large for success in life makes him tragic. That is his distinction over Farfrae who has the right balance of resources for success. Hardy's skilful feat here (as in his characterisation of Eustacia) is to portray Henchard as mainly unattractive and then to turn our sympathies toward him in the end when he becomes a tragic figure.

In a conversation with Farfrae early in the novel, Henchard, in describing the mood he was in when he met Lucetta, shows where he wants to end up. '"I sank into one of those gloomy fits I sometimes suffer from ... when the world seems to have the blackness of hell, and, like Job, I could curse the day that gave me birth"'. '"Ah, now, I never feel like it"', says the well-adjusted Farfrae (ch. XII, p. 60). In the end Henchard, having refused to attend Elizabeth-Jane's wedding, bungles his return to the wedding in such a way as to bring upon himself even more pain through her rejection of him. He neglects to give her the caged bird he brought as a gift, but finding it dead a few days later, Elizabeth-Jane extends its pathos to Henchard, so that 'her heart softened towards the self-alienated man', always 'one of his own worst accusers' (ch. XLV, p. 251). And finally he fulfils his deepest wish in the terrible Job-like epitaph he prescribes for himself as his will: '"& that I be not bury'd in consecrated ground. /... & that no man remember me"' (ch. XLV, p. 254). By obeying his directions, Elizabeth-Jane allows Henchard his tragic ending undiluted with sentimentality.

> She knew the directions to be a piece of the same stuff that his whole life was made of, and hence were not to be tampered with to give herself a mournful pleasure, or her husband credit for large-heartedness.
>
> (ch. XLV, p. 255)

To return to my original argument about Henchard's lack of sexual feeling, he finds little to interest him sexually in Susan and Lucetta, his love of Farfrae is at most homo-erotic for a while before it turns into bitter rivalry masking a love that grows increasingly spiritual; while his eventual love for Elizabeth-Jane is paternal and spiritual, with no sexual component suggested. Indeed Henchard demonstrates a large capacity for asexual love; the sign of this is the implied comparison with the initiation into love of King Lear, a man too old for sexual emotions. Having been rejected by his 'daughter', Henchard like Lear wanders alone attended only by his faithful fool (Abel Whittle). One finds the pattern of the Lear–Cordelia story in Henchard's rejection of the loving Elizabeth-Jane when he learns she is not his biological daughter and when their subsequent reconciliation is followed by his final heartbreak after she, in an analogue to Cordelia's death, rejects him.

How sexual are the other major characters? Both Donald Farfrae and Elizabeth-Jane are cool sexually, or at least their sexual emotions do not interfere with the clarity of their thinking. The only sexually passionate character in the novel is Lucetta, who dies because her unreserved passion for Farfrae gets mixed up through exposure in the skimmity-ride with the consequences of her earlier unreserved passion for Henchard. '"I'd let people live and love at their pleasure!"' says the amorous Lucetta (ch. XXIII, p. 124).

Farfrae's character is exemplified by his ability to bring tears to the eyes of himself and others with songs of his native Scotland even though he has no intention of returning there. '"It's well you feel a song for a few minutes"', he says to Elizabeth-Jane after his performance at The Three Mariners,

> 'and your eyes they get quite tearful; but you finish it, and for all you felt you don't mind it or think of it again for a long while. O no, I don't want to go back! Yet I'll sing the song to you wi' pleasure whenever you like.'
>
> (ch. XIV, p. 72)

Such shallow emotions are an advantage for succeeding in the acquisition of money and power; and this aspect of Farfrae's character is displayed again at the end, when Henchard from the street hears Donald at his wedding singing 'a song of his dear native country that he loved so well as never to have revisited it' (ch. XLIV, p. 247). The repetition, through the ears of the fallen Henchard, discredits Farfrae in comparison with Henchard whose lack of moderation, of control over his emotions, is one of the flaws that make him a tragic hero. 'Character is Fate, said Novalis, and Farfrae's character was just the reverse of Henchard's' (ch. XVII, p. 88).

Most revealing of all is Lucetta's analysis of Farfrae's character. Speaking of Scotsmen generally, she says on first meeting him, '"We common people are all one way or the other – warm or cold, passionate or frigid. You have both temperatures going on in you at the same time."' The narrator speaks of the curious mixture in Farfrae of 'the commercial and the romantic' (ch. XXIII, pp. 122–3). Sure enough Farfrae interrupts his first meeting with Lucetta to attend to a customer, but not before he has pleased Lucetta and himself by hiring a young carter with his old father so as to keep the carter in the vicinity near his sweetheart. Farfrae is both practical and sentimental, a not unusual combination among people who do not let the sentimental get in the way of the practical.

Farfrae's coolness is shown by his notable lack of response to Henchard's warm feelings for him of love and rivalry. He easily drops his courtship of Elizabeth-Jane after Henchard indicates displeasure over it; and after Henchard drops his objection, he comes to court Elizabeth-Jane but turns to Lucetta instead, showing in his susceptibility to her blandishments little understanding of women. After his wife Lucetta's death, there is no emphasis on his grief for her and their unborn child, but only on his swift recovery so he can turn his attention back to Elizabeth-Jane. Farfrae has the right amount of sexual feeling for success in life, since he is attracted to women as Henchard is not, but sex does not interfere with his other faculties. In Henchard, instead, the powerful passionateness that displaces sexual feeling does interfere with his other faculties.

Elizabeth-Jane's case is more complicated, for though her sexuality is measured and moderate, she does fall in love with Farfrae almost at first sight and she remains steadfastly in love with him. She begins, however, as a colourless, priggish maiden with a quite unromantic rage for respectability. 'Elizabeth-Jane', Hardy wrote in a letter, 'was, of course, too estimable to be piquant.'[10] In fact Elizabeth-Jane *discovers* her womanliness, her sexuality evolves in the course of the novel. If *The Mayor of Casterbridge* is, on the one hand, about the moral 'feminisation' of Henchard, it is, on the other hand, about the biological feminisation of Elizabeth-Jane.

Under the secure shelter of Henchard's financial support, Elizabeth-Jane's womanliness begins to blossom. 'With peace of mind came development, and with development beauty' (ch. XIV,

p. 66). In her newly acquired finery, she begins to draw admiration, including Farfrae's. 'Sex', we are told, 'had never before asserted itself in her so strongly, for in former days she had perhaps been too impersonally human to be distinctively feminine.' Yet she still doubts whether she is sufficiently feminine to justify such frivolous clothing: '"Good Heaven"', she whispered, '"can it be? Here am I setting up as the town beauty! ... If they only knew what an unfinished girl I am. ... Better sell all this finery and buy myself grammar-books and dictionaries and a history of all the philosophies!"' (ch. XV. p. 74). There remains throughout her story the obstacle to feminisation which Hardy calls her impersonal humanity and we might call her introspective intellectuality. At first 'her budding beauty' went unregarded, for 'when she walked abroad she seemed to be occupied with an inner chamber of ideas' (ch. XV, p. 73). When at a dance Farfrae alludes to a question he would like to ask her that very night, 'instead of encouraging him she remained incompetently silent'. Wondering later how permanent was the impression she had made on him, she thought that 'by this time he had discovered how plain and homely was the informing spirit of that pretty outside' (ch. XVII, pp. 84, 86). Hardy takes a cue from George Eliot's Dorothea in portraying a beautiful woman who does not *feel* beautiful and compensates with intellectuality.

Elizabeth-Jane's asexual intellectuality is developed through contrast with Lucetta, who, when Elizabeth-Jane settled into her house, deposited herself on the sofa in the pose of Titian's Venus. Instead, 'Elizabeth's mind ran on acquirements to an almost morbid degree. "You speak French and Italian fluently, no doubt", she said. "I have not been able to get beyond a wretched bit of Latin yet"' (ch. XXII, p. 116). We can hear Elizabeth-Jane's unspoken criticism when later Lucetta asks for help in choosing her new wardrobe. '"I wouldn't think so hard about it"', says Elizabeth-Jane. Depending on your choice, Lucetta explains, '"You are that person" (pointing to one of the arrangements), "or you are *that* totally different person" (pointing to the other)'. She finally decided to be 'the cherry-coloured person at all hazards' (ch. XXIV, p. 127). As a result Farfrae 'passed from perception of Elizabeth into a brighter sphere of existence than she appertained to' (ch. XXIV, p. 130) – he saw only the cherry-coloured Lucetta. Hardy, however, gives us with Elizabeth-Jane a heroine in whom beauty and goodness triumph in reconciliation with intellectuality. When Farfrae courts her again in the end, he presents her with many books, thus recognising her difference from Lucetta.

There is another reason for Elizabeth-Jane's intellectuality and sobriety. These are appropriate qualities for her other function as the novel's observer, Hardy's nearest approach so far to a Jamesian central intelligence (he will go even farther in *The Well-Beloved*). 'The position of Elizabeth-Jane's [back] room – rather high in the house ... afforded her opportunity for accurate observation of what went on' in the hay-stores and granaries where Donald was running Henchard's business. 'Her quiet eye' (ch. XIV, p. 69) – she is called 'that silent observing woman' (ch. XVI, p. 85) – expresses the quality of her observation throughout. After Donald's dismissal, she moves to a front chamber overlooking the street. And when she moves in with Lucetta, she is afforded windows 'looking out upon the market' (ch. XXII, p. 117) where Donald and Henchard do business. Although her eye is mainly on Donald out of love for him, her erotic voyeurism does not, as in the earlier novels, disturb the accuracy of her observation. This may be one reason Hardy makes her erotic temperature run low.

The quality of Elizabeth-Jane's love is described in the following passage:

> Thus she lived on, a dumb, deep-feeling great-eyed creature, construed by not a single contiguous being; quenching with patient fortitude her incipient interest in Farfrae, because it seemed to be one-sided, unmaidenly, and unwise.
>
> (ch. XX, p. 102)

'Unwise' is the key word, showing that her emotions are never allowed to exceed the boundaries of reason (we hear only of her 'incipient interest in Farfrae'). Her erotic watching, as she moves from one point of observation to another, is pursued emotionally but calmly.

Thus, she fulfils her dual function of lover and observer. Even in dealing with her rival Lucetta, where her own vital love interest is at stake, she can be remarkably perspicacious. From the data at hand she can divine a meeting between Donald and Lucetta she has not attended, the first in which sparks flew, so that the scene 'could be held as witnessed' (ch. XXIV, p. 131), the way the author would witness it. And 'surveying ... from the *crystalline sphere of a straightforward mind*, [Elizabeth-Jane] did not fail to perceive that her father, as she called him, and Donald Farfrae became more desperately enamoured of her friend every day' (ch. XXV, p. 137, my italics). Henchard is not really enamoured but stimulated by competition; Elizabeth-Jane is perceptive but not omniscient. Note the contrast between the serenity of her perceiving mind and the passionate material perceived, material especially relevant to Elizabeth-Jane's own desire.

Elizabeth-Jane's detachment can be maintained because she can assimilate her disappointment at losing Donald to the lesson of renunciation she had long since learned. And just as Donald took with relative equanimity his early loss of her and his later loss of Lucetta, 'so she viewed with an approach to equanimity the now cancelled days when Donald had been her undeclared lover, and wondered what unwished-for thing Heaven might send her in place of him' (ch. XXV, p. 137). But we see in the following passage another reason for her detachment. At a moment of tension among Lucetta, Henchard and Farfrae, 'Elizabeth-Jane, being out of the game, and out of the group, could observe all from afar, like the evangelist who had to write it down' (ch. XXVI, p. 139). Through much of the book she acts as surrogate for the author.

Even when after Lucetta's death she marries Donald, Elizabeth-Jane takes this turn of fortune with only a little livelier equanimity than her earlier misfortune, absorbing it into her philosophy of endurance. Henchard is surprised to find her dancing at her wedding; for she 'had long ago appraised life at a moderate value' and knew 'that marriage was as a rule no dancing matter' (ch. XLIV, p. 248).

> As the lively and sparkling emotions of her early married life cohered into an equable serenity, the finer movements of her nature found scope in discovering to the narrow-lived ones around her the secret (as she had once learnt it) of making limited opportunities endurable.
> (ch. XLV, p. 255)

These are not the views of a heroine whom love has taken by storm. Such views are expanded in the novel's final sentence in which Elizabeth-Jane, in the midst of her happiness, shows a clear-eyed understanding that 'happiness was but the occasional episode in a general drama of pain' (ch. XLV, p. 256). One is reminded of the choruses in *Oedipus Rex*. As the author's surrogate Elizabeth-Jane expresses the tragic view of life which accounts for and makes endurable the spectacle of Henchard's fall. Hardy thought tragedy inherent in the nature of things and not an aberration.[11]

Elizabeth-Jane might, with her colourless sobriety, be considered a dull heroine (Hardy describes her as 'our poor only heroine', ch. XLIII, p. 236) were it not for her perceptive intelligence and consistent dignity (her 'countenance whose beauty had ever lain in its meditative soberness', ch. XLI, p. 255). George Eliot's Dorothea seems by comparison colourful and romantic. The nearest precedent might be Jane Austen's Fanny Price in *Mansfield Park*, whose stance for morality and respectability is not swept away by erotic emotion. But Elizabeth-Jane is more intellectual and more tragic-minded than Fanny, because of her role as observer and author's surrogate; she emerges therefore as a new kind of heroine.

Hardy's intention to write a tragic novel may explain the reversal of his usual concern with sexuality. He minimises the sexuality of his major characters, except for Lucetta, in order to throw the emphasis on moral judgement, since Eros creates its own laws of judgement, making us forget moral questions as we sympathise with love for its own sake. (The erotic Lucetta is, compared to the other major characters, too trivial to command such sympathy.) Hardy reveals his tragic intention in his journal where, two days after noting that he has finished the last page of *The Mayor of Casterbridge*, he writes: 'The business of the poet and novelist is to show the sorriness underlying the grandest things, and the grandeur underlying the sorriest things' (*Life*, p. 171).

From Robert Langbaum, *Thomas Hardy in Our Time* (Basingstoke, 1995), pp. 127–41.

NOTES

[Robert Langbaum reads Hardy as a distinctly modern, if not proto–modernist writer. Acknowledging the interest of Hardy for a range of politicised critics, Langbaum reassesses the tragic dimensions of *The Mayor of Casterbridge*. The purpose of this rereading is to explore how, exceptionally in comparison with Hardy's other novels, there is a significant playing down of sexuality, which, the critic argues, is in keeping with the moral design of the novel. Ed.]

1. J. Hillis Miller, *Thomas Hardy: Distance and Desire* (Cambridge, MA, 1970); T. R. Wright, *Hardy and the Erotic* (New York, 1989).

2. Ian Gregor, *The Great Web: The Form of Hardy's Major Fiction* (London, 1974), p. 119.

3. In an earlier draft Henchard has recently married Lucetta, but annuls the marriage after Susan's reappearance (MS, f. 112, 114); a still earlier version suggests an illicit sexual relation with Lucetta (MS, f. 167). Hardy's revisions minimise the sexual element in Henchard's relation with Lucetta. (Manuscript in Dorset County Museum, Dorchester.)

4. Thomas Hardy, *The Mayor of Casterbridge*, ed. James K. Robinson (New York, 1977), ch. XIII, p, 63. [All subsequent quotations from the novel are from this edition – Ed.]

5. In the published novel and in manuscript Henchard says: '"It [wife-selling] has been done elsewhere – and why not here?"' (p. 10). Excised after 'elsewhere' in the manuscript: '"Why, Jimmy Clay, sold his wife, didn't he, for thirty shillings? And wasn't it done at Southampton the year before last?"' (MS, f. 17). Hardy read about actual wife sales in old issues of the *Dorset County Chronicle*.

6. Max Weber, *The Protestant Ethic and the Spirit of Capitalism* (1904–5; 1920), trans. Talcott Parsons (New York, 1958). See especially ch. v: 'Asceticism and the Spirit of Capitalism'.

7. John Goode, *Thomas Hardy: The Offensive Truth* (Oxford, 1988), p. 82.

8. Dale Kramer, *Thomas Hardy: The Forms of Tragedy* (Detroit, 1975), pp. 86–7. [Further references are cited parenthetically in the essay – Ed.]

9. Elaine Showalter, 'The Unmanning of the Mayor of Casterbridge', in *Critical Approaches to the Fiction of Thomas Hardy*, ed. Dale Kramer (London, 1979: pp. 99–115), pp. 101–2. [Further references are cited parenthetically in the essay – Ed.]

10. Thomas Hardy, 21 October 1897, *The Collected Letters of Thomas Hardy*, vol. 2: 180. Edited in seven volumes by Richard Little Purdy and Michael Millgate (Oxford, 1978–88).

11. Commenting on Hegel's rationalism in May 1886, the month *Mayor* appeared in volume form, Hardy wrote: 'These venerable philosophers seem to start wrong; they cannot get away from a prepossession that the world must somehow have been made to be a comfortable place for man' (Florence Emily Hardy, *The Life of Thomas Hardy 1840–1928* [London and Basingstoke, 1982], revised and ed. Michael Millgate as *The Life and Work of Thomas Hardy* [London and Athens, GA, 1985], p. 179. [Any further references are cited parenthetically as *Life* – Ed.]).

7

The Mayor of Casterbridge: Made of Money

JOE FISHER

'I haven't more than fifteen shillings in the world, and yet I am a good experienced hand in my line. I'd challenge England to beat me in the fodder business; and if I were a free man again I'd be worth a thousand pound before I'd done o't. But a fellow never knows these little things till all chance of acting upon 'em is past.'

(MC, p. 10)

'Very well,' said Henchard quickly, 'please yourself. But I tell you, young man, if this holds good for the bulk, as it has for the sample, you have saved my credit, stranger though you be. What shall I pay you for this knowledge?'

(MC, p. 49)

'Then the wheat – that sometimes used to taste so strong o' mice when made into bread that people could fairly tell the breed – Farfrae has a plan for purifying, so that nobody would dream the smallest four-legged beast had walked over it once. Oh yes, everybody is full of him, and the care Mr Henchard has to keep him, to be sure!' concluded this gentleman.

'No, he won't do it for long, good-now,' said the other.

'No!' said Henchard to himself behind the tree. 'Or if he do, he'll be honeycombed clean out of all the character and standing that he's built up these eighteen year!'

(MC, p. 107)

When Susan Henchard and her daughter arrive in Casterbridge Michael Henchard is at the height of his power and influence in the town, celebrating his mayoral authority at the banquet at the King's Arms. The narrative thus contains two opposed extremes, both contained in the novel's principal character. At Weydon-Priors he got drunk and sold his wife and daughter to a sailor; at Casterbridge he is the most prominent figure in the town. There is no clear narrative continuity offered to explain the two versions of the subtitled 'Man of Character'; and consequently narrative stability gives way almost from the first to the 'staging' devices of *The Return of the Native*. Hardy's dangerous dare here is contained in the subtitle, and notions of stable character are replaced by the 'elemental' capitalist instabilities of cash and credit. Character and narrative are sacrificed to these non-humanistic imperatives. The bourgeois liberal fictional trick is displaced at its roots (which are, literally, the fertile roots of Henchard's trade, his 'character' and his 'credit'). As Goode shows,

> All Henchard's decisive acts are theatrical and the story is constructed around them – the auction, the oath, the banquet, the meeting with Susan in the arena, the embrace of Farfrae, the visit to the soothsayer, the greeting for the royal personage, the reading out of Lucetta's letters, his meeting with her in the arena, the fight with Farfrae, the last exit. The self-begotten, arranged significant and egocentric gesture is the dominant unifying force of the narrative. Susan and Elizabeth-Jane enter Casterbridge as though it were a theatre ... There is even a band to welcome them and their first glimpse of Henchard is in tableau, performing a role.
>
> This theatricality does not enter and transform the novel: it is the very condition of its existence. We have no indication of the details of Henchard's rise from journeyman to Mayor and are surely not intended to think that being teetotal is a guarantee of such success.[1]

We see Henchard at Casterbridge through Susan and Elizabeth-Jane's arrival. We follow the two women into the town in order to see, as they see, that an alchemical change has taken place in Henchard. Like them we are given no psychological data to help analyse the change. And like them we do not see the change but are asked to construct it from the two analogues of alchemical change Hardy offers: the changing of wife into cash at Weydon-Priors fair and Farfrae's changing of grown wheat to wholesome.

These two transactions are absolutely connected and they order the making of the whole fiction. Farfrae is the instigator of Henchard's downfall, and thus of almost all the novel's dramatic action. Henchard is the drama: Farfrae is the staging machinery.

This function is nearly as blatant as Dare's in *A Laodicean*. Farfrae *causes* so much of the novel because he contains the allegorical proposition it devotes itself to falsifying, that it is possible to make grown wheat wholesome, to reverse malign (organic?) processes which have already taken place. The sample has been changed by Farfrae's alchemical process, so that the remaining question is whether the same process will hold good for the bulk. The novel's full title is *The Life and Death of the Mayor of Casterbridge*. Henchard is mayor for less than a third of its length, and what we really see is the process by which Henchard loses his power and Farfrae gains it. The point is that the mayor is *seen* to be created by the trading practices which enforce the power of money, and Casterbridge, over the field. In terms of the traded text Henchard's ascent to power, which we do not see, is assumed to be an earlier version of Farfrae's: Henchard is the 'rule o' thumb sort of man' and Farfrae his technological successor. Henchard's emotional need for Farfrae naturalises, even physicalises, one stage of a historical, material process trying to retain its power against a successor. The proposition that this is 'A Story of a Man of Character' actually proposes the question of whether the individual is stronger than the material process which makes him, and whether character can overcome the cash which in every sense creates him. 'Character', 'credit' and 'standing' become virtually coterminous. Plainly this strikes at the heart of all notions of liberal 'individualism'.

> 'You must be, what – five foot nine, I reckon? I am six foot one and a half out of my shoes. But what of that? In my business, 'tis true that strength and bustle build up a firm. But judgement and knowledge are what keep it established. Unluckily, I am bad at science, Farfrae; bad at figures – a rule o'thumb sort of man. You are just the reverse – I can see that, I have been looking for such as you these last two year, and yet you are not for me. Well, before I go, let me ask this: Though you are not the young man I thought you were, what's the difference? Can't you stay with me just the same? Have you really made up your mind about this American notion? I won't mince matters. I feel you would be invaluable to me – that needn't be said – and if you will bide and be my manager I will make it worth your while.'
>
> (MC, pp. 49–50)

But the 'rule o'thumb' is far more than this, Henchard's judgement is based on guesswork and superstition. These are the qualities which have built his 'character', 'credit' and 'standing' in

Casterbridge. In terms of the historical moment of the novel's production, as opposed to its earlier setting, this represents an appeal to fatalism which was part of the workfolk's response to the 1880s agricultural depression: Kerr cites the example of *Raphael's Book of Fate*, a best-seller guaranteed to 'tell the fate of anyone'.[2] This becomes the vehicle of the authorial will to power. Henchard's failed gamble on harvests and prices when he tries to overpower Farfrae and retain control without his new ally resembles a real transaction Kerr also refers to. A plausible part-model for Henchard is Shadrach Dunn of Gillingham (1799–1867), a self-made seed merchant and pioneer of artificial grasses reputed to have made £10,000 from grain deals in 1848, having bought cheap after the good summer of 1846 and held his stock until the 1848 harvest was washed out by summer rains.[3] Henchard's failure to capitalise in the same way seems to be attributable to his superstition, and Farfrae's consequent success to the lack of it.

This brings into play a whole alternative structure based on the essentially volatile discourses (in terms of the 'rational' constructs of 'science' and 'history') of magic and witchcraft. In the traded text these devices are used to colour and validate a Wessex setting and a 'Wessex' protagonist, the superstitious countryman faced with a centralising cash economy and its threatening scientific devices. In the counter-text Henchard is 'made of money' at Casterbridge after he has been magically created at Weydon-Priors. Hardy's use of the Wild Man figure is again central in this process. Like the mock Wild Man brought out of the woods in a pageant to greet Elizabeth I at Kenilworth in 1575,[4] Henchard comes out of the wilderness and approaches the margin of civilisation at a fair. The fair becomes the Victorian communal equivalent of the individualised, mythologised medieval Wild Man in terms of its dangerous marginality. It is both inside and outside socio-economic structure. As Stallybrass and White put it:

> the fair, like the marketplace, is neither pure nor outside. The fair is at the crossroads, situated at the intersection of economic and cultural forces, goods and travellers, commodities and commerce. It is a gravely over-simplifying abstraction therefore to conceptualise the fair purely as the sight of communal celebration.[5]

Hardy's fair at Weydon-Priors is also at an intersection of historical perspective. Malcolmson quotes an 1875 petition against the two annual fairs at Sawbridgeworth which encapsulates the Victorian bourgeois attempt to suppress the threatening 'low' culture of the fair:

> But whilst these Fairs are of the smallest possible conceivable worth in a commercial point of view, indefensibly and indisputably they are the prolific seed plots and occasions of the most hideous forms of moral and social evil – drunkenness – whoredom – robbery – idleness and neglect of work ...[6]

This is a remarkably transhistorical gesture. Ebbatson points to Hardy's use elsewhere, notably in 'On the Western Circuit', of the fair's machinery of misrule to express the erotic and sexual activity which the bourgeois onlookers cannot.[7] In *The Mayor of Casterbridge* the device is turned on the bourgeois reader in terms of a more elemental and heretical fertility. The Sawbridgeworth petitioners' 'seed plots' (presumably) unwittingly link the fair to its more general and older source as a subversive celebration of fertility, in which the Wild Man was an essential figure. Bernheimer refers to the early christian writings of St Peter Chrysologus (d. 450) and Caesarius, Bishop of Arles (d. 542), denouncing pagan and part-christian carnivals and their Wild Men, culminating in their (unsuccessful) suppression by decree at the Second Trullan Council in 692.[8] The attempt to remove the individuated figure of the Wild Man becomes the attempt to remove 'moral and social evil' in 1875.

Hardy starts with a reading of the historical moment of *The Mayor of Casterbridge*'s production: the Wild Man, once indispensable, joins the fair as it is about to close. Bernheimer gives this account of the Wild Man's foreknowledge of the land's fertility, which is also the basis of Henchard's 'rule o'thumb':

> as a demon he shares nature's secrets and is thus in a position to give advice about the weather, the harvest prospects, medical herbs, and even about processes in the dairy business. Accordingly he tells the peasants when to sow and to gather the rye, and thus is responsible for the ensuring abundance.[9]

He goes on to say that making the Wild Man drunk reveals his secrets. The secret we are told at Weydon-Priors when Henchard gets drunk is the Wild Man's potential to exploit a cash economy: 'if I were a free man again I'd be worth a thousand pound before I'd done o't.' Then at Casterbridge Henchard protects his secret that he sold his wife and child (the human expressions of the same fertility), and the magical predictive skill which built his character and his credit, by abstaining from alcohol.

But the drink at Weydon-Priors has been mixed in a witch's cauldron. This is presented with a minimum of ambiguity.

> At the upper end [of the tent] stood a stove, containing a charcoal fire, over which hung a large three-legged crock, sufficiently polished round the rim to show that it was made of bell-metal. A haggish creature of about fifty presided, in a white apron, which, as it threw an air of respectability over her as far as it extended, was made so wide as to reach nearly round her waist. She slowly stirred the contents of the pot. The dull scrape of her spoon was audible throughout the tent as she thus kept from burning the mixture of corn in the grain, flour, milk, raisins, currants, and what not, that composed the antiquated slop in which she dealt. ...
>
> But there was more in that tent than met the cursory glance; and the man, with the instinct of a perverse character, scented it quickly. After a mincing attack on his bowl he watched the hag's proceedings from a corner of his eye, and saw the game she played. He winked to her, and passed up his basin in reply to her nod; when she took a bottle from under the table, slily measured out a quantity of its contents, and tipped the same into the man's furmity. The liquor poured in was rum. The man as slily sent back money in payment.
>
> (MC, pp. 8–9)

Casterbridge is made up of (apparently) stable structures and a stable market (and a stable Man of Character); Weydon-Priors is the portable structure of a portable market. Although the assumed exchange of the fair is a trade in livestock and workfolk, like the trade at Casterbridge and Greenhill fairs in *Far From the Madding Crowd*, the exchange we actually see is the purchase of rum-laced furmity for cash. This magical transaction creates Henchard's Casterbridge in the counter-text, because the act of making the Wild Man drunk and engaging him with the cash economy on the margin of the wilderness (repeated in a Casterbridge where 'Country and town met at a mathematical line' [MC, p. 29]) reveals the means by which his 'character' and 'credit' will be established. The most notable constituents in the furmity, 'to those not accustomed to it', are 'grains of wheat, swollen as large as lemon-pips, which floated on its surface' (MC, p. 9). These grains, and the smuggled rum which is part of the heretical 'low' law and culture of Mixen Lane (a street name which reprises Mrs Goodenough's act of mixing the contents of her cauldron; and naturally enough, she comes to Mixen Lane when she comes to Casterbridge) are the main constituent elements of this version of Casterbridge. Furmity is possibly the only drink in which seeds are literally planted and which therefore plants seeds in the drinker.

In this way corn and rum are mixed inside Henchard. The effect is immediate. Having used cash to buy rum he gets drunk and in this uninhibited state he sells his wife and frees himself. The buyer who emerges, not entering the tent until the auction is under way and Henchard is already drunk, is a sailor. Rum is traditionally a sailors' drink, and it has (presumably) been smuggled to Weydon-Priors from the sea. This connection is repeated when Susan and Elizabeth-Jane arrive in Casterbridge. Henchard, having abstained from alcohol ever since the wife-selling, has risen to eminence by corn-trading. The narrator observes that 'Time the magician had wrought much here' (MC, p. 35). When the two women come to the King's Arms and see the banquet, which celebrates the success of an economy built on the corn trade, the diners at Henchard's table are preparing to drink rum. The narrator makes this a parody of the christian ritual overthrown (by witchcraft and the breaking of christian marriage) at Weydon-Priors:

> Three drinks seemed to be sacred to the company – port, sherry, and rum; outside which old-established trinity few or no palates ranged.
> A row of ancient rummers with ground figures on their sides, and each primed with a spoon, was now placed down the table, and these were promptly filled with grog at such high temperatures as to raise serious considerations for the articles exposed to its vapours.
> (MC, pp. 35–6)

And when Henchard and Susan finally meet again they do so at an inn called the Three Mariners. Farfrae arrives at Casterbridge at the same time as the two women, and these arrivals signal the breaking of the spell cast in the tent. Henchard's 'rule o'thumb' judgement begins to fail and he is forced to visit Conjurer Fall in order to guess at the weather and harvest prospects.

This 'magical' disruption of 'realism' is equally a disruption of class and gender structures. In terms of the sexing of property it immediately overturns the notions of male planting of male seed (which inform Casterbridge's entirely male government) at the centre of Victorian evolutionary theories of patriarchy and the beginnings of property: the Henchard created at Weydon-Priors has been mixed in a female witch's cauldron, in which seeds are stirred (and scraped, or potentially aborted) as if they were in a womb. By selling his wife and daughter Henchard becomes a self-dispossessed patriarch, so that Hardy's usual pattern of a fatherless woman is replaced by a wifeless and daughterless man without the human fertility to perpetuate his power structures. His business is to control, buy and sell other people's seed, but he has given up control of his own.

Henchard's chief magistracy at Casterbridge has been achieved, in effect, by a repudiation of paternity which he tries to make good as his 'high' law collapses when it is challenged by the 'low' law of the furmity-woman and Mixen Lane. In regaining his wife and (non-biological) daughter, these power structures collapse. And Henchard's anti-realistic conception, or transformation, at Weydon-Priors produces a class antagonism which adumbrates the basis of his trading success in Casterbridge. As Wotton puts it:

> Henchard negates the festive and celebratory nature of the fair by his egotism. What the people perceive as a joke permissible under the rules of topsy-turvy, the licence of the temporary release from the world of work, Henchard means seriously and in that act which refuses the spirit of the festival he places himself in a position of antagonism to the workfolk, an antagonism which grows with time.[10]

The placing of money, the notes and coins which Newson (a surrogate new son who takes over the patrilinear inheritance Henchard is surrendering) counts out as payment for Susan, in Henchard's magical transformation is an additional and very fundamental subversion of a fiction which makes a claim to 'realism'. As John Vernon argues, potent comparisons can be made between the nineteenth-century novel's claim to represent reality and paper money's claim to represent 'things of (presumably) enduring value: gold and silver'.[11] In this sense the novel's opening at Weydon-Priors uses the dice-throwing on the heath in *The Return of the Native* as its point of departure. Both fallacies are in the hands of a witch in *The Mayor of Casterbridge*.

Hardy makes this connection clear when Henchard visits Conjuror Fall. A conjuror is traditionally a male witch, often regarded as a white witch and a repository of communal wisdom. Conjuror Minterne and Conjuror Trendle are mentioned on this basis at Talbothays dairy in *Tess of the d'Urbervilles*. An additional meaning is that a conjuror may be a priest of the old religion,[12] and

the sources of both Minterne and Trendle suggest this more dia-
bolic function. John Minterne was reputed to have made a pact
with the devil which enabled him to jump on horseback from
Batcombe Down over the church at Batcombe. A pinnacle of the
church could not be made to stand and it was said that the hoof of
Minterne's horse removed it. Minterne was buried against a church
wall because he 'vowed to be buried neither in nor out of church'.[13]
Waring connects this with the medieval legend of the church-build-
ing devil, in which an architect makes a pact with the devil to assist
him in building a church and cheats the devil of his reward, at
which the devil kicks an irreparable hole in the church as he
departs. This suggests striking connections with Hardy's novelistic
practice as an antinomian architect. The Trendle comes from the
mummers' play: in the Dorchester play the devil says

> Here comes I, Beelzebub –
> And over my shoulders I carry a club
> And in my hand a frying-pan
> And I think myself a jolly old man.[14]

The Trendle is the club, also brandished by the Cerne Abbas giant.
  The narrator's account of Henchard's visit to Conjuror Fall is
heavily laden with counter-meanings:

> In a lonely hamlet a few miles from the town – so lonely that what
> are called lonely villages were teeming by comparison – there lived a
> man of curious repute as a forecaster or weather-prophet. The way
> to his house was crooked and miry – even difficult in the present un-
> propitious season. One evening when it was raining so heavily that
> ivy and laurel resounded like distant musketry, and an out-door man
> could be excused for shrouding himself to his ears and eyes, such a
> shrouded figure on foot might have been perceived travelling in the
> direction of the hazel copse which dripped over the prophet's cot.
> The turnpike-road became a lane, the lane a cart-track; the cart-track
> a bridle-path, the bridle-path a footway, the footway overgrown. The
> solitary walker slipped here and there, and stumbled over the natural
> springs formed by the brambles, till at length he reached the house,
> which, with its garden was surrounded with a high dense hedge. The
> cottage, comparatively a large one, had been built out of mud by the
> occupier's own hands, and thatched also by himself. Here he had
> always lived, and here it was assumed he would die.
>   He existed on unseen supplies; for it was an anomalous thing that
> while there was hardly a soul in the neighbourhood but affected to
> laugh at this man's assertions, uttering the formula 'There's nothing

in 'em', with full assurance on the surface of their faces, very few of them were unbelievers in their secret hearts. Whenever they consulted him they did it 'for a fancy'. When they paid him they said, 'Just a trifle for Christmas', or 'Candlemas', as the case might be.

He would have preferred more honesty in his clients, and less sham ridicule; but fundamental belief consoled him for superficial irony. As stated, he was enabled to live: people supported him with their backs turned. He was sometimes astonished that men could profess so little and believe so much at his house when at church they professed so much and believed so little.

(MC, pp. 185–6)

The setting of Conjuror Fall's house has striking similarities with a widely reported incident in 1863, in which a wiseman from Sible Hedingham called Dummy, who lived alone in a self-built mud hut on the outskirts of the village, was ducked, and later died, because he was thought to have cursed the landlady of an inn which refused him accommodation.[15] Again we are taken to the margin of the wilderness through a series of obscuring devices. The turnpike-road turning to overgrown footpath is either an invitation to the reader, or a dangerous dare, which moves from the main turnpike-road of the traded text to the concealed creative strategies which make the counter-text. Hardy specifically characterises an authorial position in Conjuror Fall: the authorial project of producing *The Mayor of Casterbridge* is, very fundamentally, to conjure a fall. In asking how the harvest will grow from the seed Henchard is asking for foreknowledge of his own story, of the seed planted at Weydon-Priors. In this sense the tempest and disaster Conjuror Fall forecasts also accurately foretells Henchard's own future. And Conjuror Fall has, inevitably, predicted Henchard's arrival at his house and set a place for him at his table. Once more cash is exchanged before secrets are revealed, just as cash is exchanged before the reader can reproduce the fiction.

'Then take this,' said Henchard. ''Tis a crown piece. Now, what is the harvest fortnight to be? When can I know?'

'I've worked it out already, and you can know it at once.' (The fact was that five farmers had already been there on the same errand from different parts of the country.) 'By the sun, moon and stars, by the clouds, the winds, the trees and grass, the candle flame and swallows, the smell of the herbs; likewise by the cats' eyes, the ravens, the leeches, the spiders, and the dung-mixen, the last fortnight in August will be – rain and tempest.'

'You are not certain, of course.'

'As one can be in a world where all's unsure. 'Twill be more like living in Revelations this autumn than in England. Shall I sketch it out for 'ee in a scheme?

(MC, p. 187)

There is no need to sketch out any scheme, because the reader already has it in the pages which follow. The harvest and its sequels, foretold by the invocation of pagan, pantheistic signs, will create another anti-christian Revelation of St John Power the Divine. When the rains come, after Henchard has acted against Conjuror Fall's advice and already lost heavily, and it becomes clear that the prediction will come true, the 'Man of Character's overwhelming egotism in the traded text is juxtaposed with a sense of his counter-textual creation. This threatens narrative dislocation on a major scale.

> From that day and hour it was clear that there was not to be so successful an ingathering after all. If Henchard had only waited long enough he might at least have avoided loss though he had not made a profit. But the momentum of his character knew no patience. At this turn of the scale he remained silent. The movements of his mind seemed to tend to the thought that some power was working against him.
>
> 'I wonder,' he asked himself with eerie misgiving; 'I wonder if it can be that somebody has been roasting a waxen image of me, or stirring an unholy brew to confound me! I don't believe in such power; and yet – what if they should ha' been doing it!' Even he could not admit that the perpetrator, if any, might be Farfrae.
>
> (MC, p. 190)

And so as the spell breaks, a self-knowledge which also threatens to break the traded text begins to emerge. Because this threat is located in a self-creative and self-destructive central protagonist, it is possible to bury the counter-text and the author's concealed will to power in a way which appears to strengthen the traded text; Henchard's overwhelming (and at this point almost paranoid) egotism seems to account for his instinct that he may have been cursed. The introduction of these discourses of magic represents a very important progression from *A Laodicean*, where a surprisingly similar project, in terms of its critique, weakens its traded text because its counter-textual discourses dealing with the technology of perception must necessarily be displayed on the surface of the text without the same potential for integration. *A Laodicean* attempts the integration and fails. The most important change between these two novels is the shift from a counter-text concerned, like *The Hand of Ethelberta* and *The Return of the Native*, with the *destruction* of fictional representation and perception, to a counter-text concerned with a genuine alternative mode of *creation*. In this sense the production of *The Mayor of Casterbridge* is Hardy's first truly revolutionary act, which puts his earlier subversions into context as localised attacks and overthrowings in the campaign of gradual erosion which has made this revolution possible.

Lucas argues that in *The Mayor of Casterbridge* 'the bare fact matters, because [Hardy] isn't writing fable or allegory. On the contrary, actuality is all important.'[16] The point is that because Hardy's heretical creative discourses in this novel create a writing based on *fundamentally* anti-realistic fable and allegory, he is free for the first time to deal with socio-economic actuality. Although Henchard comes from nowhere, his encounter with the outside edge of structure at Weydon-Priors has a firm material basis. Henchard and his family become a paradigm of the landless workfolk his business at Casterbridge sets him against. When Henchard and Susan come to civilisation from the field they need work and somewhere to live. Weydon-Priors can offer neither: five houses were cleared away last year and three this. They only go to the fair after learning this information.

All that remains of the fair is 'the clatter and scurry of getting away, the money o' children and fools' (MC, p. 8). When Susan and Elizabeth-Jane arrive at Casterbridge, the image is repeated and institutionalised; they come to the town just as the shops are closing and the curfew is being sounded. As in *A Laodicean*, the end of day signals the start of an analytical *walpurgisnacht*. In Casterbridge Susan and Elizabeth-Jane go to a hotel, civilisation's image of comfort and welcome, where at Weydon-Priors the Henchards go to a tent. Again the repetition is clear: the choice of the Three Mariners rather than the King's Arms echoes the choice of the shabby furmity tent rather than the opulent-looking beer tent.

At the moment when natural light is lost Casterbridge is brought gradually into focus, as a preparation for its stage lighting. Because the counter-text is now creative rather than destructive, Casterbridge is made revelatory after sunset where Edgon Heath was made obscure. The narrator begins by supporting Elizabeth-Jane's comment about the town's antiquity ('naturalising' it historically in the 'traded' text) and its visual sense of geometric artifice as

an imposition placed in the field, like the Baptist chapel in
A Laodicean:

> Its squareness was, indeed, the characteristic which most struck
> the eye in this antiquated borough, the borough of Casterbridge – at
> that time, recent though it was, untouched by the faintest sprinkle of
> modernism. It was compact as a box of dominoes. It had no suburbs
> – in the ordinary sense. Country and town met at a mathematical
> line.
>
> To birds of the more soaring kind Casterbridge must have ap-
> peared on this fine evening as a mosaic-work of subdued red,
> browns, greys and crystals, held together by a rectangular frame of
> deep green. To the level eye of humanity it stood as an indistinct
> mass behind a dense stockade of limes and chestnuts, set in the midst
> of miles of rotund down and concave field. The mass became gradu-
> ally dissected by the vision into towers, gables, chimneys, and case-
> ments, the highest glazings shining bleared and bloodshot with the
> coppery fire they caught from the belt of sun-lit cloud in the west.
>
> (MC, p. 29)

The 'level eye of humanity' capable of mathematical definition and
dissection is a significant change from Clym's ophthalmia and
Dare's corrupt photography. Because Henchard's Casterbridge has
been made in Mrs Goodenough's cauldron, or in Conjuror Fall's
mud hut, there is no need to obscure it. First we see a general shape
and the emphasised margin of the mathematical line; then we see
the town from the height of a bird, perceiving only abstract colour
and image; then human vision focuses more closely, seeing specific
architectural features as Susan and Elizabeth-Jane come up one of
the avenues which run out from the town into the surrounding
cornland; then we see people; then we hear voices; then we hear
Henchard's name. The stage is set. Now that the arrival at Weydon-
Priors has been repeated in an arrival at the more permanent structure the tents adumbrate, the results of the Wild Man's witching
can be revealed.

> The lamplights now glimmered through the engirdling trees, con-
> veying a sense of great smugness and comfort inside, and rendering
> at the same time then unlighted country without strangely solitary
> and vacant in aspect, considering its nearness to life. The difference
> between burgh and champaign was increased, too, by sounds which
> now reached them above others – the notes of a brass band. The
> travellers returned into the high street, where there were timber-
> houses with overhanging stories whose small paned lattices were

screened by dimity curtains on a drawing-string and under whose
barge-boards old cobwebs waved in the breeze. There were houses of
brick-nagging which derived their chief support from those adjoining. There were slate roofs patched with tiles, and tile roofs patched
with slate, with occasionally a roof of thatch.

The agricultural and pastoral character of the people on whom the
town depended for its existence was shown by the class of objects
displayed in the shop windows. Scythes, reap-hooks, sheep-shears,
bill-hooks, spades, mattocks, and hoes, at the ironmongers: bee-
hives, butter-firkins, churns, milking-stools and pails, hay-rakes,
field-flagons, and seed-lips, at the cooper's; cart-ropes and plough-
harness at the saddler's; carts, wheelbarrows, and mill-gear at the
wheelwright's and machinist's; horse-embrocations at the chemist's;
at the glover's and leather-cutter's hedging-gloves, thatcher's knee-
caps, ploughmen's leggings, villagers' pattens and clogs.

(MC, pp. 30–1)

The 'celebration' of Susan and Elizabeth-Jane's arrival by fairy lights
and a brass band marks the point where Henchard and Casterbridge
cease to be fused by the breaking of the witch's spell. For Casterbridge
and its economic future it is a genuine celebration, because Farfrae
arrives the same night; the tainted bread which threatens civilisation's
power over the field can be made good. For Henchard it is ironic;
because it marks the start of alienation from the trading process
which has made him. The images of trade and selling are contradictory. The narrator suggests that they show 'the agricultural pastoral
nature of the people', invoking the anthropological Myth of Wessex;
but their very profusion re-emphasises the self-conscious artifice of
Casterbridge and its trade. In the counter-text these are really stage
settings for the analytical drama which follows. Once the curfew has
been rung and the shops closed, the reader and the two women are
inside the revelatory theatre. A physically revelatory image follows:

> In an open space before the church walked a woman with her
> gown-sleeves rolled up so high that the edge of her under-linen was
> visible, and her skirt tucked up through her pocket-hole. She carried
> a loaf under her arm, from which she was pulling pieces of bread
> and handing them to some other women who walked with her,
> which pieces they nibbled critically. The sight reminded Mrs
> Henchard-Newson and her daughter that they had an appetite; and
> they enquired of the woman for the nearest baker's.
>
> 'Ye may as well look for manna-food as good bread in
> Casterbridge just now', she said.

(MC, pp. 31–2)

The increasingly focused, evolving close-up shot of Casterbridge has produced an increasingly rigorous analysis of its function. The relationship between human and agricultural fertility is crucial at Weydon-Priors and it is equally crucial when the two are brought together again. We see the woman walking with her under-linen visible, bringing us close to a source of human fertility (in the non-patriarchal history of Mrs Goodenough's cauldron; and the woman goes on to explain that she has been wife and mother) and this suggests that we are very close to a primary explanation, since the narrator has been stripping layers of misrepresentation and false explanation from Casterbridge just as he has been stripping her clothes. The revealed under-linen has no other conceivable purpose. The woman is carrying bread, and distributing it, and so she exactly describes Casterbridge's business. The town is able to trade, to build itself and to continue trading because it takes corn from the country and turns it into bread. The bread is bad; the man to blame is the man at the centre of the transaction, the corn-factor; the corn-factor is Henchard; and Henchard is the mayor of Casterbridge.

Henchard's business is the very fundamental capitalist transaction which places a cash value (and *makes* and *alters* that value) on the primary process of growing food to eat. The business of trading in corn, of paying a cash price to the grower (Henchard's main creditor at this bankruptcy is a Mr *Grower*) and selling on to the miller and the baker is the paradigm business which can be made to stand for all the further levels and degrees of business which could not otherwise be carried on. Henchard's corn-factoring becomes the primary transaction which enforces the laws of cash on the field, and his monopoly is emphasised: Susan and Elizabeth-Jane learn that 'he's the man that our millers and bakers all deal wi'' (MC, p. 32). It is the transaction which makes possible the changing of the workfolk's labour into cash; and so this is the alternative alchemy analysed at Casterbridge. This was the state of alienation Henchard was in when he came to Weydon-Priors, and so his position at Casterbridge follows necessarily from the nature of his transformation at Weydon-Priors.

After his fall has been conjured, his fellow bourgeois on the town council set Henchard up in a seed-merchant's shop. This is a set-up in both senses (and an ironic precursor of the twentieth-century notion of 'seedbed' capital). The un-wild Wild Man has grown and husbanded money instead of crops, and a bad harvest of the latter has also been a bad harvest of the former. Without his credit, character and standing he has no trade. In his little shop, Henchard is using Casterbridge's capital rather than his own to sell the seeds which created him at Weydon-Priors, and in this way the town's power over him is established. He is forced to sell the seeds of new fertility and history when the seeds of his own history have germinated, flourished and overgrown, like the 'growed' wheat. The public display of this cash-alienation comes in the royal personage's visit. The Wild Man is drunk, and the secret he reveals now is the extent of his alienation from the bourgeois hegemony he personified when Susan and Elizabeth-Jane first came to Casterbridge. This was the 'real' secret of his position when he came to Weydon-Priors looking for work and shelter.

When Henchard meets the witch again the only remaining product of the spell is his magistracy. The 'high' law he upholds once protected his economic interests and now it reinforces his alienation. The cauldron and Casterbridge both contain the same dialectic, in which evolutionary patterns of 'natural' law and history are replaced by a conflict between 'high' and 'low', between the materially powerful and the materially powerless. The skimmington-ride is the clearest example of the attempt to negotiate law and government on this basis. Hole attributes the skimmington's prevalence in the nineteenth century to 'the primitive notion that incest, adultery or immortality blighted the crops',[17] represented in *The Mayor of Casterbridge* by loaves 'as flat as toads, and like suet pudden inside' (MC, p. 32). She also gives the instance of participants in a skimmington in Hedon in 1889 making the claim that it had become 'legal' because the victim's effigy had been carried three nights in succession, as if the anti-rational and 'superstitious' discourses of *The Mayor of Casterbridge's* counter-text can gain hegemonic control of the traded text by insistent covert practice. This is plainly a notional victory when a bourgeois fiction must be traded for the counter-text to exist at all, but it nonetheless indicates a radical shift in the power relations which structure the fiction's competing discourses.

The counter-text comes close to the surface allegorically in the Roman remains at Casterbridge. Bernheimer shows that, as for instance in *Gorboduc*, Wild Men were often identified in England as pre-Anglo-Saxon Britons (and in this sense Henchard supersedes the earlier Aeneas figures, founding England from Rome).[18] In this sense, with the conflict between magical and material histories at issue, the Roman amphitheatre, where Henchard has two critical meetings, becomes a dangerous middle ground between past and present. And the Roman remains are also very much an authorial 'dare': the townspeople of Casterbridge, like the reader of the traded text, regularly dig up Roman antiquities without any sense of their interest or value.

The one building in Casterbridge which does not have a direct relation to corn-trading is Lucetta's house, the unambiguously-named High-Place Hall.

> The Hall, with its grey *façade* and parapet, was the only residence of its sort so near the centre of the town. It had, in the first place, the characteristics of a country mansion – birds'-nests in the chimneys, damp nooks where fungi grew, and irregularities of surface direct from nature's trowel ... The house was entirely of stone, and formed an example of dignity without great size. It was not altogether aristocratic, still less consequential, yet the old-fashioned stranger instinctively said, 'Blood built it, and Wealth enjoys it,' however vague his opinions of those accessories might be.
>
> Yet as regards the enjoying it, the stranger would have been wrong, for until this very evening, when the new lady had arrived, the house had been empty for a year or two, while before that interval its occupancy had been irregular. The reason of its unpopularity was soon made manifest. Some of its rooms overlooked the marketplace; and such a prospect from such a house was not considered desirable or seemly by its would-be occupiers ... Elizabeth trotted through the open door in the dusk, but becoming alarmed at her own temerity, she went quickly out again by another which stood open in the lofty wall of the back court. To her surprise she found herself in one of the little-used alleys of the town. Looking round at the door which had given her egress, by the light of the solitary lamp fixed in the alley, she saw that it was arched and old – older even than the house itself. The door was studded, and the keystone of the arch was a mask. Originally the mask had exhibited a comic leer, as could still be discerned; but generations of Casterbridge boys had thrown stones at the mask, aiming at its open mouth; and the blows thereon had chipped off the lips and jaws as if they had been eaten away by disease. The appearance was so ghastly by the weakly lamp glimmer that she could not bear to look at it – the first unpleasant feature of her visit.
>
> (MC, p. 140–2)

Under Lucetta's tenancy High-Place Hall, which overlooks the corn market, becomes the source of a female overview of a male trade in the seeds of fertility. The house looks two ways, forward to the market, the source of 'blood' and 'wealth's' continuing power and back, through the leering arch, to an alternative history of squalid intrigue. In this sense it is also the analogue of Hardy's cultural power when his fictions enter bourgeois society from the front door and the non-bourgeois sources of the fictions. The leering mask, in the context of the house's pretensions to 'naturalise' power, represents the erosion this duplicity has achieved.

The mask was originally the representation of a human face, just as the novel is originally concerned to represent human behaviour. It is always described as a mask, never as a face; it is plainly a pretence. It is in any case part of a house, not a human body, and its meaning must therefore really refer to the structure, not the conceit that the structure is pretending to be a person. Over the years the face has been eroded, almost to the point of becoming featureless, by thoughtless attack. The mask is the keystone of the arch over the back door of High-Place Hall. In the literal surface of the text, the mask's meanings refer to the world behind, or below, the house, to 'low life' and intrigue: but the placing of the mask means that it can equally be read as referring to the world inside, and in front of, the house. If the arch can be used to go in one direction, it can also be used to go in the other; the intrigue and erosion might equally be said to refer to the market, and the exchanges between Lucetta, Henchard and Farfrae which encompass Henchard's downfall in the traded text.

Farfrae's conquest over the trade in fertility is enforced by his conquest over Henchard's women, first a putative wife and then a putative daughter. And the fertility ritual of the Wild Man's fair is also repeated ironically as part of this process: Henchard's dancing, his attempt to bring the fair to town, is virtually ignored in favour of Farfrae's.

When Henchard and Susan re-court and re-marry, a period of impossible equipoise is introduced. Henchard and Farfrae operate in tandem and it seems that grown wheat can be made good. But the equipoise is based on the belief that Elizabeth-Jane is the daughter Henchard sold. If the new contract with Susan was permanent or productive (if, in other words, Elizabeth-Jane was Henchard's daughter rather than Newson's, and there was a biological link between Weydon-Priors and Casterbridge), it would be possible for an individual to break his contract with state and society, to have the benefits of operating without the hindrances of the contract, and then to re-contract on his own terms; or, more directly, to have had the use of the capital obtained from the exchange of fertility for cash without penalty. This is not possible. Susan is moribund when she arrives in Casterbridge and Elizabeth-Jane is Newson's daughter. In terms of Mrs Goodenough's mixture she is the daughter of rum, not corn. She is Henchard's by incantatory narrative, not 'natural' blood.

Henchard's second attempt at marriage in Casterbridge is to Lucetta, and since her 'honour' has already been compromised by Henchard this is another attempt to make grown wheat wholesome. This contract would establish a connection which looks forward rather than backward (hence the ambivalent dual aspects of High-Place Hall) because it represents an alliance between new trade and old wealth. Henchard's trade is already superseded when he tries to marry Lucetta, and she marries Farfrae, who has become the newer personification of the corn trade. (Their marriage is witnessed by the ubiquitous Mr Grower.) Farfrae's new horse-drill, literally an image of agricultural efficiency and allegorically an image of sexual proficiency, epitomises this. Lucetta's pseudo-active choice is, more blatantly than elsewhere, simply between the attraction of past and future stages of capitalism: the two suitors' 'characters' rise and fall as their 'credit' rises and falls. Human fertility is for sale and she falls, like Susan at Weydon-Priors, to the highest bidder.

Lucetta is duly impregnated by the man with the horse-drill, but she dies while she is carrying Farfrae's child, leaving the alliance between trade and wealth unachieved and without issue. Henchard is indirectly responsible for the death, and for this seed failing to grow, because the return of his love-letters leads to the skimmington. Then Henchard sees his own effigy, as if it were his dead body, floating in the river; and this image moves the marriage plot to its concluding stage. The marriage between Farfrae and Elizabeth-Jane has nothing to do with Henchard. He is neither Elizabeth-Jane's father nor the progenitor of Farfrae's business, which has grown up quite independently as a result of his failure. The patriarchal structure has overthrown the Wild Man's transgression, and Henchard's last gift to Casterbridge is a caged bird, which ought to live on seed, starving to death for the lack of it.

All that remains is Henchard's will, the egotistical force which created his business and his 'character' in the traded text. He is not left with no contract, no issue and no business. He is in early middle age and of robust constitution, and there is no practical reason why he should die so quickly. Even a temperance novelist could not expect such a precipitate death from drink, and the narra-

tor offers no evidence that drink kills him. But the vow of abstinence has the counter-textual meanings established at Weydon-
Priors and now rum has succeeded corn. Henchard is a drinking
man and a field-labourer once more, not a teetotaller buying and
selling fields and field-labourers and their produce. His life only
existed in terms of his analytical journey from Weydon-Priors to
Casterbridge; so now he returns to Weydon-Priors before returning
to his obscure origins to die. Once his character and credit are gone
he literally ceases to exist. His will represents the necessity of this
self-negation: his consciousness, or his willpower, extends only to
obliterating the evidence of his own life.

'Michael Henchard's Will.
'That Elizabeth-Jane Farfrae be not told of my death, or made to
grieve on account of me.
'& that I be not bury'd in consecrated ground.
'& that no sexton be asked to toll the bell.
'& that nobody is wished to see my dead body.
'& that no murners walk behind me at my funeral.
'& that no flours be planted on my grave.
'& that no man remember me.
'To this I put my name.

'Michael Henchard.'
(MC, p. 333)

From Joe Fisher, *The Hidden Hardy* (Basingstoke, 1992),
pp. 115–35.

NOTES

[Joe Fisher's study focuses on hidden patterns in Hardy's writing which
produce alternative 'texts' to the ostensible narratives concerned with rural
Victorian England. His purpose in reading these submerged texts is to
politicise the reading of Hardy so as to produce fissures in the novels, from
which can be read ideological concerns. *The Mayor of Casterbridge* is read
for those submerged elements of mythical and magical discourse, which
challenge the rationalist, economic base of Victorian life. All references to
The Mayor of Casterbridge are to the Oxford World's Classics edition, ed.
Dale Kramer (Oxford, 1987), and are cited parenthetically in the essay as
MC. Ed.]

1. John Goode, *Thomas Hardy: The Offensive Truth* (Oxford, 1988),
   p. 79.

2. Barbara Kerr, *Bound to the Soil: A Social History of Dorset 1750–1918* (Wakefield, 1975), p. 243.

3. Ibid., pp. 188–91.

4. Richard Bernheimer, *The Wild Man in the Middle Ages* (Cambridge, MA, 1952), pp. 73–4.

5. Peter Stallybrass and Allon White, *The Politics and Poetics of Transgression* (London, 1986), pp. 28–9.

6. Robert Malcolmson, *Popular Recreations in English Society, 1700–1850* (Cambridge, 1973), p. 151.

7. Roger Ebbatson, *Hardy: The Margin of the Unexpressed* (forthcoming), MS, pp. 85–6. [*Hardy: The Margin of the Unexpressed* (Sheffield, 1992) – Ed.]

8. Bernheimer, *The Wild Man*, p. 71.

9. Ibid., p. 25.

10. George Wotton, *Thomas Hardy: Towards a Materialist Criticism* (Dublin and Totowa, NJ, 1985), pp. 63–4.

11. John Vernon, *Money and Fiction: Literary Realism in the Nineteenth and Early Twentieth Centuries* (Ithaca, NY, 1984), p. 7.

12. Christina Hole, *Witchcraft in England* (London, 1945), p. 48.

13. Edward Waring, *Ghosts and Legends of the Dorset Countryside* (Tisbury, Wilts, 1977), pp. 38–9.

14. Ibid., p. 47.

15. Hole, *Witchcraft in England*, p. 151.

16. John Lucas, *The Literature of Change: Studies in the Nineteenth-Century Provincial Novel* (Brighton, 1977), p. 159.

17. Christina Hole, *English Folklore* (London, 1940), p. 24.

18. Bernheimer, *The Wild Man*, p. 120.

8

Haunting Casterbridge, or 'the persistence of the unforeseen'

JULIAN WOLFREYS

The Mayor of Casterbridge is haunted. Spectres are everywhere, even in the faces or actions of the living. The town of Casterbridge is a haunted place, its topographical, architectural and archaeological structures resonating with the traces of the spectral. The ghosts of other textual forms, of which the tragic is only the most persistent or obvious, haunt the very structure of the novel. Michael Henchard particularly is troubled by the past, by a certain spectral revenance. The Mayor of Casterbridge is haunted.

HAUNTING

From one perspective, haunting might best be described as the ability of forces that remain unseen to make themselves felt in everyday life. Such an oscillation causes us to anticipate, to fear, to act or to respond in ways which we do not fully comprehend, supposing that we understand them at all. As Keith Wilson suggests, 'all the major characters [in the novel] reveal a capacity ... of responding to experience as the working-out of inevitable courses'.[1] This assessment catches the sense of a spectral movement of the invisible within the visible. Such haunting can also cause us to feel unsafe, uneasy, in places where we had always felt at home.

Haunting creates the sense of the unfamiliar within the familiar. Its operation is thus a structural disturbance. Haunting inhabits and, in creating an uncanny response, manifests itself as not as arriving from elsewhere, but instead 'surfacing ... in a return of the repressed as a foreign element that strangely seems to belong to the very domain that renders it foreign'.[2] As I shall argue, haunting, ghosting, spectrality are all necessary traces in *The Mayor of Casterbridge*. Barely comprehensible and supplementary to the logic of the narrative, they nonetheless inhere, haunting the very places, narratives and forms they make possible. Haunting, as we shall see, is written into the novel's constant concern with economy, households, architecture and habitation.

CRITICAL APPARITIONS

The persistence of the past in the present of *The Mayor of Casterbridge* is acknowledged by several critics of the novel.[3] In this *New Casebook*, J. Hillis Miller, Bruce Johnson, and Tess O'Toole consider the question of what returns from the past to disturb the calm sense of the present. In common they seem to acknowledge the configuration of universal recurrence, the sense that events leave their imprint on time only to recur, albeit it in a different manifestation. Or, there is figured that Freudian spectre, the return of the repressed, which creates in the disturbed subject the sense of the uncanny, described appropriately by Mark Wigley as that 'uneasy sense of the unfamiliar within the familiar, the unhomely within the home'.[4] Most recently amongst Hardy critics, Suzanne Keen has offered a sustained consideration of 'the return of the repressed' in relation to 'centuries-old tradition'. She considers also the persistence of 'residual' customs and forms, along with the 'archaic survival' of equally 'archaic practices' as a temporal trace within the social spaces of Casterbridge and its environs in the novel's present.[5] And Keen's sense of the return moves in the direction of the spectral, when she suggests that Newson is 'merely a ghost, or a memory' before his undeniable reappearance.[6]

Other brief moments of spectral recognition are to be found in criticism of *The Mayor of Casterbridge*. The question of uncanny resonance is considered, albeit in passing, by Raymond O'Dea.[7] Tess O'Toole (in essay 3) also acknowledges the haunting trace: 'as a "spectre", the genetic product is at once the reincarnation of a figure from the past and an image that has been raised by a guilty party's imagination'.[8] In reading the images of ghosts and the ghostly trace of heredity from Hardy's poem 'San Sebastian', O'Toole connects subjective perception and external manifestation, as does Miller (essay 1), in his reading of Hardy's poetry, although he makes it clear the spectral is no mere subjective invention.[9] Robert Langbaum (essay 6) emphasises Susan Henchard's lack of sexuality by acknowledging the doubleness of her ghostly quality; for she is 'the ghost of a past crime, the wife-sale, [and] ... ghostly in her lack of sexual vitality'.[10]

Despite these tantalising apparitions of critical acknowledgement of the spectral, however, no critic of Hardy, to my knowledge, has offered an extended analysis of the spectral in *The Mayor of Casterbridge*. This is, in part, doubtless because, as Jacques Derrida suggests, 'Ghosts always pass quickly ... in an instant without duration, presence without presence of a present which, coming back only *haunts*. The ghost ... appears only by means of figure or fiction, but its appearance is not nothing, nor is it mere semblance.'[11] The ghost is not a likeness, not a simple copy or representation. It has an explicitly textual relationship to that which it haunts. To reiterate and return to a point made earlier, the spectral is that which inhabits structure or identity in such a way as to displace or disrupt the propriety of the form from within.

Both J. Hillis Miller and Jim Reilly acknowledge this quality of Hardy's writing. Stating that, 'Hardy's is a haunted art ... [in which] material reality is displaced as the goal of representation by shadowy and spectral unrealities',[12] Reilly reads Hardy as working within a fictional paradigm that is not indebted to a form of mimetic realism. Both Reilly and Miller comprehend the world of Hardy's novels, in the latter's words as a world 'not of copies but of what Deleuze calls "simulacra" or "phantasms"'.[13] This is hardly a new or modish discovery reflecting the interests of literary theory, given the instances of spectral persistence in Hardy's own poetry. What it suggests however, is that it is important that we begin to take the spectral in Hardy seriously, if for no other reason than that the novelist appears to anticipate the interests of theory, and thus to haunt the critical text.

THAT WHICH RETURNS

One aspect of the spectral is that manifestation or persistence of the past in the present, though never as a presence as such. Instead, the ghost of and from the past leaves its trace in the structures of the present of *The Mayor of Casterbridge*. When we speak of the 'past' in relation to *The Mayor of Casterbridge*, this might signal equally a number of traces, none with any precedence over any others. Of personal returns and manifestations of the past there are those who come back from Henchard's personal past: Susan, Lucetta, Elizabeth-Jane, even Newson. There is also the furmity-woman, through whom the wife-sale returns to haunt Henchard's public identity, even as it has perpetually haunted his private sense of self. The impersonal past of Casterbridge is acknowledged in a number of ways, not least through the mayoral office, and the surrounding land (the Ring, Mai Dun, Diana Multimammia, the history of the mayoral office). A rural past is acknowledged through and traced in the return of events such as the fair at Weydon-Priors or the skimmington-ride. Then there are the 'past' texts which inform the structure of the novel – Greek and Shakespearean tragedy, the Old Testament, references to French novels, to Miltonic monsters, or the novels of Walter Scott, Gothic fiction (we will return to these). The ghostly trace has the ability to disrupt not only the present moment but also any sense of identity. It may even write itself as 'dead men's traits' in the sleeping face of Elizabeth-Jane.[14]

This is not a simple or single instance in itself, for it reiterates in part an earlier moment in the novel, when Susan and her daughter return to Weydon-Priors, the mother's features being figured imperfectly in the daughter's (p. 21). Thus, ghosting returns, while the return is always ghostly. Furthermore, the earlier scene which anticipates the haunting of Elizabeth-Jane, is itself a return, as the text suggests. Reiteration is not limited to the occurrence between the faces of the two women. For as Hardy tells the reader, '[t]he scene in its broad aspect had so much of its previous character ... that it might ... have been the afternoon following the previously recorded episode' (p. 21). This is but one instance of what Dale Kramer describes as the persistence of return as evidenced through 'particularities within a continuum', which in turn establishes 'the anthropology of a location ... explicitly relating the behaviour of present individuals to that of countless predecessors'.[15]

In that we can read a doubling movement of revenance, where movement haunts moment, we can suggest that the entire order of the novel is predicated on the troping of return as the spectral persistence disordering order and identity from within, as an otherness within the text. Even as Elizabeth-Jane's face is haunted by Susan's, and even as this recalls the earlier moment of return on the part of the two women, so that moment of return, in recalling the supposedly 'initial' scene of arrival at the Fair and the subsequent wife-sale, implies the continuous structural movement of displacement and disjointing. To this can be added a reading of the wife-sale itself, not as some simple or single originary event generating the unfolding of the narrative but as itself a moment of what Suzanne Keen calls a form of 'archaic survival' which, in turn, belongs to forms of economic 'traffic' which 'structure the novel'.[16]

The spectral can be seen on occasions in acts of uncanny doubling, a form of return, as when Elizabeth-Jane, on visiting her mother's grave, encounters a figure 'in mourning like herself ... [who] might have been her wraith or double' (p. 134). Lucetta – she is the 'wraith' – is also an uncanny double of Susan Newson/Henchard on one occasion, the 'double of the first' (p. 250). Elizabeth-Jane is herself a double of sorts. Not Henchard's but Newson's Elizabeth-Jane, she doubles even as she is haunted by the dead child whose place she has taken, whose identity is signed and simultaneously displaced in the reiteration of the name. That 'Elizabeth-Jane' is a proper name given to two characters sharing the same mother (whose features 'ghost' the second daughter's face) is important. For it alerts us to the importance of textual haunting, of haunting as textual, where even the act of writing can return, though never quite signifying that which it had done. This is a sign of repetition *and* displacement, return *and* disturbance. In addition, Henchard sees in Farfrae's face the double of his dead brother, as is well known (p. 49). Finally, Henchard is doubled (as is Lucetta) by the skimmington-ride effigy which, as Suzanne Keen so appositely suggests, comes 'back to haunt him'.[17]

Keith Wilson speaks of the effects and figures of doubling in his introduction to the novel.[18] Such patterns and the 'phantasms' of which they are composed (for all involve the images and memories of the dead), do nothing so much as signify the operations of each other, rather than intimating either a 'reality' beyond the text or an origin or source of which the text is a copy. Indeed, the uncanny mo(ve)ment of revenance and disturbing reiteration comes from within a figure or face to disturb identity and disconcert the subject. In this operation, the ghostly trace, which in reiterating constantly operates in a manner similar to the *simulacrum*, 'calls into question the authority and legitimacy of its model'.[19] Such doubling and the rhythm of return of which it is a part destabilise more than the identity of particular characters. It is disruptive of what Scott Durham calls 'distinct domains and temporalities ... [to] the extent to which they increasingly appear as the echoes of doubles of one another'.[20] To put this another way, with direct reference to *The Mayor of Casterbridge*, it is not only a question of particular characters being haunted. The various spatial and temporal boundaries of the novel that are found increasingly to be permeable and capable of being transgressed (as Marjorie Garson makes clear in her essay in this collection), signify one another's functions and potential interpretative roles in the novel.

This is the case whether one is speaking of the 'haunting' of the present by the past, signalled in the numerous returns discussed above, all of which permeate arbitrarily defined temporal boundaries. This can be read at the level of particular words themselves. Through archaic, untimely words such as 'burgh and champaign' (p. 30), the present of the narrative is disrupted. Words such as 'furmity' and 'skimmington' also signify an anachronic haunting; traces of other times and other modes of expression, they remain ruinous and fragmentary, giving no access to some originary discourse. There is also spatial movement across boundaries, which involves a temporal emergence of residual archaic practices, as in the eruption of Mixen Lane into the 'proper' or familiar space of Casterbridge, as Suzanne Keen argues.[21]

Such haunting therefore, while a form of return, is not simply a straightforward temporal arrival from some identifiable prior past. As J. Hillis Miller puts it, '[t]hese are underground doublings which arise from differential interrelations among elements which are all on the same plane. This lack of ground in some paradigm or archetype means that there is something ghostly about the effects of this ... type of repetition'.[22] Speaking of Hardy's fiction in general, Miller motions towards a reading which acknowledges the reiterative, the reciprocally interanimated, and the effect of doubling that articulates Hardy's text. There is that which returns, though never as itself. In its untimely, not to say anachronistic fashion, this spectral trace articulates disymmetry, non-identity within identity.

THE GOTHIC

If *The Mayor of Casterbridge* is haunted by the trace of the tragic text, it is also disturbed by manifestations of another textual form:

the gothic. Gothic, which might be described as the 'low other' to tragedy's high portentousness, involves the arrival of some apparently external figure which disturbs and makes abject the subject, through the subject's registration of fear and even terror. The gothic relies on making apparent those effects which are often only imminent or otherwise underplayed in tragedy, or otherwise in some manner 'vulgarises' them according to the gothic context (the witches in *Macbeth* might easily, in another narrative context, be only all too gothic). There is a question here of a certain spectral trace read as a discursive and structural slippage between supposedly discrete forms, a haunting transference across boundaries.

This slippage is, of course, perpetually at work in Hardy's novel, but it is interesting to observe the extent to which Hardy relies on the discourse of the gothic throughout the novel. The ghosting of *The Mayor* with the traces of gothic textuality serves to produce what Derrida calls a 'ghost-text'. For it is not simply a question of the ghost of another text haunting and inhabiting the familiar structure of the nineteenth-century novel. Rather, the very identity of the novel, its familiar shape, and the reader's familiarity with that, is disturbed from within, as the traces of the gothic 'phantomise the text itself' for, as Derrida suggests, a phantom-text is that in which 'references, or citations ... leave only traces'.[23]

The phantom-text is everywhere. There is the doxical acknowledgement of Susan as '"The Ghost"' (p. 83), a 'mere skellinton ...' (p. 85). Almost immediately upon her death, Susan is reported as having something of a headstone-appearance by Mrs Cuxsom: 'And she was as white as marble-stone' (p. 120). Susan is immediately replaced in this comment, her face equated with – and ghosted by – the second- or third-hand signification of a material which will form the architectural symbol of her being dead. Of Henchard, Nance Mockridge comments, in that knowing, prescient manner peculiar to working women in gothic novels, 'There's a bluebeardy look about en; and 'twill out in time' (p. 86). Not of course, that the Mayor has a dungeon, nor does he chain Susan in it, yet his figure is haunted by a powerful figure drawn from the gothic. Moreover, Nance's prediction points to the 'persistence of the unforeseen' (p. 334), as Hardy will put it on almost the final page (which statement, I would argue, is where all the spectral traces return from and to where they might be read as leading us). Her phrase is both economical and excessive: it is an utterance belonging to the cheapest of gothic thrills, while also resonating in a somewhat uncanny, if not haunted fashion. Structurally, therefore, her phrase, having to do with time, is disturbed from within, being both timely and untimely, having to do with the persistence of un-readable traces as a condition of temporal disturbance, with which the novel is so concerned.

Other characters are also marked in ways which suggest gothic convention. Newson is given a ghostly quality in relation to the question of the return. Specifically, he disturbs Henchard: '[t]he apparition of Newson haunted him. He would surely return' (p. 300). Conjuror Fall lives outside the town, and therefore outside the boundaries of society, as is typical of figures associated with alchemy and the black arts. His habitation and narrative preparation for the encounter between Henchard and Fall confuse discursive boundaries, intermixing the gothic, the folkloric and fairy-tale. The way to Fall's house is 'crooked and miry' (p. 185), and Henchard's approach to Fall's home is suggestively eerie: 'One evening when it was raining ... heavily ... a shrouded figure on foot might have been perceived travelling in the direction of the hazel copse which dripped over the prophet's cot' (pp. 185–6). Even the furmity-woman gets in on the gothic act, for, upon her return, it is remarked that she 'had mysteriously hinted ... that she knew a queer thing or two' (p. 202). Of course, what she knows is merely the information concerning Henchard's past, but her return is part of the general movement of return in the text, while Hardy carefully frames her ominous comment in a manner designed to amplify its portentous aspect.

What will return in this instance is the narrative which already haunts Henchard, as the furmity dealer's citation. While the old woman returns, what returns through her is the trace of the past and, with that, the suppressed truth as that which haunts. As Derrida makes clear in reading the spectral in Freud, repressed or suppressed, the truth-as-hauntedness nonetheless 'exists and *returns*, as such'; what returns 'comes down to spectral truth ... The truth is spectral, and this is its part of truth which is irreducible by explanation'.[24] The gothic is one mode of production which allows for an economy of explanation, a logic of representation, to order and rationalise, even as it relies on the non-rational. Yet within that mechanism, there is always that spectral element. Gothic convention is precisely this: convention, structure and law. Within such convention however, is that which is irreducible by explanation, as Derrida puts it. What cannot be explained is that the return happens, and that it happens not as the return of some presence to the present, but as the haunted trace. The truth of Henchard's past is coincidental to the general movement of spectral revenance, which the Mayor of Casterbridge is incapable of reading, and which *The Mayor of Casterbridge* barely glimpses.

The technique of repetition at work throughout the novel provides this barely seen spectral condition, even while, within the structures of the text, such reiteration is locally domesticated through the recourse to particularly familiar textual forms, such as the gothic. Not only are characters read and written as if in a gothic context, therefore. They behave as though they were characters from a gothic novel, even as the narrative voice mimics or is haunted by the trace of the gothic. Elizabeth-Jane is 'startled by the apparition of Farfrae' (p. 136). Lucetta's face is altered by an encounter with Farfrae also: her face 'became – as a woman's face becomes when the man she loves rises upon her gaze like an apparition' (p. 178).

There are other gothic traces too, improper references and ghostly citations without specific origins. The keystone-mask above Lucetta's door (p. 142) and the decaying sign of the Three Mariners (pp. 42–3) have a certain gothic appeal. Furthermore, their ruined decaying qualities hint at the uncanny, the unfamiliar within the familiar. Suggesting forms of temporal persistence, of the past's ability to return and to disturb, they both signify a certain sinister ineffability which gives the lie to the familiarity and homeliness of the structures – the public house and Lucetta's home – of which they are synecdochic figures. Both serve economically in tracing that 'structural slippage from *heimliche* [homely] to *unheimliche* [unhomely] [in which] that which supposedly lies outside the familiar comfort of the home turns out to be inhabiting it all along'.[25] Most immediately however, their function is to create that *frisson* so typically desired in the gothic. Both the sign and the keystone serve a textual, that is to say a haunting function, in that they remind us that a 'house is not simply an object that may be represented, but is itself a mechanism of representation'.[23]

One can read such effects at work when the reader is told how Jopp's cottage is 'built of old stones from the long-dismantled priory, scraps of tracery, moulded window-jambs, and arch-labels, being mixed in with the rubble of the walls' (p. 221). Those scraps, the ruins of the priory, long since gone, operate as references in a number of ways. Priories are of course favourite ruined sites, often haunted, in gothic discourse. There is in this image, with its fragments of clauses, the return of the past in the present structure once more, the structure of the cottage and the structure of the sentence. The former is structurally (dis-)composed by the material traces of a former structure; the latter is structurally (dis-)composed by the haunting traces of gothic discourse which, in their phantomatic inscription, enact a ghostly transference in the image of the cottage, from its being simply an object to be represented, to being a mechanism of representation, as Mark Wigley puts it. In this, the text does nothing so much as displace itself, endlessly. For the operation of haunting signals not simply a prior moment, if that is even the purpose. Instead, it serves to signal a certain spectral dislocation that belongs to the novel as a whole, signalling the ruins of other ruins, the keystone, the decaying sign, the Ring (ch. XI), even as they in turn signify other traces, and the other of the trace.

This movement, the gothic 'oscillation', is not merely an intertextual feature; it is of a different – spectral – order. This order is summed up in a discussion of Hardy's use of topography by J. Hillis Miller. Miller notes that reading the novel as a map of a series of places articulates a chain-like structure, any link of which 'may be placed at any position in the sequence. Any link presupposes the others as its determining causes, but in its turn is cause of the others'.[27] There is no stable or stabilising locus, no originary or central feature, event, character or textual referent (tragedy, the gothic), by which the reading of the novel can be calmed, or from which can be generated the idea of a meaning or identity. Each figure can be substituted for any other, maintaining both the process of signification and the concomitant disorganisation of the process, prohibiting its coming to rest.

There still remains, though, one further question pertaining to the trace of the gothic, and why the gothic persists in Hardy's text. Is the imposition of the Gothic, like that of the tragic, an effort to make the unfamiliar familiar once again, to keep the ghosts at bay, to give haunting a familiar, even a proper identity? Do the literary allusions and gothic moments seek to impose a limit on that which haunts, that which will not be forgotten but which nags at the memory and thereby becomes an obsession? In addition, who is haunted precisely? Is it Casterbridge? Is it Henchard? Or is it Hardy himself, who, having returned home to Dorchester in 1883, to build himself a home – Max Gate – with the help of his family – in his home, begins to be haunted in the very moment of being at home? What causes Hardy to dig into local archives, seeking stories of wife-sales, even as the laying of foundations for Max Gate reveals the bones of the long dead? What returns for Hardy, even as Hardy returns?[28]

THE UNCANNY

Freud defines the uncanny in his well-known essay of the same name (*Das Unheimliche*, 1919). In reading the ways in which the sensation of the uncanny is produced, Freud demonstrates how the supposedly separate terms – *heimliche* and *unheimliche* – are always already deconstructed by the internal slippage from one to the other.[29] What this makes apparent for Freud is that the uncanny is structural in nature, and that the uncanny moreover, is that sense of the unfamiliar, the disturbing, which is not caused by some external phenomenon but rather arises as something indefinable from within the self. Identity is thus always already haunted from within and haunting is inextricably connected to habitation.

Other aspects of the uncanny experience are what Freud calls the 'phenomenon of the "double"', which results in a 'doubling, dividing and interchanging of the self' and the 'constant recurrence of the same thing', described by Freud as the 'repetition of the same features or character-traits or vicissitudes ... or even the same names through several consecutive generations'.[30] We have seen already how *The Mayor of Casterbridge* is endlessly articulated by devices of doubling and repetition which are intrinsic to its structure and identity, and yet which disturb that very form from within. Thus, arguably, the entire novel may be considered as an exploration of the uncanny, of that 'something which is secretly familiar [*heimliche–heimisch*], which has undergone repression and then returned from it'.[31]

In one sense, Hardy's own return to Dorchester, his research of decades-old newspapers, his discovery of Roman burial remains in the land where he was to build Max Gate, is highly suggestive, were we to seek a correlation between the author's desire for home after a serious illness and the subsequent uncanny and haunted persistence manifesting itself in the novel. There is a persuasive psychobiographical reading hovering here. However, regardless of what may have turned Hardy's attention to these issues, what is apparent in *The Mayor of Casterbridge*, beyond any reading of Henchard as a psychological character study, beyond any character-orientated reading; indeed, beyond a reading of the story or the novelist's intertextual indebtedness, there is the uncanny sense that the novel is haunted. Such an impression must however remain exactly that, an impression which is uncanny precisely because it cannot be either validated or repudiated.

At more immediate and local levels, however, there are numerous instances of the experience of the uncanny in the novel. Henchard feels haunted by Newson, as we know already. Moreover, the reader is told repeatedly that he is a superstitious man. Henchard is first revealed as 'superstitious' though his decision to visit Conjuror Fall (p. 185). Though this moment is not in itself uncanny (though arguably Henchard's trip to Fall is meant to induce an uncanny sensation in the reader), the next instance of Henchard's superstitiousness is, and deliberately so. Henchard is ruminating on his misfortune over the reckless crop selling:

> The movements of his mind seemed to tend to the thought that some power was working within him.
> 'I wonder,' he asked himself with eerie misgiving: 'I wonder if it can be that somebody has been roasting a waxen image of me, or stirring an unholy brew to confound me! I don't believe in such power; and yet – what if they should ha' been doing it!' ... These isolated hours of superstition came to Henchard in time of moody depression ...
>
> (pp. 190–1)

While we may read the passage as remarking the residue of a superstition imbued with the discourse of folkloric mythology, the passage is notable nonetheless for its sense of the uncanny, of that internal power and the sensation of 'eerie misgiving'. Later, following the skimmington-ride, we are told that 'the sense of the supernatural was strong in this unhappy man' (p. 297). In this assessment of Henchard's response to the effigy, there is the sense that Hardy may be read as explaining away the uncanny feeling through recourse to the idea of superstition, even as Henchard experiences it. Yet, uncannily perhaps, that earlier speculation concerning the waxen image may also be read as one more example of the 'persistence of the unforeseen', while the effigy marks a form of return of Henchard's fear, and even as it physically returns via the river.

There are also clearly uncanny moments for Henchard which have little or nothing to do with superstition. Towards the end of his life Henchard is described thus:

> He rose to his feet, and stood like a dark ruin, obscured by 'the shade from his own soul upthrown'.
>
> (p. 326)

Perhaps one of the most complex and overdetermined of sentences in the novel, this delineation of Henchard addresses both his own being haunted, suffering from the disturbance of the uncanny, and the uncanny haunting to which *The Mayor* is prone. The ghostly citation with which the sentence concludes traces a double movement at least. It comes from Shelley's *The Revolt of Islam*, as does the phrase 'dark ruin', though Hardy chooses not to acknowledge this through quotation marks. While reading a citation, and one which in its signifying operation refers us to those other ghostly citations, we are impressed by the figure, not merely of the soul, but of the 'shade' also. Conventionally, the reading of that 'shade' should imply a shadow. However, there is also at work in this image the more archaic sense of 'shade', meaning 'ghost' or 'spectre'. The phrase 'dark ruin' is itself a ruin, a fragment, an improper citation which haunts the sentence and which does service as a simile for Henchard, even as it echoes beyond the image of Henchard, or, indeed, any animate creature, to hint at the Ring and other architectural sites and remnants out of which Casterbridge is composed, and by which it is haunted.

Not long before this moment, at which the return of Newson prompts Henchard's sense of being haunted again, Henchard returns to the place from where the novel begins (pp. 318–19). In this instance of reciprocal return – Henchard's return is countersigned by the return of place – so Susan's own words return to Henchard, and, uncannily, to the reader also – for her words are reported directly, from her own initial utterance, and also, adrift from her, from the grave as it were, as a disembodied voice, the voice of the other, haunts Henchard's memory (p. 319). The sense of the uncanny is quite startling here, for even as we read the words on the page, so we hear and see those words imprinted in the memory, arriving from some other place, and yet from within at the same time. In this, Susan's voice is doubly haunting for in its movement of return and address which, shockingly – uncannily – places the reader in the place of Henchard as addressee, it carries in it the anticipation of Henchard's will, which is reprinted onto the page, and there for every successive generation of readers (p. 333).

As J. Hillis Miller pointed out, the will is a 'terrifying series of negative performances, spoken from the grave',[32] and as a 'kind of ghostly negative that ...has positive existence'.[33] The will, reproduced directly before us, comes back as a fragment of Henchard's voice which, despite its commands to forget him, haunts us all the more. What this act of narration from beyond the grave suggests to Miller, quite correctly in my view, is the ghostly condition of all narrative: 'all narration is a murmur from beyond the grave ... killing it as living speech and resurrecting it at the same time as ghostly, remembered speech'.[34] Thus, Henchard's address, which comes directly to us, haunts the text while reproducing once more the sense of the uncanny in the act of reiteration.

Henchard is not the only one to be troubled uncannily however. While Henchard may walk 'restlessly, as if some haunting shade ...hovered round him and troubled his glance' (p. 298), Elizabeth-Jane encounters such moments as well: '[t]hen something happened to occur which his step-daughter fancied must really be a hallucination of hers' (p. 168) At another moment, Lucetta 'stood transfixed. Her own words greeted her, in Henchard's voice, like spirits from the grave' (p. 247). Lucetta's words disturb her because they come back in a particularly haunting fashion, as both her own and not her own. The more disturbing for Lucetta is the fact that her words return to her in her own house as if in ghostly confirmation of Freud, or, to put this another way, as if the ghost of Freud's text were to arrive from the future so as to disrupt the familiar presence of a world understood to be built on the firm foundations of the past, of tradition, of continuity. For, as Mark Wigley suggests in his discussion of Freud, the 'uncanny is literally a "not-being-at-home", an alienation from the house experienced within it'.[35]

Hardy, though, does not limit the expression of the uncanny to the experience of particular characters as their identity is disturbed in places where they feel themselves at home, as the example of Henchard's will shows. The familiarity of Casterbridge so carefully constructed by Hardy for the reader is itself disturbed. Not only does this happen with the sudden introduction of Mixen Lane. There are also occasions when the customary comfort and familiarity of the town find themselves disturbed at the margins of the world of Casterbridge. Those who appear at a given signal, a whistle, to place bridges across the brook are described thus: 'A shape thereupon made its appearance on the other side bearing the bridge on end against the sky' (p. 255). This uncanny area beyond the knowable limits of Casterbridge itself can cause the uncanny sensation, merely through atmospheric conditions: 'Beyond the stream was the open moor, from which a clammy breeze smote upon their faces as they advanced' (p. 258).

CONCLUSION

That the novel may be read as having the power to create that uncanny feeling in its readers is a sign of its being haunted. The constant pulsation engaged in the text, through doubling, reiteration and return, through textual reference, fleeting moments of citation, and the ontological confusion of heterogeneous discourses; all serve to phantomise the text, to generate the phantom-text, which in itself is never itself, and thus is all the more disturbing, all the more uncanny for that. Beginning to read such effects of ghostly troping, we may begin perhaps to read the text of Hardy not simply as a text haunted by the residual traces of the past, but as one caught between the nineteenth and twentieth centuries, between realism and modernism, as a text composed, not only of spectres from the past, but also of the traces of spectres-to-come, as a text haunted by the future.

NOTES

1. Keith Wilson, 'Introduction', in Thomas Hardy, *The Mayor of Casterbridge*, ed. Keith Wilson (London, 1997), pp. xxi–xli, p. xxxi.

2. Mark Wigley, *The Architecture of Deconstruction: Derrida's Haunt* (Cambridge, MA, 1993), p. 108.

3. See, for example, John R. Cooley, 'The Importance of Things Past: An Archetypal Reading of *The Mayor of Casterbridge*', *Massachusetts Studies in English*, 1 (1967), 17–21; W. Eugene Davis, 'Comparatively Modern Skeletons in the Garden: A Reconsideration of *The Mayor of Casterbridge*', *English Literature in Transition (1880–1920)*, 3 (1985), 108–20; Rod Edmond, '"The Past-Marked Prospect": Reading *The Mayor of Casterbridge*' in *Reading the Victorian Novel: Detail into Form*, ed. Ian Gregor (London, 1980), pp. 111–27.

4. Wigley, *The Architecture of Deconstruction*, p. 108.

5. Suzanne Keen, *Victorian Renovations of the Novel: Narrative Annexes and the Boundaries of Representation* (Cambridge, 1998), pp. 127, 132, 134, 140.

6. Keen, *Renovations*, pp. 133, 140.

7. Raymond O'Dea, 'The "Haunting Shade" That Accompanies the Virtuous Elizabeth-Jane in *The Mayor of Casterbridge*', *Victorian Newsletter*, 31 (Spring 1967), 33–6.

8. See p.42.

9. See p. 22.

10. See p. 117.

11. Derrida, *Mémoires: for Paul de Man,* rev. trans. Cecile Lindsay et al. (New York, 1989), p. 64.

12. Jim Reilly, *Shadowtime: History and Representation in Hardy, Conrad and George Eliot* (London, 1993), p. 65.

13. J. Hillis Miller, *Fiction and Repetition: Seven English Novels* (Oxford, 1982), p. 6.

14. Thomas Hardy, *The Mayor of Casterbridge*, ed. and introd. Dale Kramer (Oxford, 1987), p. 126. All further references are to this edition and are cited parenthetically in the text.

15. Dale Kramer, 'Introduction' in *The Mayor* (1987), pp. xi–xxix, pp. xxiii, xxii.

16. Keen, *Renovations*, p. 132.

17. Ibid., p. 140.

18. Wilson, 'Introduction', p. xxviii.

19. Scott Durham, *Phantom Communities: The Simulacrum and the Limits of Postmodernism* (Stanford, CA, 1998), p. 3.

20. Ibid., p. 16.

21. Keen, *Renovations*, p. 132.

22. Miller, *Fiction and Repetition*, p. 6.

23. Derrida, *Mémoires*, p. 80.

24. Jacques Derrida, *Archive Fever*, trans. Eric Prenowitz (Chicago, 1995), p. 87.

25. Wigley, *Architecture*, p. 108.

26. Ibid., p. 163.

27. J. Hillis Miller, *Topographies* (Stanford, CA, 1995), pp. 20–1.

28. The history of research and composition in relation to Hardy's return to Dorchester and the building of Max Gate is discussed by Keith Wilson and Dale Kramer in their introductions to *The Mayor of Casterbridge*, referred to in the notes above.

29. Sigmund Freud, 'The "Uncanny"', pp. 195–201 in Freud, *Writings on Art and Literature*, foreword Neil Hertz (Stanford, CA, 1997), pp. 193–233.

30. Freud, 'The "Uncanny"', p. 210.

31. Ibid., p. 222.

32. J. Hillis Miller, *Reading Narrative* (Norman, OK, 1998), p. 110.

33. Ibid., p. 112.

34. Ibid., p. 112.

35. Wigley, *Architecture*, p. 110.

9

Agon in the Marketplace: *The Mayor of Casterbridge* as Bourgeois Tragedy

MICHAEL VALDEZ MOSES

I

> Even bourgeois and pseudo-Marxist vulgar sociology have not got
> round to inventing the sub-genre of the tragic novel.
>
> (Georg Lukács, *The Historical Novel*)

The dominance of poststructuralist criticism over the last decade-and-a-half has, until very recently, banished genre studies to what has been at best a marginal position within the literary academy. The antiformalist and antifoundationalist thrust of poststructuralism necessarily reduced the question of genre to a non-status precisely because generic analyses were understood to be inherently formalist in nature and were dependent upon the proffering of structural distinctions that could not be maintained in the face of a radical epistemological critique. However, at this moment, a generic criticism which would situate itself within a historical and political framework seems both necessary and inevitable. And since the question of tragedy has always been at the heart of generic criticism, it seems only appropriate that an attempt be made to understand the history of tragedy in political terms. Of paramount concern to such a study would be how decisive changes in the political basis of Western civilisation are to be related to corresponding changes in tragic form. In particular, the gradual collapse of aristo-cratic polities and the emergence of middle-class democratic regimes would have a significant bearing on the emergence of the tragic novel in the eighteenth and nineteenth centuries.

To be sure, the novel began as an essentially comic form which might be said to be in keeping with the political optimism of an emerging middle class. Nevertheless, it was not long before authors such as Richardson, Rousseau, and Goethe were attempting to give the new genre a tragic turn. By associating the novel with one of the most esteemed of traditional genres, these writers hoped to establish the literary legitimacy of the new form, as well as to claim for bour-geois existence the tragic grandeur of aristocratic life. Whatever the popular success of such novels, their authors encountered a number of difficulties, simultaneously generic, historical, and political, which have dogged the enterprise of writing tragic novels ever since. The adaptation of a traditionally dramatic form into a novelistic one turned out to be highly problematic. As a literary form which had developed out of the need to deal with the new experiences of private life and middle-class existence, the novel seemed particu-larly ill-suited for the purposes of representing tragic conflict, espe-cially as the action of traditional dramatic tragedy had dealt almost exclusively with the public deeds of aristocratic heroes.

One of the most interesting and turbid nineteenth-century at-tempts to reground tragedy on something like its traditional politi-cal basis is Hardy's *The Mayor of Casterbridge*. Formalist critics of the novel have readily seized upon those sets of parallels which Hardy developed between his hero and characters such as Oedipus, Lear, and Macbeth. Treating as decisive Hardy's use of the gods, the chorus, or the structural principles of *peripeteia* and *anagnori-sis*, these critics have eagerly accepted Hardy's own view of his artistic project, granting the archetypal equivalence between the dramatic action of Hardy's novel and that of traditional tragic dramas, as well as that between Henchard and the aristocratic heroes of such dramas.[1] Even the minority of critics who have sensed a divergence between traditional tragedy and Hardy's novel-istic variety have nevertheless persisted in understanding Henchard according to some universal and transhistorical model of the tragic hero, such as that of existential man facing an indifferent, godless universe.[2] Opposed to these formalist critical approaches which simultaneously universalise and depoliticise Hardy's novel, I will argue that Hardy's attempt to recapture, rather than simply to redefine traditional tragedy, must be understood within the specific political and historical situation in which his novel was composed, and in which its action takes place. In fact, Hardy's use of traditional dramatic tragedy as a metaphorical backdrop to his story actually interferes with or mutes its tragic impact. The patina of effects borrowed from Greek tragedy, especially the use of the gods, is symptomatic of Hardy's concern that modern life is ultimately unfruitful ground for the rebirth of traditional tragedy. Struggling to discover a source of tragic conflict in the social fabric of modern middle-class life, Hardy was only partially successful. His use of formal structures, archetypal narrative patterns, and literary allusions became a means by which he hoped to cover over what he perceived to be the deficiencies of his tragic novel. In any case, Hardy's measure of success – and it is remarkable given his historical situation that he succeeded to the extent that he did – owes much to the distinctive setting of his novel, one which allowed him to recapture more fully than in any of his other works something of the political dimension of traditional tragedy.

As a stable middle-class regime, resting upon the twin supports of parliamentary democracy and industrial capitalism, Victorian England could offer a novelist little in the way of material deserving epic or tragic treatment. Hardy's success as a tragic novelist therefore depended on his realising that he could find a corner of Victorian England which had not been fully modernised. In other words, I am suggesting a connection between Hardy as a regional novelist and Hardy as a tragic novelist. A living anachronism within Victorian England, Hardy's Wessex gave him the stage he needed for novelistic tragedy. *The Mayor of Casterbridge* unearths a residual form of life which had ceased to exist only within Hardy's lifetime and which had been conducive to a more heroic mode of existence than was generally possible in Victorian England. Henchard's story depends upon the peculiarly unmodern characteristics of Casterbridge to lend heroic grandeur and tragic dignity to what would otherwise remain a typical novelistic tale of bourgeois life.

Rather than simply grafting the forms of traditional tragedy onto the modern world, Hardy thus finds an anachronistic realm within nineteenth-century England which has many of the characteristics of the setting of traditional tragedy, especially in its Greek form, namely the *polis* or ancient city.[3] The ways in which Casterbridge resembles a *polis* provide a foundation for

Henchard's status as a hero and, as we shall see, the gradual mod-ernisation of the community precipitates his tragic fall. Before proceeding with an analysis of *The Mayor of Casterbridge*, I want to consider in some detail what distinguishes the *polis* as a form of community. Having no living examples of the *polis* before our eyes, we have lost sight of it as a political alternative and must pause to recognise the alien character of this kind of tightly knit, organic community. In the classical world, the *polis* formed the fundamental and comprehensive basis of all human relationships and all human activities. We misunderstand the *polis* as long as we translate the word as *state* or *city-state*, as if the *polis* were merely a diminutive or primitive form of the kinds of communities with which we are familiar. In fact, the *polis* and the state are fun-damentally different forms of community. *State* implies a modern set of distinctions: between state and society, state and individual, and state and church.[4] By contrast, the classical *polis* was an all-inclusive community which assimilated all other possible commu-nities and which was not included in any other whole or community. The *polis* did not distinguish between civil and reli-gious authority; in fact, authority in all matters of law and custom rested with the city. The total welfare of all citizens, both material and spiritual, was the concern of the regime. Moreover, this ancient form of political life was not conceived of as contractual, as is the modern state in the theories of Hobbes, Locke, and Rousseau. 'Individuals' in the modern sense of the term did not exist; all citizens were part of a larger communal whole and not autonomous agents who agreed to form some larger legal collec-tive entity out of their individual wills. The idea of a realm of ac-tivity – 'society' or 'culture' – which can be conceived of apart from the city was foreign to the classical understanding of politics.

In practical terms, the *polis* had to be limited in size. In terms of number of inhabitants, the ancient city would be dwarfed by modern urban centres such as London and Paris. Accordingly, po-litical relationships in the ancient city were still coextensive with what we would call personal relationships. The modern problem of *anomie*, affecting large, densely populated urban centres, was un-characteristic of ancient Athens or early republican Rome. These ancient cities remained autonomous, self-sufficient, and indepen-dent for much of their history; they were not parts of some larger nation-state, in the way that New York and Los Angeles are sub-sumed by the United States. These ancient communities were, moreover, agricultural rather than industrial, and their economies were governed largely by local considerations. Though each city had its own peculiar set of institutions, in general they were hierarchically ordered: distinctions between aristocrats and plebeians, masters and slaves, citizens and foreigners were important. Nevertheless, all inhabitants of the city were mutually interdependent, forming together one larger, comprehensive human whole.

By suggesting that Casterbridge is a modern bourgeois variant of the *polis*, I wish to argue that Hardy sought out political conditions in the contemporary world which would make possible a rebirth of traditional tragedy.[5] Animated by the conscious desire to imitate Greek models, Hardy was particularly concerned with the problem of setting. In his General Preface to the Wessex edition of 1912, Hardy argues that his decision to restrict the action of his novels to a relatively small geographic area was meant to evoke the atmosphere of ancient Greek drama:

> I would state that the geographical limits of the stage here trodden were not absolutely forced upon the writer by circumstances; he forced upon himself from judgement. I considered that the magnificent heritage from the Greeks in dramatic literature found sufficient room for a large proportion of its action in an extent of their country not much larger than the half-dozen counties here reunited under the old name of Wessex. ... So far was I possessed by this idea that I kept within the frontiers when it would have been easier to overleap them and give more cosmopolitan features to the narrative.[6]

Hardy's rejection of cosmopolitan features and his preference for a confined stage for his narratives are most evident in *The Mayor of Casterbridge*, where action takes place almost exclusively in a small provincial community, isolated, at least initially, from all outside historical movements and political forces, 'untouched by the faintest sprinkle of modernism'.[7]

Drawn from the Dorchester of Hardy's youth, Casterbridge is not merely the symbolic equivalent of a classical city, but in fact descends directly from a Roman *polis* and still retains the aura of the ancient world:

> Casterbridge announced old Rome in every street, alley, and precinct. It looked Roman, bespoke the art of Rome, concealed dead men of Rome. It was impossible to dig more than a foot or two deep about the town fields and gardens without coming upon some tall soldier or

other of the Empire, who had lain there in his silent unobtrusive rest
for a space of fifteen hundred years. ... Some old people said that at
certain moments in the summer time, in broad daylight, persons
sitting with a book dozing in the arena had, on lifting their eyes,
beheld the slopes lined with a gazing legion of Hadrian's soldiery as
if watching the gladiatorial combat.[8]

Casterbridge has preserved much of its original Roman architectural character and physical dimensions. Most striking to the visitor
first setting eyes upon Casterbridge, the community remains
bounded by its ancient defensive walls. Though they no longer serve
a military function, these defences fix a precise limit to the size of
the community, and the city's diminutive scale offers Henchard a
public stage upon which his everyday activities assume a genuine
communal significance.

The equivalent of the *agora* or public square in Casterbridge is
the *carrefour,* where the business of the community is transacted.
Hardy compares the market square to 'the regulation Open Place in
spectacular dramas, where the incidents that occur always happen
to bear on the lives of the adjoining residents'.[9] The assimilation of
Casterbridge's physical organisation to that of the stage suggests an
underlying correspondence between the public quality of life in the
ancient *polis* and that in Hardy's provincial city. Indeed, compared
to most eighteenth- and nineteenth-century novels, *The Mayor of
Casterbridge* seems remarkable for its preoccupation with the
public rather than the private aspects of middle-class life.[10] This
tendency is evident in the preponderance of pivotal scenes which
take place in public: Henchard's sale of his wife and child, his successful effort to persuade Farfrae to accept employment, his initial
conflict with Farfrae over the treatment of Abel Whittle, his competitive staging of municipal entertainments, his commercial rivalry
with his former employee, his confession in the courtroom, his
bankruptcy proceedings, his disgrace before the Royal Personage –
all are conducted in a public manner, frequently in full view of the
entire community, and quite often in the open air. Moreover, the
action of the novel turns upon a series of private relationships,
secret agreements, and intimate discussions that ultimately become
public knowledge. In a town as small as Casterbridge, Henchard's
original 'secret' marriage to Susan, Elizabeth-Jane's true parentage,
Lucetta's clandestine affair with Henchard in Jersey, and even
Elizabeth-Jane's temporary service in the Three Mariners cannot
long remain private matters.

The Mayor of Casterbridge thus marks a radical departure from the novelistic tradition Ian Watt has described:

> The world of the novel is essentially the world of the modern city; both present a picture of life in which the individual is immersed in private and personal relationships because a larger communion with nature or society is no longer available. ... [The novel] tells of an intimate world of which no one speaks out loud in ordinary life, a world which had previously found utterance only in the diary, the confession or the familiar letter.[11]

Hardy's public drama contrasts vividly with the sentimental epistolary tradition begun in England by Richardson. Hardy's 'man of character' defines himself by means of public actions and speeches, rather than by private correspondence or self-reflective moments to which the reader is made privy. Henchard customarily makes no distinction between the public and the private realms of experience.[12] If Farfrae is to be his business partner, then he must also become his trusted friend; if Henchard is to marry Susan or Lucetta, it is with an eye toward his social reputation and financial status within the community; if he is to serve as Elizabeth-Jane's father, it is primarily out of a sense of public duty and social propriety.

Henchard fits M. M. Bakhtin's model of the public man of classical biography, who lives his life in the *agora*, always before the eyes of his fellow citizens:

> The square in earlier (ancient) times itself constituted a state ... it was the highest court ... the entire people participated in it. ... [Within it] the laying bare and examination of a citizen's whole life was accomplished, and received its public and civic stamp of approval. ... Here the individual is open on all sides, he is all surface, there is in him nothing that exists 'for his sake alone', nothing that could not be subject to public or state control and evaluation. Everything here, down to the last detail, is entirely public.[13]

According to Bakhtin, the novel's preoccupation with the representation of inner life and the purely private realm of experience developed after the collapse of the *polis* and the emergence of new forms of political life which lacked the comprehensive and unified communal character of the ancient city. In this respect, *The Mayor of Casterbridge* restores in some measure the tragic potential of literature by once again portraying a small community in which all 'individual' matters sooner or later become matters of public concern. Within such a political context, the novel's customary depiction of the inner life of bourgeois man gives way to the dramatic representation of the 'man of character', who objectifies his inner being by means of his public conduct.

The relevance of Henchard's actions to the community is assured not only by the limited size and public character of Casterbridge, but also by the town's virtual political, economic, and social autonomy. To be sure, Casterbridge is officially part of a larger political entity: Great Britain. But, paradoxically, the extent and power of Great Britain make possible the relative independence of its provincial agricultural townships. Though not at liberty to pursue an independent foreign policy, Casterbridge can safely ignore political matters beyond its local horizons. Unlike ancient Athens or republican Rome, it has no need to defend itself against hostile powers. In certain respects, then, Casterbridge is more completely autonomous and absorbed in its local affairs than any ancient *polis* could afford to be: in Hardy's Casterbridge, royal and parliamentary authority are remote. The presence of the central government in London makes itself felt only once, during the exceptional and largely ceremonial visit of a Royal Personage to Casterbridge. Hardy shows the provincial life of Casterbridge during an age when almost all political and economic matters of concern to the citizenry are addressed by the local magistrates and the town council. Under such circumstances, a member of the town council, chief local magistrate, and church warden such as Henchard possesses more genuine political power and civic responsibility than any other individual with whom a citizen of Casterbridge would ordinarily come into contact.

The agricultural basis of life in Casterbridge further contributes to the city's autonomous character. In the days before the repeal of the Corn Laws (1846), the existence of tariffs on imported grain effectively localised the English grain markets. Protected by these tariffs, an agricultural community such as Casterbridge depended upon its own harvests and local weather conditions for its economic livelihood. Consequently, the economic prosperity of the entire community turned on the fortunes of a few prominent farmers and grain merchants. Henchard's sale of bad grain early in the story adversely affects the daily diet of the entire community. His scheme to drive Farfrae out of business by means of competitive bidding and selling similarly depends on the existence of a purely local grain market subject to the manipulation of a single powerful trader. Since the repeal of the Corn Laws neutralised the impact that any one merchant could have on the availability and price of grain, their elimination at an earlier date would have made Henchard's plan to ruin Farfrae inconceivable and thus forestalled his tragedy.

The agricultural and provincial character of Casterbridge also ensures its social isolation, or what we might term its cultural autonomy. The rustic city has been largely unaffected by the advances in the arts and sciences and in social manners which characterise London. Unaware of their lack of refinement, the citizens of Casterbridge are unself-consciously content with their rural existence. Before the arrival of Farfrae, Elizabeth-Jane, and Lucetta, a representative Casterbridge inhabitant such as Solomon Longways can unreservedly esteem Michael Henchard as a social ideal, 'a pillar of the town', though by the standards of London, Henchard – even as mayor – lacks taste, social grace, education, and breeding. Yet in a community cut off from the cosmopolitan world of fashion, social snobbery, formal education, and refined entertainment, the most eminent men in Casterbridge feel no need to distance themselves from the agricultural source of their wealth and power. The exclusive residential section of the city juxtaposes barns and private homes, and the 'street ruled by a mayor and corporation' echoes 'with the thump of the flail, the flutter of the winnowing fan, and the purr of the milk into the pails'.[14] Even the most socially elevated man in Casterbridge mingles with his labourers, visits his barns and fields, and lives in daily contact with the heat of the sun, the smell of the livestock, and the din of the marketplace. Casterbridge thus resembles an ancient *polis* insofar as its customs, manners, and social standards are chiefly self-generated, local, and largely unaffected, at least initially, by those of other communities.

Unaware of the sophistication of London's elite, Casterbridge nevertheless generates its own social distinctions. Ostensibly a middle-class community which excludes monarchs and aristocrats, as well as slaves and serfs, Casterbridge in fact preserves a strict order among its inhabitants. One may, for example, roughly determine the social status of someone in Casterbridge according to which of three inns he frequents: the King's Arms, the Three Mariners, or Peter's Finger.[15] The pre-eminent citizen in Casterbridge is of course the mayor, who belongs to 'an elective dynasty dating back to the days of Charles I'; directly beneath him are the 'Peerage of burghers' – the aldermen and members of the Corporation – followed in turn by the other chief businessmen and professionals, then the small shopkeepers and skilled tradesmen, and finally the unskilled labourers and menials.[16] From a broad historical perspective, the distinction between a corn factor and a skilled tradesman might seem relatively fine, since both belong to what may roughly be termed the bourgeoisie. However, the diminutive size and insularity of Casterbridge magnify and exaggerate the smallest differences in social status, thereby producing a stratified community out of a seemingly homogeneous one.

In Casterbridge no individual or class can afford to ignore the troubles of any other. Economically interdependent, the populace retains 'the primitive habit of helping one another' in the face of a potentially disastrous harvest.[17] Unlike Manchester or Liverpool, Casterbridge has yet to experience the divisive and alienating effects of industrial capitalism. All citizens remain in close touch with each other and with the means of production; a common preoccupation with agriculture impedes the divergence of political interests along strict class lines.[18] Accordingly, the relationships between members of different social strata remain personal, direct, and subject to mood, unmediated by fixed bureaucratic procedures, legal statutes, union contracts, and corporate regulations. Rather than summarily dismiss a perpetually tardy workman for a violation of his contractual obligations, as would a modern corporate officer, Henchard personally humiliates Abel Whittle before his co-workers and fellow townsfolk in order to teach him a lesson and reform his work habits.[19] Henchard secretly compensates for his severity by supplying Whittle's poor aged mother with coals and potatoes during the winter. In turn, Whittle never resents Henchard's paternalism; he remains doggedly loyal to his old master, accompanying him into self-imposed exile and sheltering him in his last days as an outcast on Egdon Heath. Given the archaic class relationships in the city, Henchard's tragic fall has an immediate and palpable effect upon his fellow citizens. As Casterbridge loses one of its ablest magistrates and its chief commercial benefactor, Farfrae's assumption of Henchard's political and economic power signals the beginning of a new age of lower pay and more arduous work for the ordinary labourers.[20] The organic interdependence of all classes and individuals lends a concrete public importance to the fall of a middle-class businessman and small-town politician.

II

For all of its archaic features, Casterbridge is only a modern equivalent of an ancient *polis* and therefore in several crucial respects is quite different from a community like republican Rome or ancient Thebes. The effects of modernity manifest themselves even in a provincial backwater like Casterbridge, where the ethos is distinctly bourgeois. The activities of its inhabitants are limited by a middle-class concern with commerce, agriculture, marriage, and family. Thus far I have considered the ways in which the setting of Hardy's novel provides a public context for Henchard's tragedy. But Hardy's greatest challenge – and one which he only partially succeeded in meeting – was to locate and dramatise whatever heroic elements persisted in bourgeois existence. The political activities of the traditional hero – the foundation or preservation of a regime, and above all the exercise of martial virtue – are no longer available to Hardy's hero. Politics in its provincial and modern form in Casterbridge has lost much of its mortal seriousness and epic glory. Hardy nevertheless endeavours to dramatise a heroic substratum of bourgeois life still discernible in the early Victorian period. The chief form in which Henchard expresses his Achillean temperament is 'commercial combat'.[21] Henchard pursues success in the market-place with the same volcanic intensity with which Achilles pursues glory on the battlefield: economic competition becomes Henchard's form of heroic endeavour.

Henchard's economic form of heroism should be understood in light of the philosophic foundations of the modern middle-class regime. Hobbes and Locke championed commercial enterprise over traditional aristocratic pursuits as the chief activity for the modern citizen. They regarded commercial activity as a means of taming man's vainglorious pursuits and aggressive impulses. In their view, men would no longer fight over elevated matters such as religious salvation and political glory; the modern state would redirect men's contentiousness into more prosaic and productive channels. Later economic theorists such as Adam Smith and David Ricardo understood commercial competition within a free market as a means by which the wealth of all could be increased.[22] The modern liberal tradition was founded upon the hope that the pursuit of happiness would consist of a peaceful striving for material gain and personal security and not a violent struggle for national glory, aristocratic honour, and religious salvation. Like Robinson Crusoe, to whom

Hardy compares his hero, Henchard is a fictional reflection of these philosophic and economic developments.

Henchard begins, as does Defoe's shipwrecked hero, a penniless and isolated individual, forced to rely on his own initiative to survive in an inhospitable world. When he leaves the furmity woman's tent at Weydon-Priors, Henchard enters into a solitary landscape and hostile environment in which he must make his fortune by means of raw physical strength, determination, ingenuity, and courage. Pitted against the indifferent but ultimately fruitful world of nature, initially lacking membership in any social group, Henchard, like Crusoe, ultimately makes himself the leader of an entire community. In an early stage of pre-industrial capitalism, Henchard's acquisitiveness can thus appear in a heroic light.[23] Nevertheless, Hardy is careful to omit the eighteen years of Henchard's life during which, in a long and presumably arduous struggle, he rises from penury and obscurity to wealth and eminence. This narrative elision lends greater credibility and force to one of the governing myths of bourgeois culture: the heroic tale of the self-made man.[24] Unlike Defoe, Hardy covers over the prosaic details: the drudgery of physical labour, the painstaking process of capital accumulation, the mundane commercial disappointments and successes, in short, the ordinary and unheroic tenor of economic enterprise which must have characterised two decades of his hero's life. Hardy omits exactly the material which was the traditional subject matter of the bourgeois novel from Defoe to Dickens: the gradual rise of a character, first into the middle class and then into prominence within that class. Hardy's economic hero emerges suddenly, after two decades of presumed commercial activity, fully formed, already wealthy, powerful, and successful, seemingly unsullied and unburdened by the prosaic demands of economic life, as if his inner heroic resolve were in itself sufficient to transform him instantaneously into a great public figure.

While Hardy's structural innovation lends heroic stature to his protagonist, it does not provide the basis for a tragic conflict. Within the parameters of middle-class beliefs, the successful businessman might appear courageous and heroic, but he does not normally seem tragic. This is precisely what the philosophic founders of the modern commercial state had envisioned: a taming of the heroic impulse, replacing the potential for tragic conflict in society with the potential for harmonious cooperation. Henchard ultimately deviates, however, from the course which modern liberal philosophy and economics prescribe for bourgeois man. He refuses to limit his economic activity to achieving personal security and prosperity. Though not averse to the pleasure and comfort wealth provides, Henchard does not pursue business solely for the sake of his material well-being; rather, Hardy's hero often conceives of trade as a contest of strength, a struggle for recognition and prestige in which he can compel others to acknowledge his superiority.[25] It is as if Henchard were striving to reconvert commercial enterprise back into Achillean endeavour, rather than allowing the sublimation of his aggressive impulses into non-violent economic undertakings.

Henchard's commercial war with Farfrae provides the basis of his tragedy. Hardy's description of this conflict makes explicit the way in which financial competition becomes a substitute for mortal combat:

> A time came when, avoid collision with his former friend as he might, Farfrae was compelled, in sheer self-defence, to close with Henchard in mortal commercial combat. He could no longer parry the fierce attacks of the latter by simple avoidance. As soon as their war of prices began everybody was interested, and some few guessed the end. It was, in some degree, Northern insight matched against Southern doggedness – the dirk against the cudgel – and Henchard's weapon was one which, if it did not deal ruin at the first or second stroke, left him afterwards well-nigh at his antagonist's mercy.[26]

What distinguishes this particular commercial combat from the everyday variety of business competition is Henchard's desire for prestige and personal revenge, rather than material gain.[27] In principle, Henchard and Farfrae could both do business and make a comfortable living in Casterbridge. But far from seeking personal security or greater prosperity, Henchard risks his entire fortune and financial reputation simply for the sake of crushing a hated rival. In the manner of a Homeric contest or classical agon, this struggle, though carried out in an economic market, remains an intensely personal confrontation between enemies known intimately to each other.[28]

Though he risks all he values, Henchard is not capable of acting according to a strictly aristocratic ethic. In the end, he always draws back from the destructive act that would forever place him beyond the pale of middle-class morality. When he actually locks with Farfrae in physical combat, and has the power, opportunity, and motive to take his enemy's life, Henchard recoils from the deed, conscience-stricken and completely unmanned. Though 'in a modern sense' he may have 'received the education of Achilles', Henchard has never learned to kill.[29] He lacks the pagan ferocity and aristocratic disdain for weakness and mere life that characterise the Homeric hero. In fact, Henchard is capable of kindness, pity, and forgiveness: given an opportunity to deny the furmity woman's accusation in court and be taken at his word, Henchard makes the humanitarian gesture and confesses his transgression. Moreover, he chooses not to justify his former actions, but instead accepts the moral disapprobation of an ethic he earlier dismissed as conventional. Above all, he has no aristocratic pathos of distance; he willingly grants that he is morally equivalent to a wretched creature from the lowest ranks of society.[30]

The fact that Henchard ultimately remains bound by the limits of bourgeois morality suggests how one might apply to Hardy's novel Hegel's conception of tragedy as the conflict of two forms of value or ethical life. *The Mayor of Casterbridge* dramatises not the conflict between an aristocratic hero and a democratic middle-class community – and hence not the clash of two antithetical systems of value – but instead the internal conflict between values contained within a single ethical system. The bourgeois ethic may at first sight seem straightforward and uncomplicated, but it contains potential sources of tension: values such as devotion to business and devotion to family are not always fully compatible. *The Mayor of Casterbridge* reveals a rift at the heart of bourgeois existence; it pits the values of financial success, commercial competition, and economic dynamism against those of domestic tranquillity, paternal responsibility, and lasting friendship. Torn between a fierce drive for commercial success and a need for companionship and domestic happiness, Henchard ends by ruining both his business and his personal life.[31]

Henchard's economic drives work against his domestic impulses and destroy his chances for happiness as a family man. His domestic affairs are subject from the very beginning to his tendency to view family members as personal possessions and in extreme cases as marketable commodities. His sale of his wife and child at Weydon-Priors vividly reveals a crude capitalist psychology which reifies the human beings to whom Henchard ought to be most intimately attached. Twenty years after his fateful bargain with Newson, Henchard 'tacitly' repurchases his family for five pounds.

Though his marriage to Susan lacks even the faintest spark of sentiment, family life domesticates Henchard to a limited degree; over time he develops a fatherly attachment to Elizabeth-Jane. However, for the sake of striking at a commercial competitor, Henchard blocks a potential match between Elizabeth-Jane and Farfrae, simultaneously alienating his stepdaughter and freeing Farfrae eventually to compete for Lucetta's affection. With Susan's death, Henchard's 'craving ... for [the] tenderest human tie' momentarily intensifies, and he draws closer to Elizabeth-Jane. But when he discovers his stepdaughter's true parentage, Henchard's propensity to reify a personal attachment reasserts itself: he displays 'a positive distaste for the presence of this girl *not his own*'.[32] In effect driving Elizabeth-Jane from his home through neglect and misuse, Henchard once more isolates himself and intensifies his desperate hunger for the love of a domestic companion. The eventual reunion of father and daughter is, however, largely a by-product of Henchard's financial collapse, and takes the form of an obsessive emotional dependence on Henchard's part. Far from discovering some deep spiritual accord with his daughter, Henchard sinks into a state of financial dependence and emotional servitude. Having completely compromised the basis for a genuine personal relationship with his stepdaughter, Henchard must sever all domestic ties and banish himself from Casterbridge once Newson and Farfrae supplant him in Elizabeth-Jane's heart.[33]

This violent inner conflict between domestic and commercial interests has disastrous consequences for Henchard's relations with Farfrae. While Henchard's preoccupation with business and his willingness to manipulate or sacrifice family ties for the sake of commercial ends undermine his chances for domestic happiness, his obsessive insistence on treating Farfrae as either an intimate friend or personal enemy brings about Henchard's financial ruin. Initially Henchard needs only a skilled manager to assist him in a growing business, but upon hiring Farfrae, he insists that the young man become his closest friend and confidante. This personal relationship, whether harmonious or antagonistic, henceforth clouds Henchard's otherwise lucid business sense and leads to a series of ruinous decisions. Their very intimacy makes Henchard distrust his employee and contributes to unnecessarily strained working relations. When Farfrae gradually supplants the mayor as the most admired man in Casterbridge, Henchard dismisses his highly talented and productive manager in a fit of pique and jealousy, thereby creating a commercial rival for himself. Moreover, Henchard's efforts to frustrate Farfrae's courtship of Elizabeth-Jane prevent a natural rapprochement between the two men that would have led to a mutually profitable commercial merger. His preoccupation with a personal rivalry fuelled by Farfrae's romantic interest in Lucetta culminates in Henchard's unnecessary and disastrous commercial war against the Scot. Even after this economic catastrophe, Henchard persists in allowing personal considerations to dictate his business conduct, with the result that his half-hearted attempts to recover from bankruptcy meet with continual frustration. Having first refused Farfrae's offer of financial assistance, Henchard eventually accepts an offer of employment as a common labourer, only to end up assaulting his employer for what the former mayor regards as a series of affronts to his dignity. Though only in his midforties at the close of the novel, Henchard finds himself too exhausted to rebuild his ruined fortune; having devoted all his energies to a financially ruinous personal rivalry, he lacks the strength, energy, and determination that once made him a successful entrepreneur.

III

While a tragic tension between the commercial and the domestic aspects of middle-class life manifests itself as an inner division within Hardy's hero, it is also mirrored in Casterbridge's economic, social, and political history. Thus far I have offered a synchronic view of the tragic conflict at the heart of Hardy's novel, as if the hero vacillated between two equally available ethical options. I want to turn now to the diachronic dimension of Henchard's tragedy, and to discuss the ways in which a 'heroic' phase of early capitalism dialectically produces a second 'domestic' phase which is antithetical to the first, thus contributing to the hero's fall.[34] As chapter 3 begins, Henchard is firmly ensconced in a position of financial affluence, political power, and social prominence. For all of his faults, he has, in the opinion of the citizenry, ruled well as mayor, judged wisely as a magistrate, and acted prudently as a businessman. We have little reason to suspect that Henchard, after many years of success, is on the verge of social disgrace and financial collapse. In fact, he exemplifies the rugged masculine character of an insular community which regards commerce and agriculture as the most important human activities. Content with the status quo, the populace rarely questions the uncultivated character of provincial life, the relatively stratified hierarchy which governs social relations, the primitive condition of agricultural methods, or the basically masculine ethos of the city.

However, this seemingly static state does not last; a series of outsiders arrives in Casterbridge, who gradually transform the community. Farfrae, Elizabeth-Jane, and Lucetta each contribute in varying degree to the modernisation, domestication, and sophistication of Casterbridge in ways that subtly undermine Henchard's authority. The fact that Henchard is largely responsible for these individuals remaining in Casterbridge reveals that he is the author of his own downfall. The limited horizons of his original situation in Casterbridge make possible many years of success, but also give rise to desires and hopes whose fulfilment undermines the foundation of his success.

Prior to Farfrae's arrival in Casterbridge, Henchard's economic triumphs depended upon his own skill and energy, but after many years, Henchard's business has become too large for one man to manage by himself. His very success thus forces Henchard to rely upon the help of another for the first time. Farfrae offers technical and managerial skills, as well as a secret scientific process by which Henchard's bad grain can be restored, or at least by which the impurities of the grain may be disguised.[35] Critics have long noted the Faustian aspects of the bargain Henchard strikes with Farfrae: because he challenges the restraints imposed by nature on the farmer and merchant (that grain, once gone bad, cannot be restored to its original state), and because he seeks to overcome the limits of a small, self-sufficient commercial enterprise, Henchard becomes a kind of middle-class overreacher.[36] His need for greater technical and managerial skill thus illustrates the Faustian dimension of capitalism itself. Economic progress entails a relentless dialectical process: man overcomes the material restraints imposed by nature and convention, and the very success of primitive methods of doing business eventually makes necessary more advanced technological and commercial practices which then make prior modes of economic activity obsolete. For Henchard, this means that his desire for ever greater economic success eventually produces a competitor whose superior commercial talents allow him to supplant Henchard as the leading businessman in the community.

Were Henchard simply to accept these new economic developments, he could avert commercial disaster: instead, he resists the new technologies and managerial practices inaugurated by Farfrae. Their disagreements over the introduction of a seed drill and the treatment of a tardy worker point to the difference between a primitive, personal and despotic form of doing business and its technological, bureaucratic, and rational counterpart. By contrast with Henchard, who repeatedly allows personal, non-economic considerations to dictate his business practices, Farfrae never deviates from his temperate and fully rationalised system of 'small profits frequently repeated'.[37] He wins the commercial war with Henchard precisely because he never allows a desire for revenge or honour to affect his financial judgement. Having rejected the advanced business practices his manager pioneers, Henchard reverts to a trust in superstitious folklore, personal vitality, and rash courage. Rather than depend on the advice of a modern businessman, Henchard in the end relies on the auguries of a local weather prophet in making his fateful financial decision.

While Farfrae's rationalised form of doing business is obviously less heroic than Henchard's, it might seem odd that his concept of impersonal economic activity could in any way be conducive to greater domesticity. Rationalised commercial activity would appear to be the antithesis of family life. But this very separation of the public world of commerce from the private world of family offers a form of inviolability to the latter. While personal considerations no longer affect business, commercial concerns correspondingly no longer interfere, at least directly, with domestic affairs. As an epitome of the successful Victorian businessman, Farfrae lives an existence in which the domestic ('romantic') and the commercial are mutually dependent but clearly distinct: 'The curious double strands in Farfrae's thread of life – the commercial and the romantic – were very distinct at times. Like the colours in a variegated cord those contrasts should be seen intertwisted, yet not mingling.'[38] Initially the communal character of Casterbridge as *polis* does not require men like Henchard to discriminate between what are later distinguished as public and private affairs. As a public man without a family, Henchard is at first in harmony with a regime in which the domestic is subsumed by the communal. To put this another way, initially in Casterbridge the world of commerce and agriculture takes priority over, and indeed barely recognises the world of domestic affairs. However, the economic development of Casterbridge tends to subvert the comprehensive communal character of the city, allowing for the cultivation of an autonomous domestic sphere.[39]

Elizabeth-Jane and Lucetta contribute to the increasing domestication and refinement of Casterbridge's everyday life. Elizabeth-Jane is remarkable for her interest in books, her efforts to educate herself, her desire for a measure of female independence, and her seeming indifference to commercial affairs. Lucetta introduces new fashions, and promotes greater interest in matters of taste, decorum, and sociability. Both women speak out for the importance of sentiment and the centrality of domestic life; each thus partially represents the dynamic process of social evolution which subtly transforms the nature of Casterbridge.

Farfrae's attention to matters of particular concern to the women of Casterbridge (song, dance, books, fashion, sentiment, love) enables him to become what we might term the first successful public relations man in the town. Although apparently quite impersonal when doing business, Farfrae nevertheless wins the support and admiration of the community by playing to its sentimental and nostalgic longings, made all the more acute by the fact that the city is experiencing the first effects of modernisation. By assuming the romantic posture of a Highlander filled with a deep lyric attachment to his distant and pre-industrial homeland, Farfrae capitalises on the anxieties and desires of the burgeoning domestic element within the community and thereby makes a name for himself, laying the foundation for his eventual commercial success. Hardy reveals that Farfrae's performance is chiefly calculated to capture the public sympathy, and not meant to reveal the man's 'true' or 'inner' self. His staging of genteel and domesticated forms of public entertainment, for which he charges admission, epitomises both his rational economic calculation and his corresponding attention to what the buying public desires. Like the presidents of major American corporations who enter our domestic lives through personal appearances in television advertisements, Farfrae, regaled in his Scottish garb, becomes a self-promoting public relations symbol for his own commercial enterprise. As opposed to Henchard, who is always himself no matter what the occasion, Farfrae adopts the role most appropriate to the two worlds of commercial and domestic life which have become increasingly divergent and equally important. Farfrae thus becomes a pioneer of 'domesticated' capitalism in Casterbridge in two important respects: he rationalises economic activity, stripping it of whatever lingering heroic potential it possessed, and he responds to and encourages the development of the increasingly important domestic life of the community through a calculated appeal to the sentimental needs of his market.

Whether the tragic conflict of the novel is understood as taking place within the hero himself, or between two phases of economic and social life, the tension between two aspects of middle-class existence – the commercial and the domestic – provides the basis for a bourgeois tragedy grounded firmly in political realities. Casterbridge experiences not simply a succession of mayors, but an important and decisive change in its political identity. After Henchard, business will no longer be run in despotic fashion. Under Farfrae the opinions and desires of all classes and both genders are deemed relevant in all civic and commercial matters. In every sense of the term, Farfrae's rule is more popular than Henchard's. The hero's fall is thus the harbinger of a more egalitarian and more commercialised age in Casterbridge.

By the close of Hardy's novel, the archaic character of Casterbridge has been compromised in every respect: over the course of just five or six years, the city experiences the first effects of the revolution in modern technology, the rationalisation of commercial activity, the growth of the social and economic influence of women, the introduction of new fashions and social manners, the democratisation of political life, and the erosion of local autonomy. The ceremonial visit of the Royal Personage signals the increasing integration of Casterbridge into modern British life: Farfrae and the town council welcome the royal guest as a representative of economic and scientific progress in Victorian England. Henchard's individual destruction is an emblem of the passing away of a residual communal existence which ultimately succumbs to the forces of the dominant form of modern bourgeois life.

IV

We have seen the ways in which Hardy recovered some of the power and prestige of traditional dramatic tragedy for the novel. However, in certain respects, both thematic and formal, Hardy's attempt at a tragic novel is in the end not entirely satisfactory. As Florence Hardy reports, Hardy seemed particularly concerned about the adverse effects that serialisation had on *The Mayor of Casterbridge*:

> Hardy fancied he had damaged [*The Mayor of Casterbridge*] more recklessly as an artistic whole, in the interest of the newspaper in which it appeared serially, than perhaps any other of his novels, his aiming to get an incident into almost every week's part causing him in his own judgement to add events to the narrative somewhat too freely.[40]

In the first English edition of the novel, published in two volumes in 1886, Hardy attempted to correct some of these faults by a series of excisions, including the removal of most of the penultimate chapter, which he felt particularly weakened the end. Though in later editions, beginning with that of 1895, Hardy was persuaded to restore this excised chapter, his initial judgement was probably correct: the cut contributed to the dramatic compression and hence to the tragic effect of the novel. I shall return to the specific problems posed by this penultimate chapter, but first I want to consider how Hardy's difficulties with serialisation point to a larger problem with his plotting.

Comic novels, like comic dramas, often derive their humour from farcically rapid plot developments and an abundance of narrative events. Episodic novels such as *Don Quixote* and *Tom Jones* depend for their comedy to some extent on many adventures taking place in a brief period of time. By contrast, tragedy requires a selective representation of events. To overload a tragic novel with too many calamities is to risk producing bathos and an unintended farcical effect, for it taxes the reader's credibility and powers of empathy to subject a hero to a seemingly endless series of personal misfortunes. In *The Mayor of Casterbridge*, in addition to his economic and political fall, Henchard must endure within the space of just a few years the death of his wife, the discovery that Elizabeth-Jane is in fact not his daughter (his real daughter having died years before), the loss of his stepdaughter's affection (twice), the frustration of his matrimonial designs upon Lucetta, the collapse of his friendship with Farfrae, the double defeat dealt him by Farfrae for the affections of Elizabeth-Jane and Lucetta, the bafflement of his plans first to revenge himself upon Lucetta and then to preserve her name from public scandal, the supplanting of himself in Elizabeth-Jane's affections by Newson, and so on.

As Norman Friedman and Irving Howe have argued, one consequence of Hardy's narrative excess is a disjunction in his plot. *The Mayor of Casterbridge* contains in fact two superimposed but separate plot lines, one involving Henchard, Susan, Elizabeth-Jane, and

Newson, the other involving Henchard, Farfrae, and Lucetta.[41]
These two plot lines only appear to converge; actually they culm-
inate in two distinct catastrophes: one domestic and personal,
brought about in large part by the furmity woman's revelation of
Henchard's past; the other economic and political, the result of
Henchard's commercial war with Farfrae. As Howe puts it, 'there is
no necessary or sufficiently coercive reason why the consequence of
a personal sin should coincide in time and impact with the climax
of socio-economic failure'. There are of course many ways in which
these two plot lines may be *thematically* related; we have seen that
the conflict between the domestic and economic strains of middle-
class life provides the basis for both catastrophes. But though the
novel possesses thematic unity, it lacks structural integrity, and to
some degree this structural defect, once recognised, diminishes the
tragic effect of the novel as a whole. The novel does not possess the
unity of action and tight dramatic logic characteristic of Sophoclean
or Shakespearean tragedy, in which the hero's death almost always
grows directly out of the same forces which led to the turn in his
fortunes. The concatenation of tragic events in *The Mayor of
Casterbridge* must seem to some degree artificially and arbitrarily
imposed by Hardy rather than the result of an inevitable causal
sequence.[42]

Anticipating this kind of structural critique, I have emphasised the
plot line involving Henchard and Farfrae, since it constitutes for me
the essence of Henchard's tragedy. For it is the commercial rivalry
between the two men which gives Henchard's tragedy its public and
political character. To be sure, Henchard's original transgression at
Weydon-Priors is economically motivated (insofar as it frees him to
pursue his mercantile ambitions) and the furmity woman's revelation
leads to the hero's social disgrace. But were it not for his conflict with
Farfrae ending in bankruptcy, Henchard might well have survived
the scandal in the courtroom without undue loss of economic and
political power.[43] By the same token, Henchard would have been
financially ruined even without the fresh revelation of his past mis-
conduct. To the degree that other causes contribute to Henchard's
economic collapse, they are unrelated to the furmity woman's accusation. In a seldom noted passage, Hardy relates that Henchard's commercial credit is overthrown because the bad harvest has bankrupted
his chief debtor (on whom Henchard had depended to cover his own
disastrous speculation) and, simultaneously, because in desperation
Henchard misrepresents the quality of his grain, failing to preserve

the strict correspondence between bulk and sample. Henchard's fall as corn factor and mayor thus remains firmly rooted in the economic and political facts of middle-class life, rather than, as some critics have argued, in an abstract and metaphysical principle of retribution that demands the hero's punishment for his transgression of divine or natural law.[44]

The way I have tended to neglect Hardy's use of structural and thematic elements from Greek drama (in particular, his reworking of Sophocles' *Oedipus Rex*) is consequently justified by my conviction that Hardy has merely hung the trappings of Greek tragedy upon the essentially modern story of a middle-class businessman and politician. If other critics have insisted upon understanding *The Mayor of Casterbridge* on the model of Greek tragedy, it is the result of their having in effect been taken in by Hardy's artistic sleight-of-hand. For the novel's disjunctive plot results from Hardy's desire to present a modern serialised novel in the guise of traditional Greek tragedy. The double plot answered the demands of the Victorian reader for a significant event in every newspaper instalment, while still leaving the reader with the impression that Henchard's story – though concerned with the middle-class pursuits of business and local politics – somehow neatly recapitulates that of a traditional aristocratic hero like Oedipus.

In Marxist terms one could regard the superimposition of the story of Oedipus on that of Henchard as an ideological feint, an attempt to mask the contradictions in bourgeois existence Hardy had uncovered by overlaying them with the aura of Greek myth. The very lack of structural integrity in the novel can be said to reveal a fissure between the idealised portrait of the bourgeois mayor – elevated to tragic status by the mythic background – and the sordid economic and political realities out of which his self-destructive career emerges. One might go so far as to view this strategy as economically motivated on Hardy's part (that is, an attempt to sell the novel by appealing to the prejudices, which he shares, of his middle-class audience) and even economically circumscribed by the modes of production (serialisation) governing fiction during the Victorian period. All this would suggest Hardy's complicity in perpetuating a reigning ideological dogma; though his novel actually reveals the contradictions that riddle bourgeois existence, he succeeds in making that form of economic life palatable to his middle-class readers by assimilating it to the prestigious patterns of traditional Greek myth and tragedy.

The issue of the mythic background raises doubts about the success of *The Mayor of Casterbridge* as a tragic novel. The short-comings of grafting the forms of Greek tragedy onto a novel expressly concerned with the economic middle-class politician become especially evident toward the end. The chapters following Henchard's abortive suicide seem particularly weak and contrived as an attempt at a traditional tragic denouncement; the conclusion of the novel increasingly loses sight of Henchard as a public figure and accordingly concerns itself with the unfortunate domestic fate of a private individual utterly cut off from political life. The central plot of the novel, concerned with the deeds of a political and economic hero, reaches its climax with Henchard's bankruptcy in chapter 31. The next ten chapters may still be regarded as contributing to the tragic effect, insofar as they chronicle Henchard's vain attempts to reassert his heroic identity in the face of political and financial collapse: Henchard's violent confrontation with Farfrae in the hayloft, and his subsequent attempt to drown himself, are two potential tragic endings to a heroic economic existence. But, in the end, Henchard draws back from these potentially fatal steps, sparing first Farfrae and then himself. In one of the strangest scenes in the novel, Henchard sees his double beneath the surface of the water into which he proposes to throw himself. The image of his tragic destiny rises before him, but he chooses to interpret this sign as an admonition against suicide, rather than as a confirmation of his tragic fate.

By contrast, traditional tragic heroes, when finally faced with catastrophe, display a heroic integrity of character. For the Shakespearean hero, a moment usually comes when he must fulfil his tragic destiny and reassert or reclaim his heroic identity through a heroic death. In *Othello*, this is the moment when the hero kills Desdemona and then himself, emphatically drawing attention to his heroic past:

> And say besides that in Aleppo once,
> Where a malignant and a turban'd Turk,
> Beat a Venetian and traduc'd the state,
> I took by th' throat the circumcised dog,
> And smote him – thus.[45]

Henchard instead chooses to live with the consequence of his public humiliation, hoping to find in his relationship with Elizabeth-Jane a form of domestic happiness that will compensate for his total loss of wealth, power, and prestige.

The Henchard who makes this decision has already ceased to be a hero. He has become 'a fangless lion', 'an inoffensive old man', willing to submit to 'snubbings and masterful tongue-scourgings'.[46] From the moment of his financial collapse, Henchard's life becomes a gradual process of degeneration and decline.[47] Taking once more to drink, he pays no heed to his increasingly shabby appearance, returns to the lowly vocation of haytrusser, and depends completely upon his stepdaughter for economic and emotional support. This gradual collapse of Henchard's character is deeply affecting and elicits our sympathy; nevertheless, the growth of our pity for Henchard comes at the expense of our admiration for his strength and wilfulness and hence our sense of him as a heroic figure.

Henchard's self-imposed exile from Casterbridge would seem to be a final effort to reassert his heroic identity. However, the ostensible reason for his self-banishment is not public shame or financial ruin or loss of political power; it is rather the fear that he will lose Elizabeth-Jane's affection to Farfrae and Newson. Now that the main socio-economic and political action has drawn to its close, the concluding chapters once more take up the secondary plot line, with its overlay of motifs borrowed from Greek tragedy. Henchard's actions in this section are not motivated by public or political considerations – they are purely private and personal. Consequently, Hardy once again feels called upon to invoke the spectre of Oedipus and to lend his story the aura of sacred Greek drama. But Henchard's desperately histrionic gesture of self-banishment is, as Hardy himself seems to have realised, undercut by his subsequent return to Casterbridge in the penultimate chapter. The restoration of this chapter, motivated by Hardy's desire to please one of his American readers and admirers,[48] makes necessary a second self-imposed sentence of exile, which inevitably cheapens the effect of the first, and reveals both acts as empty theatrical gestures. For the second act of self-banishment makes all too evident that Henchard's exile has always been revocable, and completely without the force of a legal sentence.

Exile in *The Mayor of Casterbridge* lacks the political significance which lends tragic dignity to the banishment of Oedipus. I have suggested that Casterbridge possesses something of the autonomy and insularity of a *polis*, but by the close of the novel, this autonomy has been compromised, and in any case the city's political authority has never been absolute, nor has it extended to such matters as ostracism. The mayor of Casterbridge, whoever he may be, has never possessed the authority to banish anyone. Given the fact that labourers in Victorian England regularly wandered from town to town seeking work, as Henchard himself does in the opening chapters, banishment from a given township, even if it were legally permissible, would not be the cruel and terrifying sentence it was in the ancient world.

Indeed there are no external reasons, no political or economic obstacles, which prevent Henchard from once more launching forth on a new commercial enterprise:

> And thus Henchard found himself again on the precise standing which he had occupied a quarter of a century before. Externally there was nothing to hinder his making another start on the upward slope. ... But the ingenious machinery contrived by the Gods for reducing human possibilities of amelioration to a minimum – which arranges that wisdom to do shall come *pari passu* with the departure of zest for doing – stood in the way of all that.[49]

Hardy's reference to the gods here is a particularly telling instance of his invoking the machinery of Greek drama at precisely that point at which his hero's tragedy has become politically ungrounded: he offers a purely psychological tragedy which is projected outward onto an indifferent universe in the form of Henchard's superstitious belief in a malevolent deity. The futile gesture of self-banishment by a man only forty-six years old and in perfect health is a psychological, not a political necessity. Having long ceased to be a public figure when he finally withdraws from Casterbridge, Henchard loses nothing he has not already forfeited. The fact that only Elizabeth-Jane is present at Henchard's first departure from Casterbridge, and that no one at all is at his second, further reveals that banishment in the novel lacks a political context. The concluding drama of Henchard's life, centring on his relationship with Elizabeth-Jane and her acceptance or rejection of him as a father, thus becomes a purely domestic affair, only incidentally related to the hero's earlier political and economic career.

One might argue that *Oedipus at Colonus* and *King Lear* are nonetheless tragic for their treatment of the relationship between father and daughter, and that we should not find fault with the conclusion of Hardy's novel for its similar preoccupation. However, neither Sophocles nor Shakespeare loses sight of the political dimension of his hero's tragedy. In *Oedipus at Colonus*, the relationship between Oedipus and his two daughters is finally subordinated to the political relationship between the hero and Theseus. Oedipus leaves his daughters, refusing them access to the site of his apotheosis so that Theseus's beloved Athens might be protected from its enemies. As for Shakespeare's play, though Lear develops an inner depth of character after he has lost his throne, and though this deepening owes much to his newfound appreciation of his private relationship with Cordelia, he ignores the exigencies of political life only at his peril. Even as Lear proposes to Cordelia 'Come let's away to prison, / We two alone will sing like birds i' th' cage', Edmund plots their deaths. Indeed, with the murder of Cordelia, Lear must once more assert his kingly authority and re-enter the bloody political arena: he slays his daughter's assassin in a fit of royal anger.

Above all, unlike Henchard, Lear remains the focus of the attention of his political community until the moment of his death. Henchard, on the other hand, ceases to have any effect on Casterbridge after his fall from power.[50] With characteristic irony, Hardy contrasts the happiness of Elizabeth-Jane, Farfrae, Newson, and the wedding guests with the misery of the outcast Henchard. Long before Henchard's death, Casterbridge has achieved a renewed equilibrium and communal identity which bears little trace of the former mayor's rule. Henchard's last will and testament merely confirms what he already knows – he has become irrelevant to the community he once ruled. The fall of a bourgeois politician and businessman cannot have the convulsive and catastrophic effects on a community that, for example, Lear's abdication has in Britain. The political apparatus of a modern bourgeois state is, after all, designed to transfer power peacefully and smoothly from one official to the next, without civil strife or political turmoil. Casterbridge as it emerges under Farfrae's governance has become a community capable of continual and incremental economic and social progress.[51]

Thus, whereas traditional tragedy does not lose touch with the political context of the hero's existence, Hardy's novel gradually contracts its focus until the hero appears exclusively in his domestic and private capacity. No doubt Hardy's difficulties with the tragic novel arose in part because he understood that Henchard's economic and political failure, while complete, was not in and of itself fatal. In the modern world, businessmen regularly suffer bankruptcy and local politicians lose elections without their resorting to murder, suicide, or self-imposed exile, and without our feeling that their lives are fit material for tragic treatment. The superimposition of the two plot lines reflects Hardy's concern that the story of the socioeconomic ruin of a bourgeois character ultimately lacks the high seriousness of traditional tragic drama. In short, Hardy ran up against the limitations placed upon the would-be tragic writer by the changed conditions of the modern world. For the disjunction of the two plots mirrors a bifurcation in contemporary life between the political and the tragic. Insofar as Henchard's story is about a political man, it ends with his economic ruin and public disgrace, and hence is not fully tragic, but insofar as it ends with the hero's exile and death, it is about a private individual who suffers a series of domestic disappointments and hence is not fully political.

While killing Farfrae and himself would not, strictly speaking, have been the necessary outcome of his financial and political ruin, Henchard might, like Julien Sorel, at least have maintained a tragic dignity after his fall by acting *as if* the end of his public career were something worth killing and dying for. But this is not Henchard's or Hardy's decision. As Casterbridge gradually conforms to the facts of modern economic and political life, Henchard lingers, just beyond the margins of the city, becoming with the passage of time a human anachronism, alienated from the community and the new historical age.[52] Within the quickly changing economic and political conditions of Victorian England, the hero's fall robs him of his stature and dignity without putting an end to his life.

From *South Atlantic Quarterly*, 87:2 (Spring 1988), 219–49.

NOTES

[Michael Valdez Moses' reading seeks to politicise the reader's comprehension of the tragic dimensions of *The Mayor of Casterbridge*, initially through an examination of Casterbridge as a Victorian bourgeois version of the Greek *polis*. Somewhat typical of New Historicist modes of analysis, Moses' essay analyses the ways in which the novel effects containment of potentially subversive or antagonistic forces, while the bourgeois rewriting of tragedy determines Henchard's fall though denying him full tragic status by leaving him alive after the collapse of his business and his removal from the office of Mayor. Ed.]

1. See, for example, D. A. Dike, 'A Modern Oedipus: The Mayor of Casterbridge', *Essays in Criticism*, 2 (1952), 169–79; John Paterson, '*The Mayor of Casterbridge* as Tragedy', *Victorian Studies*, 3 (1959),

151–72; Frederick Karl, 'The Mayor of Casterbridge: A New Fiction Defined', *Modern Fiction Studies*, 6 (1960), 195–213; Robert Heilman, Introduction to *The Mayor of Casterbridge* (Boston, 1962); Michael Millgate, *Thomas Hardy: His Career as a Novelist* (London and New York, 1971); Laurence Lerner, *Thomas Hardy's The Mayor of Casterbridge: Tragedy or Social History?* (London, 1975); and Jeanette King, *Tragedy in the Victorian Novel* (Cambridge, 1978). For an attempt to trace the structural features of the novel as tragedy without reference to Greek models, see Dale Kramer, *Thomas Hardy: The Forms of Tragedy* (Detroit, 1975).

2. See Lawrence Starzyk, 'Hardy's *Mayor*: The Antitraditional Basis of Tragedy', *Studies in the Novel*, 4 (1972), 592–607; Ted R. Spivey, *The Journey Beyond Tragedy: A Study of Myth and Modern Fiction* (Orlando, FL, 1981). The two approaches to *The Mayor of Casterbridge* I have outlined are not strictly separable.

3. For a different account of Casterbridge as a 'primitive hierarchic society', see Paterson, '*Mayor of Casterbridge* as Tragedy', 162–3. Noorul Hasan, in *Thomas Hardy: The Sociological Imagination* (London, 1982), pp. 68–72, analyses Casterbridge in terms of Ferdinand Töonies' sociological categories of *Gemeinschaft* and *Gesellschaft*.

4. See Aristotle, *Politics*, 1253a–b, and, for the distinction between the ancient city and the modern state, see Harry Jaffa, 'Aristotle', in *History of Political Thought*, ed. Leo Strauss and Joseph Cropsey (Chicago, 1972), especially pp. 65–7.

5. I do not mean to imply that the *polis* is the only possible setting for tragedy, or that its historical demise effectively ended the possibility of tragedy. The *polis* is not a necessary precondition of tragedy, but it is a particularly favourable – perhaps even the most favourable – ground for its emergence and development.

6. Thomas Hardy, General Preface to the Wessex Edition of 1912, in *The Mayor of Casterbridge*, p. 378. All references are to this edition of the novel.

7. Ibid., p. 59.

8. Ibid., pp. 100–2.

9. Ibid., p. 192.

10. For a similar view, see Ian Gregor, Introduction to *The Mayor of Casterbridge* (1974), p. 15.

11. Ian Watt, *The Rise of the Novel* (London, 1957), pp. 185, 198.

12. For a similar view, see Irving Howe, *Thomas Hardy* (New York, 1967), pp. 94–5.

13. M. M. Bakhtin, *The Dialogic Imagination*, trans. Caryl Emerson and Michael Holquist (Austin, TX, 1981), p. 132. See pp. 132–6.

14. Hardy, *Mayor of Casterbridge*, p. 121.

15. See Millgate, *Thomas Hardy*, pp. 223–4; Hasan, *Sociological Imagination*, p. 71; and Lerner, *Tragedy or Social History?* p. 79.

16. Hardy, *Mayor of Casterbridge*, pp. 268, 162.

17. Ibid., p. 219.

18. See Howe, *Thomas Hardy*, p. 92.

19. Ibid.

20. Hardy, *Mayor of Casterbridge*, pp. 224, 333, 245.

21. Ibid., p. 143. See D. A. Dike, 'A Modern Oedipus: *The Mayor of Casterbridge*', *Essays in Criticism*, 2 (1952), 169–79, 172.

22. For a general history of this development, see Albert O. Hirschman, *The Passions and the Intellects: Political Arguments for Capitalism Before its Triumph* (Princeton, NJ, 1977) and Leo Strauss, *The Political Philosophy of Hobbes* (Chicago, 1952), pp. 113–22. For the philosophic foundations of this trend of thought, see in particular the discussion of 'the passions that incline men to peace' at the end of ch. 13 of Hobbes's *Leviathan* and Adam Smith's contrast of the modern labourer with the traditional warrior in *The Wealth of Nations* (New York, 1937), pp. 734–5.

23. See Dike, 'Modern Oedipus', 177.

24. In his introduction, Heilman argues that Hardy 'anticipates' the 'Horatio Alger myth' (p. xxxiii).

25. Alexandre Kojève explains how the activity of the free worker, as opposed to that of the slave, becomes an expression of the desire for recognition. See Kojève, *Introduction to the Reading of Hegel*, trans. James Nichols, Jr (New York, 1969), p. 230.

26. Hardy, *Mayor of Casterbridge*, p. 143.

27. See Heilman, Introduction, p. vii.

28. See Dike, 'Modern Oedipus', 172.

29. Hardy, *Mayor of Casterbridge*, pp. 297, 106.

30. Ibid., pp. 44, 227.

31. See Dike, 'Modern Oedipus', 173–8, for a discussion of the conflict between the 'Market' and the 'Home'; see also Juliet Grindle, 'Compulsion and Choice in *The Mayor of Casterbridge*', in *The Novels of Thomas Hardy*, ed. Anne Smith (New York and London, 1979), pp. 93–5, and Elaine Showalter, 'The Unmanning of the Mayor

of Casterbridge', in *Critical Approaches to the Fiction of Thomas Hardy*, ed. Dale Kramer (London, 1979), pp. 99–115.

32. Hardy, *Mayor of Casterbridge*, pp. 153, 160; emphasis mine.

33. For a sociological interpretation of Henchard's final 'alienation' from Casterbridge as the 'logical extension of the irresponsible individualism' inherent in market capitalism, see Dike, 'Modern Oedipus', 178. Though one of the best analyses of Hardy's novel with which I am familiar, Dike's interpretation tends to reduce *The Mayor of Casterbridge* to a crude sociological fable which merely exposes the evils of a market economy.

34. For a different analysis of the changes in economic and social conditions in Casterbridge, see, for example, Howe, *Thomas Hardy*, pp. 92–6. The transformation of an epic culture into a bourgeois capitalist culture is discussed in general theoretical terms by Theodor Adorno and Max Horkheimer, who see modern bourgeois man already prefigured in Homer's Odysseus. See *Dialectic of Enlightenment*, trans. John Cumming (New York, 1972), pp. 43–80.

35. See Millgate, *Thomas Hardy*, p. 227.

36. On the Faust motif in the novel, see Paterson, '*Mayor of Casterbridge* as Tragedy', 153, 159, and Starzyk, 'Hardy's *Mayor*', 597–8.

37. Hardy, *Mayor of Casterbridge*, p. 186. See Lerner, *Tragedy or Social History?* pp. 77–8.

38. Hardy, *Mayor of Casterbridge*, p. 187.

39. See Showalter, 'Unmanning the Mayor', 113, for a feminist interpretation of how this domestic sphere comes into being.

40. Florence Hardy, *The Life of Thomas Hardy, 1840–1928* (London, 1962), p. 179.

41. Norman Friedman, 'Criticism and the Novel', *Antioch Review*, 18 (1958), 348–52, and Howe, *Thomas Hardy*, pp. 98–9.

42. For a similar view, see Howe, *Thomas Hardy*, pp. 90–2, and James R. Baker, 'Thematic Ambiguity in *The Mayor of Casterbridge*', *Twentieth Century Literature*, 1 (1955), 13–16.

43. Heilman, Introduction, p. xix, notes that Hardy dismisses Casterbridge's reaction to the furmity woman's revelation in a single cursory paragraph. It would appear that Hardy has little interest in working out the public ramifications of Henchard's domestic misdeeds.

44. See, for example, Paterson, '*Mayor of Casterbridge* as Tragedy', 152, 158–62. My reading of the novel is based on the assumption that Hardy did not believe in the gods he invoked as a novelist, and that

their appearance can usually (though not always) be explained in terms of Henchard's superstitious beliefs, which he projects outward. What has not hitherto been adequately explained is why Hardy chose to make use of the gods when he obviously had no belief in them except as dramatic machinery.

45. See Lerner, *Tragedy or Social History?* pp. 69–72, for an attempt to assimilate Henchard's death to the pattern of a Shakespearean tragic hero, using this very speech (V. iii. 352–6) from *Othello*.

46. Hardy, *Mayor of Casterbridge*, p. 330.

47. See Showalter, 'Unmanning the Mayor', pp. 112–14.

48. See Carl J. Weber, *Hardy of Wessex* (London, 1965), pp. 151–3. The admirer was Rebekah Owen of New York City.

49. Hardy, *Mayor of Casterbridge*, p. 340.

50. Karl, 'A New Fiction Defined', p. 206, argues that 'the townspeople themselves are under no pall of tragedy ... Only Henchard is tragic, only Henchard really suffers'.

51. Kramer, *Thomas Hardy*, pp. 71–91, argues that Henchard's tragic fall is only one phase in the socially progressive cycle of Casterbridge life.

52. For an analysis of Henchard's anachronistic status, see Hasan, *The Sociological Imagination*, pp. 61–3.

Further Reading

The Mayor of Casterbridge first appeared in twenty weekly parts in the *Graphic*, between 2 January and 15 May 1886. It was published simultaneously in instalments in the USA in *Harper's Weekly*. Both serial publications featured Robert Barnes' illustrations, which are reproduced and discussed in the Penguin 1995 edition (ed. Keith Wilson). Hardy began work on the novel in the early part of 1884, the year after he had moved back to Dorchester. He finished composition in April 1885. He pursued an active period of research, gathering details from local newspapers such as the *Dorset County Chronicle*, and from other sources.

Full details of the composition history and its initial publication are to be found in Simon Gatrell's *Hardy the Creator: A Textual Biography* (Oxford: Clarendon Press, 1988), pp. 75–81, which also provides an interesting account of the editorial schedule, along with questions of editorial censorship, particularly over Hardy's use of swear-words. Gatrell also offers a comprehensive note on the text of the novel, following his introduction to the Oxford World's Classics edition (pp. xxxi-xliv; see below for details of the text). Three articles give details of Hardy's research, and related matters concerning the manuscript and the history of composition; these are: Christine Winfield, 'The Manuscript of Hardy's *The Mayor of Casterbridge*', *Papers of the Bibliographical Society of America*, 67 (1973), 33–58; Christine Winfield, 'Factual Sources for Two Episodes in *The Mayor of Casterbridge*', *Nineteenth-Century Fiction*, 25 (1970), 224–31; William Greenslade, 'Hardy's "Facts" Notebook: A Further Factual Source for *The Mayor of Casterbridge*', *The Thomas Hardy Journal*, 2:1 (January 1986), 33–5. For a study of Hardy's work and revision processes between serial and novel form, see Mary Ellen Chase, *Thomas Hardy from Serial to Novel* (Minneapolis: University of Minnesota Press, 1927; rpt. New York: Russell and Russell, 1964). The standard study of Hardy's work, with respect to questions of writing, editing and publication, is Richard Little Purdy, *Thomas Hardy: A Bibliographical Study* (Oxford: Oxford University Press, 1954).

The bibliography which follows provides the reader with selected editions of the novel; books and articles divided according to the principal areas of study – the novel as tragedy and the novel as social history or sociological narrative – and other articles, essays, extracts from chapters and books which address *The Mayor of Casterbridge*.

EDITIONS OF *THE MAYOR OF CASTERBRIDGE*

The standard edition is:

The Life and Death of the Mayor of Casterbridge: A Story of a Man of Character (London: Macmillan, 1912, Wessex Edition, vol. v). Reprinted in the USA in the 'Anniversary Edition' of *The Writings of Thomas Hardy* (New York: Harper and Bros., 1920). The pagination of the American edition is the same as its British counterpart for most of the novels, although some of the pages were reset.

Modern editions recommended are:

The Mayor of Casterbridge, ed. Martin Seymour-Smith (London: Penguin, 1985).
The Mayor of Casterbridge, World's Classics, ed. Dale Kramer (Oxford: Oxford University Press, 1987).
The Mayor of Casterbridge, ed. Robert B. Heilman (Boston: Houghton Mifflin, 1990).
The Mayor of Casterbridge, ed. Keith Wilson (Harmondsworth: Penguin, 1995). This edition provides the reader with both Hardy's prefaces to the novel, from 1895 and 1912, Chapter XLIV as it appeared in the American first edition, and which was subsequently restored in modified form to the 1895 edition, and the illustrations by Robert Barnes which accompanied the novel's serial publication in the *Graphic*.
The Mayor of Casterbridge, ed. Norman Page (Peterborough, Ontario: Broadview Press, 1997). This edition offers footnotes rather than end-notes, as is the case with the Oxford and Penguin editions. It also provides eleven appendices, dealing with: dialect words and expressions; place-names; wife-selling; the Corn Laws; Prince Albert's visit to Dorchester; Maumbury Ring and the Execution of Mary Channing; the Skimmington Ride; Henchard's Bankruptcy; The First Book of Samuel; Hardy's 'General Preface' from 1912; contemporary reviews of the novel.

THE MAYOR OF CASTERBRIDGE AND TRAGEDY

Aschkenasy, Nehama, 'Biblical Substructures in the Tragic Form: Hardy, *The Mayor of Casterbridge*, Agon: And the Crooked Shall Be Made Straight', *Modern Language Studies*, 13: 1 (1983), 101–10.
Brooks, Jean R., *Thomas Hardy: The Poetic Structure* (London: Elek, 1971).
Dike, D. A., 'A Modern Oedipus: The Mayor of Casterbridge', *Essays in Criticism*, 2 (1952), 169–79.
Edwards, Duane D., '*The Mayor of Casterbridge* as Aeschylean Tragedy', *Studies in the Novel*, 4 (1972), 608–18.
Guerard, Albert J., *Thomas Hardy: The Novels and Stories* (Cambridge, MA: Harvard University Press, 1949).
Karl, Frederick, '*The Mayor of Casterbridge*: A New Fiction Defined', *Modern Fiction Studies*, 6 (1960), 195–213.

King, Jeanette, *Tragedy in the Victorian Novel: Theory and Practice in the Novels of George Eliot, Thomas Hardy and Henry James* (Cambridge: Cambridge University Press, 1978).

Kramer, Dale, *Thomas Hardy: The Forms of Tragedy* (Detroit: Wayne State University Press, 1975).

Lerner, Laurence, *Thomas Hardy's The Mayor of Casterbridge: Tragedy or Social History?* (London: University of Sussex Press, 1975).

Levine, George, *The Realistic Imagination* (Chicago: Chicago University Press, 1981).

Millgate, Michael, *Thomas Hardy: His Career as Novelist* (London: Bodley Head, 1971; rev. edn Basingstoke: Macmillan, 1994).

Paterson, John, 'The Mayor of Casterbridge as Tragedy', *Victorian Studies*, 3 (1959), 151–72.

—, 'Hardy, Faulkner and the Prosaics of Tragedy', *Centennial Review*, 5 (1961), 156–75.

Schweik, Robert C., 'Character and Fate in *The Mayor of Casterbridge*', *Hardy: The Tragic Novels* ed. R. P. Draper (London: Macmillan, 1975), pp. 133–47.

Spivey, Ted R., *The Journey Beyond Tragedy* (Orlando: University Press of Florida, 1980).

Starzyk, Lawrence, 'Hardy's *Mayor*: The Antitraditional Basis of Tragedy', *Studies in the Novel*, 4 (1972), 592–607.

THE MAYOR OF CASTERBRIDGE AS SOCIAL HISTORY AND SOCIOLOGY

Brown, Douglas, *Thomas Hardy: The Mayor of Casterbridge* (London: Edward Arnold, 1962).

Hasan, Noorul, *Thomas Hardy: The Sociological Imagination* (London: Prometheus, 1982).

Maxwell, J. C., 'The Sociological Approach to *The Mayor of Casterbridge*', in *Imagined Worlds: Essays on Some English Novels and Novelists in Honour of John Butt*, ed. Maynard Mack and Ian Gregor (London: Methuen, 1968), pp. 225–36.

Widdowson, Peter, *Hardy in History: A Study in Literary Sociology* (London: Routledge, 1989).

Williams, Merryn, *Thomas Hardy and Rural England* (London: Macmillan, 1972).

OTHER ESSAYS AND ARTICLES ON *THE MAYOR OF CASTERBRIDGE*

Bair, Judith, 'The Mayor of Casterbridge: "Some Grand Feat of Stagery"', *South Atlantic Bulletin*, 42.2 (1977), 11–22.

Baker, James. R., 'Thematic Ambiguity in *The Mayor of Casterbridge*', *Twentieth Century Literature*, 1 (1955), 13–16.

Casagrande, Peter J. and Lock, Charles, 'The Name "Henchard"', *Thomas Hardy Society Review*, 1 (1978), 115–18.

Chapman, Raymond, 'The Reader as Listener: Dialect and Relationships in *The Mayor of Casterbridge*', *The Pragmatics of Style*, ed. Leo Hickey (London: Routledge, 1989), pp. 159–187.

Cooley, John R., 'The Importance of Things Past: An Archetypal Reading of *The Mayor of Casterbridge*', *Massachusetts Studies in English*, 1 (1967), 17–21.

Davis, W. Eugene, 'Comparatively Modern Skeletons in the Garden: A Reconsideration of *The Mayor of Casterbridge*', *English Literature in Transition (1880–1920)*, 3 (1985), 108–20.

Draper, R. D., '*The Mayor of Casterbridge*', *Critical Quarterly*, 25 (1983), 57–70.

Edmond, Rod, '"The Past-Marked Prospect": Reading *The Mayor of Casterbridge*', *Reading the Victorian Novel: Detail into Form*, ed. Ian Gregor (London: Vision, 1980), pp. 111–27.

Epstein, Leonora, 'Sale and Sacrament: The Wife Auction in *The Mayor of Casterbridge*', *English Language Notes*, 24.4 (1987), 50–6.

Fussell, D. H., 'The Maladroit Delay: The Changing Times in Thomas Hardy's *The Mayor of Casterbridge*', *Critical Quarterly*, 21.3 (1979), 17–30.

Grindle, Juliet M., 'Compulsion and Choice in *The Mayor of Casterbridge*', *The Novels of Thomas Hardy*, ed. Anne Smith (London: Vision, 1979), pp. 91–106.

Haig, Stirling, '"By the Rivers of Babylon": Water and Exile in *The Mayor of Casterbridge*', *The Thomas Hardy Yearbook*, 11 (1984), 55–62.

Hartveit, Lars, 'Thomas Hardy, *The Mayor of Casterbridge*: The Persuasive Function of Character', in *The Art of Persuasion: A Study of Six Novels* (Oslo: Universitatsforlaget, 1977), pp. 50–70.

Heilman, Robert B., 'Hardy's *Mayor* and the Problem of Intention', *Criticism*, 5 (1963), 199–213.

——, 'Hardy's *Mayor*: Notes on Style', *Nineteenth-Century Fiction*, 18 (1964), 307–29.

Hennelly, Mark M., Jr, 'The Unknown "Character" of *The Mayor of Casterbridge*', *Journal of Evolutionary Psychology*, 16: 1–2 (1995), 92–101.

Higbie, Robert, 'The Flight of the Swallow in *The Mayor of Casterbridge*', *English Language Notes*, 16 (1979), 311–12.

Ingersoll, Earl G., 'Troping and the Machine in Thomas Hardy's *The Mayor of Casterbridge*', *University of Hartford Studies in Literature: A Journal of Interdisciplinary Criticism*, 22:2–3 (1990), 59–67.

——, 'Writing and Memory in *The Mayor of Casterbridge*', *English Literature in Transition (1880–1920)*, 33.3 (1990), 299–309.

Keily, Robert, 'Vision and Viewpoint in *The Mayor of Casterbridge*', *Nineteenth-Century Fiction*, 23.2 (1968), 189–200.

Moore, Kevin Z., 'Death against Life: Hardy's Mortified and Mortifying "Man of Character" in *The Mayor of Casterbridge*', *Ball State University Forum*, 24:3 (1983), 13–25.

Moynahan, Julian, '*The Mayor of Casterbridge* and the Old Testament's First Book of Samuel: A Study of Some Literary Relationships', *PMLA*, 71 (1956), 118–30.

O'Dea, Raymond, 'The "Haunting Shade" That Accompanies the Virtuous Elizabeth-Jane in *The Mayor of Casterbridge*', *Victorian Newsletter*, 31 (1967), 33–6.

Peck, John, 'Hardy and Joyce: A Basis for Comparison', *Ariel*, 12 (1981), 71–85.

Showalter, Elaine, 'The Unmanning of the Mayor of Casterbridge', *Critical Approaches to the Fiction of Thomas Hardy*, ed. Dale Kramer (London: Macmillan, 1979), pp. 99–115.

Solimine, Joseph, '"The Turbid Ebb and Flow of Human Misery": "Love among the Ruins" and *The Mayor of Casterbridge*', *Studies in Browning and his Circle: A Journal of Criticism, History, and Bibliography*, 8:2 (1980), 99–101.

Taft, Michael, 'Hardy's Manipulation of Folklore and Literary Imagination: The Case of the Wife-Sale in *The Mayor of Casterbridge*', *Studies in the Novel*, 13.4 (1981), 399–407.

Notes on Contributors

Joe Fisher is a literary critic and screenwriter. He lives in London.

Marjorie Garson is Associate Professor of English at the University of Toronto. She has published articles on Swift, Dickens, Thackeray, Scott, Keats, Munro and Austen, and is the author of *Hardy's Fables of Integrity: Woman, Body, Text* (1991).

Simon Gatrell is Professor of English at the University of Georgia. He has written two books on Hardy: *Hardy the Creator* (1988) and *Thomas Hardy and the Proper Study of Mankind* (1993). He has edited critical editions of *Tess of the d'Urbervilles*, *The Return of the Native* and *Under the Greenwood Tree* and was general editor of the Oxford University Press World's Classics series of Hardy texts. He has also completed a biography of the Irish poet William Allingham, and is writing (for Macmillan) a study of the genesis, nature and effect of Wessex in Hardy's writing.

Bruce Johnson is Professor Emeritus and Senior Faculty Associate at the University of Rochester. He did his PhD at Northwestern with the late Richard Ellmann, and has been Chair of the English Department at Rochester and past NEH Senior Fellow and Gugenheim Fellow. Much of his published work has been on Joseph Conrad. It follows naturally that today he is usually found on the beach, Sanibel Island, Florida, doing a cheap imitation of Marlow.

Robert Langbaum is James Branch Cabell Professor of English and American Literature, University of Virginia. His publications include *Thomas Hardy in Our Time* (1995), *The Poetry of Experience: The Dramatic Monologue in Modern Literary Tradition*; *Isak Dinesen's Art: The Gayety of Vision* (1995); *The Modern Spirit: Essays on the Continuity of Nineteenth- and Twentieth-Century Literature*; *The Mysteries of Identity: A Theme in Modern Literature* (1982); *The Word from Below: Essays on Modern Literature* (1987).

J. Hillis Miller is Distinguished Professor of English and Comparative Literature, at the University of California at Irvine, California. His publications include *Reading Narrative* (1998), *Topographies* (1995), *Ariadne's Thread: Story Lines* (1995), *Illustration: Essays in Art and*

Culture (1994), *Fiction and Repetition* (1985), *Thomas Hardy: Distance and Desire* (1970), *The Disappearance of God: Five Nineteenth-Century Writers* (1963).

Michael Valdez Moses is Assistant Professor of English and Affiliated Member of the Faculty in the Program in Literature at Duke University. His publications include *The Novel and the Globalization of Culture* (1995) and, as editor, *The Writings of J. M. Coetzee* (1994).

Tess O'Toole is Assistant Professor of English at McGill University, Montreal. Her publications include *Genealogy and Fiction in Hardy: Family Lineage and Narrative Lines* (1997); 'Adoption and the "Improvement of the Estate" in Craik and Trollope', *Studies in English Literature* (1997), 58–79; 'The Servant's Body: The Victorian Wet-Nurse and George Moore's *Esther Waters*', *Women's Studies* (1996), 329–49.

Julian Wolfreys is Associate Professor of English at the University of Florida. His publications include: *Writing London: The Trace of the Urban Text from Blake to Dickens* (1998), *Deconstruction • Derrida* (1998), *The Rhetoric of Affirmative Resistance: Dissonant Identities from Carroll to Derrida* (1997), and *Being English: Narratives, Idioms, and Performances of National Identity from Coleridge to Trollope* (1994). He is the co-author, with Jeremy Gibson, of *Peter Ackroyd: The Ludic and Labyrinthine Text*. He has also edited and co-edited several books on nineteenth-century literary and cultural studies and literary theory, including *The Derrida Reader: Writing Performances* (1998), *Literary Theories: A Reader and Guide* (1999), and *The French Connections of Jacques Derrida* (1999).

Index

There are no entries for characters or scenes in *The Mayor of Casterbridge*. The only reference included here is to discussion of the town itself. References in footnotes are not included.